RENEWALS 458-4574
DUE

WITHDRAWN
UTSA LIBRARIES

Industries and Globalization

Globalization and Governance

General Editor: Colin Hay

Globalization has become the buzzword of the age, within political, business and academic circles alike. An ever-growing set of associations, connotations and mythologies has been created around this ubiquitous term and its supposed economic, political and cultural impact.

This series will engage in a critical interrogation, unpacking and disaggregation of the often underdeveloped, undertheorized and unduly homogeneous concept of globalization that pervades much of the existing literature and debate.

In examining the complex and multiple processes that constitute the dynamics of globalization, the series aims to contribute to the demystifying of the concept, challenging its logic of inevitability by putting the political back into the analysis of globalization.

The spirit of the series is international and interdisciplinary. It assesses the practices and processes of globalization in the cultural, political, social and economic spheres, examining the empirical evidence for the phenomenon, unpacking the ideological underpinnings of its discourse and discussing the prospects for the governance of globalization's effects and linkages.

Titles include:

Jürgen Grote, Achim Lang and Volker Schneider (*editors*)
ORGANIZED BUSINESS INTERESTS IN CHANGING ENVIRONMENTS
The Complexity of Adaptation

Colin Hay and David Marsh (*editors*)
DEMYSTIFYING GLOBALIZATION

Bernard Jullien and Andy Smith (*editors*)
INDUSTRIES AND GLOBALIZATION
The Political Causality of Difference

Globalization and Governance Series
Series Standing Order ISBN 978–0–333–79238–4 (Hardback)
978–1–4039–1906–9 (Paperback)
(*outside North America only*)

You can receive future titles in this series as they are published by placing a standing order. Please contact your bookseller or, in case of difficulty, write to us at the address below with your name and address, the title of the series and the ISBN quoted above.

Customer Services Department, Macmillan Distribution Ltd, Houndmills, Basingstoke, Hampshire RG21 6XS, England

Industries and Globalization

The Political Causality of Difference

Edited by

Bernard Jullien
Senior Lecturer in Economics, University of Bordeaux IV, France

and

Andy Smith
Director of Research, Sciences-Po Bordeaux, France

Editorial matter, selection, introduction and conclusion © Bernard Jullien and Andy Smith 2008
All remaining chapters © respective authors 2008

All rights reserved. No reproduction, copy or transmission of this publication may be made without written permission.

No portion of this publication may be reproduced, copied or transmitted save with written permission or in accordance with the provisions of the Copyright, Designs and Patents Act 1988, or under the terms of any licence permitting limited copying issued by the Copyright Licensing Agency, Saffron House, 6-10 Kirby Street, London EC1N 8TS.

Any person who does any unauthorized act in relation to this publication may be liable to criminal prosecution and civil claims for damages.

The authors have asserted their rights to be identified as the authors of this work in accordance with the Copyright, Designs and Patents Act 1988.

First published 2008 by
PALGRAVE MACMILLAN

Palgrave Macmillan in the UK is an imprint of Macmillan Publishers Limited, registered in England, company number 785998, of Houndmills, Basingstoke, Hampshire RG21 6XS.

Palgrave Macmillan in the US is a division of St Martin's Press LLC, 175 Fifth Avenue, New York, NY 10010.

Palgrave Macmillan is the global academic imprint of the above companies and has companies and representatives throughout the world.

Palgrave® and Macmillan® are registered trademarks in the United States, the United Kingdom, Europe and other countries.

ISBN-13: 978–0–230–20168–2 hardback
ISBN-10: 0–230–20168–7 hardback

This book is printed on paper suitable for recycling and made from fully managed and sustained forest sources. Logging, pulping and manufacturing processes are expected to conform to the environmental regulations of the country of origin.

A catalogue record for this book is available from the British Library.

Library of Congress Cataloging-in-Publication Data
Industries and globalization : the political causality of difference /
   edited by Bernard Jullien and Andy Smith.
     p. cm. — (Globalization and governance)
   Includes bibliographical references and index.
   ISBN 978–0–230–20168–2 (alk. paper)
   1. Industries. 2. Industrial organization. 3. Industrial policy.
   4. Globalization—Economic aspects. I. Jullien, Bernard. II. Smith, Andy, 1963 July 24–
   HD2328.I53 2008
   338—dc22   2008030088

10 9 8 7 6 5 4 3 2 1
17 16 15 14 13 12 11 10 09 08

Printed and bound in Great Britain by
CPI Antony Rowe, Chippenham and Eastbourne

Contents

Notes on Contributors	vi
Acknowledgements	viii
1 Introduction: Industries, Globalization and Politics *Bernard Jullien and Andy Smith*	1
2 European Automobile Distribution: Globalization and Incomplete Liberalization *Bernard Jullien*	29
3 Globalization Within the European Wine Industry: Commercial Challenges but Producer Domination *Andy Smith*	65
4 Shareholder Value, Political Work and Globalization in the Pharmaceutical Industry *Matthieu Montalban*	92
5 The US Defence Industry Since 1945: Globalization Refused *Sylvain Moura*	129
6 Globalization, Scottish Fisheries and 'Political Work': Global–EU–Local Dialectics *Caitríona A. Carter*	149
7 The Transformation of the French Foie Gras Industry: Globalization, Intellectual Property Rights and Industrial Domination *Bernard Jullien and Andy Smith*	182
8 Conclusion: The Politics of Industry and Globalization *Bernard Jullien and Andy Smith*	201
Notes	221
Bibliography	224
Index	235

Notes on Contributors

Caitríona A. Carter is Senior Lecturer at the Europa Institute, University of Edinburgh, and Visiting Fellow at the SPIRIT research centre in Bordeaux. Her research interest is in studying processes of institutional change both in public institutions, notably parliaments, and in industrial sectors, notably UK–EU fisheries. She has published a book on the transformation of UK–EU policy-making with S. Bulmer, M. Burch, P. Hogwood and A. Scott, *European Policy-Making Under Devolution: Transforming Britain into Multi-Level Governance* (Basingstoke: Palgrave, 2002). Her more recent publications include Carter, C., 'Identifying Causality in Public Institutional Change: The Adaptation of the National Assembly for Wales to the European Union', *Public Administration*, 86 (2): 345–361 (2008); Carter, C. and Smith, A., 'Revitalizing Public Policy Approaches to the EU: "Territorial Institutionalism", Fisheries and Wine', *Journal of European Public Policy*, 15 (2): 263–281 (2008).

Bernard Jullien is *Maître de Conférences* in economics at the GREThA research centre, attached to the University Montesquieu-Bordeaux 4, France. He is also the managing director of the GERPISA, an international network of research on the car industry. His research is centred upon the dynamics of industries from an institutionalist point of view. His work on the politics of industry has been centred upon the food industry (with A. Smith) and on car retailing and services in Europe. With V. Frigant and Y. Lung, he has published a chapter on the French car industry in Gabriel Colletis and Yannick Lung, *La France industrielle en question. Analyses sectorielles* (Paris: La Documentation Française, 2006). With Ph. Cuntigh and A. Smith, he has published the article 'Le contenu politique des régulations sectorielles et les méfaits de sa dénégation: le cas de la gestion publique des produits palmipèdes périgourdins' in *Politique et Management Public*, 23 (3): 177–199 (2005).

Matthieu Montalban is a junior lecturer in economics at the GREThA research centre, attached to the Université Montesquieu-Bordeaux 4, France. His research is centred upon the financialization of industries, especially the pharmaceutical industry, using a historical institutionalist approach (the subject of his PhD dissertation). With Marie-Claude Bélis-Bergouignan, he has published a chapter on the 'French pharmaceutical industry' in Gabriel Colletis and Yannick Lung (eds), *La France industrielle en question. Analyses sectorielles* (Paris: La Documentation Française, 2006).

Sylvain Moura is a researcher in economics at the GREThA research centre, attached to the Université Montesquieu-Bordeaux 4, France. His PhD research was centred on the defence industry, and particularly the economic consequences of national defence policy changes since the beginning of the 1990s. He has been involved in collective studies for the French Ministry of Defence and has published an article on defence sub-contractors' strategies across Europe (with V. Frigant, 2004).

Andy Smith is *Directeur de recherche* at the French Fondation Nationale des Sciences Politiques. He works at the SPIRIT research centre attached to Sciences Po Bordeaux. His initial research interests concerned European integration, a subject on which he has authored *Le gouvernement de l'Union européenne. Une sociologie politique* (Paris: LGDJ, 2004) and (with J. Joana) *Les commissaires européens: technocrates, diplomates ou politiques?* (Paris: Presses de Sciences Po, 2002) and has edited *The Politics of the European Commission* (London: Routledge, 2004). His more recent work on the politics of industry has been centred upon the food industry (with B. Jullien) Jullien B., Smith A., Organisation industrielle et politique des Indications géographiques protégées, report commissioned by the Aquitaine Regional Council, July, 2004; and on that of wine (with J. de Maillard and O. Costa), *Vin et politique: Bordeaux, la France et la mondialisation* (Paris: Presses de Sciences Po, 2007). He is currently undertaking research on the political sociology of the WTO.

Acknowledgements

This book would not have been possible without the help and encouragement of numerous colleagues from Bordeaux working in economics in the GREThA research centre and, as political scientists, within SPIRIT. More specifically, Chapter 2 benefited from research funding from the EU's framework 6 programme and translation by Marie Carpenter. Chapter 3 owes a great deal to Jacques de Maillard and Olivier Costa. Chapters 4 and 5 are based on PhD dissertations funded by the French Ministry of Research. The research behind Chapter 6 was funded by the British Academy. Finally, financed by the Aquitaine Regional Council and the EU's regional development fund, Chapter 7 benefited greatly from the input of Philippe Cuntigh and Matthieu Bécue. More generally, we would like to thank the dozens of practitioners who have accorded us interviews during our respective research projects. Without their cooperation and assistance the generation of our knowledge about industries would have been impossible.

1
Introduction: Industries, Globalization and Politics

Bernard Jullien and Andy Smith

Globalization is widely considered to cause many of the major political challenges of our time. Moreover, when defined as a set of processes that embody 'a transformation in the spatial organization of social relations and transactions, generating transcontinental or inter-regional flows and networks of activity, interaction and power' (Held *et al.*, 1999: 16), globalization is frequently said to be causing convergence in the way economies are structured and governed. More precisely, as a set of 'aggregate social consequences' (Bisley, 2007: 30), globalization is claimed to be driving homogenous and unstoppable swathes of neo-liberal transformations of contemporary economies and polities (Harvey, 2003).

Although practitioners, journalists and many academics often find the parsimony of this argument compelling, over the last few years it has come to be challenged for theoretical and empirical reasons. For instance, leading political economists have highlighted the need to abandon conceptualizations of globalization as 'a process without a subject' and study instead 'the insertion of subjects into processes' which, when analysed together, allow one to identify the phenomenon (Hay and Marsh, 2001: 6). Indeed, empirical research conducted from this perspective particularly underlines just how differently the dynamics one might synthesize as 'globalization' affect nations, states and sectors of socio-economic activity (Berger, 2006). Such research findings strongly suggest globalization should be conceptualized more as a vector for the renewal of economic, social and political diversity, than as a force causing generalized convergence (Hay, 2006).

When one restricts the scope of enquiry to change within specific industries, as we do in this book, what relationship do these processes of change have with globalization? Can one simply continue to conduct research on this question using mainstream institutionalist thinking which essentially underlines the impact of 'institutional constraints' or effects of 'path dependence' upon 'varieties of capitalism' (Hall and Soskice, 2001)? Both our research findings on contemporary industries and theoretical reflections lead us to respond negatively to the latter question in order to generate precise answers to the former. As this book seeks to demonstrate, what needs studying are the ways social and political actors work to influence change within and between the different relationships which structure daily practice in industries. More specifically, on the basis of empirical research into the way actors within industries such as automobiles and wine have interpreted globalization and intervened in order to shape its perceived effects, we have developed elsewhere an analytical approach to *The Politics of Industry* which allows one to both conceptualize these relationships (Jullien and Smith, 2008a) and study their dynamics (Jullien and Smith, 2008b). Summarized versions of arguments made in these two articles provide the basis for the central proposition made in this introduction and tested in the more empirical chapters which follow. This argues that the 'political work' carried out by actors within industries is the principal cause of the construction, maintenance, and regulation of, and challenges to, industrial orders, on the one hand, and of the specific translations of 'globalisation' which occur during this process, on the other.

By highlighting the role of political work carried out by different sets of actors, *The Politics of Industry* approach possesses three traits which increase its analytical purchase. First, it shows that grasping the dynamics of industry requires deeply interdisciplinary co-operation between economists and political scientists in order to enrich understandings of 'globalization'. Second, it encourages and structures research that is designed to generate new and in-depth knowledge about the regulation of specific industries, and this regardless of their apparent territorial implantation. Third, such an approach can also provide practitioners with improved capacity to influence interpretations and orientations of globalization within their respective industries.

This introduction unpacks these three points, transforms them into objectives and sets out how this book, and more generally *The Politics of Industry* approach, attempts to attain them. We first show how politics is omnipresent within the regulation of industries (Section 1), before developing an analytical grid designed to reveal how and why 'political work' is the independent variable which causes the changes observed within industries (Section 2). The empirical chapters are then presented, their principal findings highlighted and their validation or invalidation of the book's claims underlined (Section 3). Overall, we seek to convince the reader of the potential of the analytical framework proposed in this book for renewing research on the dynamics of industry and, in particular, for identifying whether, how and why globalization effects these processes.

1. The Politics of Industry approach: Definitions

As N. Fligstein and J. Choo underline in their analysis of 'corporate governance' (2005), the regulations which structure industries and define what economists generally call 'industrial organisation' have not been brought about by, and do not owe their continuing existence to, efficiency. Rather this organization is the consequence of sets of regulations which engender 'stable institutions that are legitimate and prevent extreme rent seeking on the part of governments and capitalists' (2005: 61). In other words, even if the sustainability of the rules which structure daily conduct within firms and industries are inevitably linked to functional issues (i.e. designing, producing and selling goods), their durability is above all a political construction. It follows that the critical condition for the stable regulation of an industry is the capacity of certain actors to impose and maintain a division of authority that rests upon justifications which are generally accepted by the practitioners concerned. Consequently, we define the regulation of industries as a set of stabilized rules which, within any industry, transform production, marketing and competition into durable and 'secure' processes.

Studying this regulation requires the development of an approach capable of simultaneously grasping the structures of an industry and the organization of its production, commercialization and competition (Section 1.1). In defining the regulation of industries in this way, one sees more clearly the concrete issues tackled by actors through their *political work* (Section 1.2). In particular, this work, and the regulation it constantly seeks to shape, will be shown to feature three processes: institutionalization (the construction and consolidation of rules), deinstitutionalization (challenges to rules) and reinstitutionalization (the creation of new rules).

1.1. Industrial organization as regulation

Undertaking research into the regulation of any industry can be broken down into three stages. The organization of an industry's regulation first needs to be studied through the *Institutionalized Relationships* around which it has emerged and evolved (Section 1.1.1). Once this knowledge has been accumulated, one is then in a position to capture the industry's specific configuration of institutionalized rules, practices and expectations: its *Institutional Order* (Section 1.1.2). Finally, analysis in terms of *Institutional Orders* enables one to grasp not only the causal processes within and between an industry's *Institutionalized Relationships*, but also their relation with institutions and regulation that are trans-industry (Section 1.1.3).

1.1.1. Institutionalized Relationships

Over time, actors within any industry have composed institutions and modes of regulation in order to manage four sets of constraints and opportunities. In turn, these have given rise to four *Institutionalized Relationships* (IRs) which concern employment, finance, production and sales.

1. The *Employment IR* is the configuration of rules, actors and expectations through which employer–employee relations are mediated. This IR obviously includes employment (or 'labour') law, but it also encompasses the range of practices for conciliating the interests of management and trade unions which are commonly called 'industrial relations'.
2. The *Finance IR* concerns the institutions which structure how the firms of an industry manage their respective capital investments and operating costs. Banking, accountancy and stock market laws are clearly of paramount importance here. Beyond such legislation, however, each industry tends strongly to have developed its own set of standardized practices and patterns of power.
3. Production of a good or service is structured by numerous factors. However, in any stabilized industry the principal mechanism through which these are collectively and publicly mediated are interfirm relations which we conceptualize as the *Purchase IR*. This is the relationship through which rules and norms are established regarding producers of raw materials and processors (e.g. wine-makers).
4. Finally, an industry's *Commercial IR* concerns the institutions that structure the selling and marketing of a good or service. Typically this IR mediates the objectives and interests of producers (e.g. car manufacturers) or wholesalers (e.g. wine merchants) on the one hand, and retailers (e.g. supermarkets) on the other.

Considered in this way, IRs possess a number of characteristics which Commons attributes to institutions (1934): they structure and liberate individual action by reducing uncertainties via collective action without which industries would be paralysed. IRs are therefore constraints on economic action but also provide the very conditions for such action. This means that each IR provides a framework for productive and commercial activity within an industry which, far from determining precisely what each individual actor will do, allows them to situate and position themselves within a broader set of considerations. More precisely, the IR enables actors to choose whether to conform with existing institutions or distance themselves from them (what we call *subscription* or *extraction*). Either option is chosen because each actor has a certain representation of the effects of their own actions and, in particular, the economic results these are likely to attain.

In our view, characterizing an industry in terms of its four IRs provides a solid starting point from which to generate studies which explicitly integrate the economic and political dimensions of an industry. By conceptualizing as IRs what neoclassical economists reduce to being a market relation regulated by price, this approach identifies why it is necessary to study the social relationships through which an industry is regulated. Consequently, our approach encourages research into an industry's normative, cognitive and symbolic (i.e. political) structure as consubstantial to its more functional dimension. Even if at certain times the regulation of an industry is 'market driven' (i.e. in response to changes in price and/or supply and demand), this occurs within a set of enduring relationships which always possess both political and functional dimensions.

This standpoint can be further explained by situating it in relation to other approaches to the study of industries. Our list of four IRs will be familiar to many economists who distinguish between fixed capital (the Finance IR), variable capital (the Purchase IR) and labour markets (the Employment IR). However, we consider that research cannot presuppose that a firm's access to its resources and its clients will systematically be determined by the market. Instead, our institutionalist perspective leads us to consider that the relationships which structure industries and the firms they contain are not just choices of types of co-ordination dictated by the nature of the goods or services being transacted. Rather these relationships stem from social and political compromises which are likely to vary considerably from one polity or period to another.

An approach similar to ours was developed some years ago by Imai and Itami (1984) when they attempted to characterize and compare Japanese and American industrial configurations. Like us, they examined four domains within industries and underlined in particular the importance of access to intermediary goods (what we call the Purchase IR). They then went on to divide each domain in terms of its market and organizational dimensions, and this from the point of view of both basic principles and modes of decision-making. They were then able to unveil important differences for each category of goods or service within both countries under study. Finally, on the basis of this analysis, Imai and Itami proposed a way of analysing the difference between varying strategies of industrial diversification, financing and innovation in terms of a firm's behaviour and its institutionalized choices (the latter conceptualized essentially as choices over modes of co-ordination). Three of our four IRs are therefore similar to theirs for three reasons:

1. Each IR has to develop its own internal coherence because all the firms concerned need to be able to fit with it in order to produce their respective goods or services.
2. Each IR has an initial need for external coherence because production, and more generally the definition of company strategies, needs to fit with all four IRs through developing 'institutional complementarity'.
3. Each IR also possesses a second need for external coherence in that the choices behind it are also inscribed in social, economic and political contexts. These structure, or at least inform, actor choices by providing them with the repertoire of legitimizing resources and legal tools which they need in order to protect and reproduce themselves.

An approach even more akin to our own has been developed by Neil Fligstein (2001), who defines industries, which he calls markets, as 'organizational fields'. More precisely, Fligstein's central question, like ours, is what determines the reproducibility of commerce and the stability of each firm's markets? For Fligstein, firms are constantly confronted with uncertainties linked to the risk that prices will fall and the fact that their internal politics are inherently unstable. In order to surmount this uncertainty, Fligstein suggests that four sets of institutions have emerged which are the product of compromises between the state and the dominant firms within its territory:

1. property rights which regulate both who controls each company and its profits;
2. governance structures made up of sets of rules which organize competition and co-operation within each sector (e.g. anti-trust regulations);

3. the rules of commerce which concern the security of transactions and the definition of product quality;
4. conceptions of control which are collective representations (or conventions) held by the managers of firms which concern how a sector is organized, the constraints they are under and the appropriate strategies for dealing with these constraints. These representations allow and cause such managers to determine which are the dominant firms and which are the dominated. Once adopted, they also shape company cultures through structuring coalitions within each organization.

If we take inspiration and support from these two sources, the meso-economic approach that is absent for Imai and Itami and explicit for Fligstein, is nonetheless much more central in our own analysis of the politics of industries. Within these authors' research agendas, the meso-level is examined essentially in order to show how macro-economic and political characteristics that are constructed elsewhere have been translated within the firm. For example, Fligstein's empirical investigations concern how macro-economic or global conceptions of control end up imposing themselves on each company and industry. He therefore avoids the question of each industry's regulatory autonomy. Consequently, one is less able to understand how macro-economic trends differentiate because of the political work carried out within each IR of each industry. Our own approach has been developed precisely to generate knowledge on this question in general, and is therefore particularly adapted to studying the relationship between industries and globalization. In short, our analysis in terms of IRs is designed to be both more conceptually solid and more empirically operational.

As Figure 1.1 highlights, the internal structure of each IR features structured and durable mechanisms which mediate between actors with differing, or even opposing, interests. Here our approach also positions itself as regards debates concerning the study of 'transactions'. With Commons (1934), but against the New Institutional Economics of Williamson (1985), we consider that the fact that these transactions concern goods and services should not lead research to forget that commerce always essentially concerns relations between people situated in societies which ascribe them rights and duties. Consequently, the internal coherence of IRs reflects the social dimension of transactions

8 Introduction

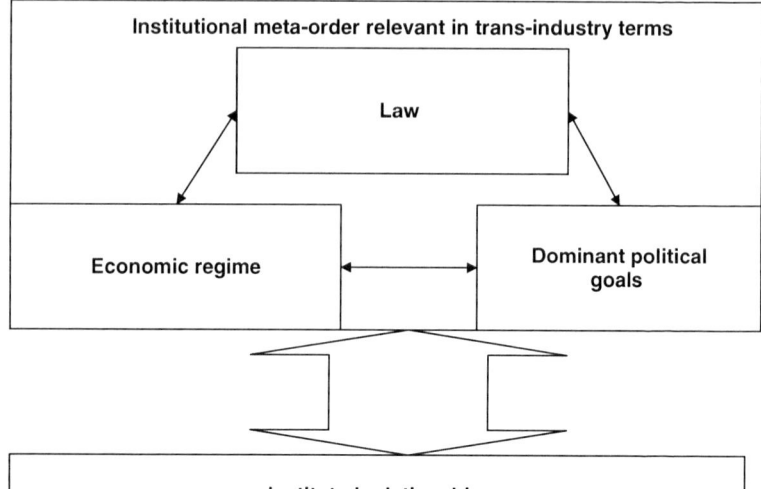

Figure 1.1 The structure of each Institutionalized Relationship

which is regulated by the institutionalization of the two sides of each relationship:

1. relations between private, collective or public representatives of rival holders and users of resources within the industry who engage in shaping its reglementation (its stakeholders);
2. relations between firms who compete for market share (its businesses).

In short, competition takes place not only directly between the firms of an industry and through markets for goods or services, but also through quests for access to resources such as intermediary goods, labour or finance. For this reason, we conceptualize first the power relations and the division between the dominant and the dominated – Fligstein's 'conception of control' – at the level of each IR (the right-hand column of Figure 1.1).

From the point of view of research, this definition of an IR obliges and enables research to unpack in three stages, and through three couples of 'Cs', how mediations within industries entail processes of cognition, powering and domination.

The first couple (*conflict–co-ordination*) concerns a fundamental economic question for both stakeholders and businesses: actors within an industry have conflicts of interest but, nevertheless, must co-ordinate in order that production and competition can take place in an environment which is not a Hobbesian 'war' of everyone against everyone else. This means studying the structural dependencies between these actors by identifying the private, collective and public actors who compete to make reglementation over the holding of resources (left-hand column), and the businesses who compete for access to these resources and clients (right-hand column). The objective of analysis here is essentially to generate thick description of the *conflicts* which occur between these protagonists and of the mechanisms of *co-ordination* that have emerged to mediate, and in many cases to 'pacify, them.

In order to delve deeper into the dynamics of an industry, a second stage of research centred upon the couple *compromise–convention* then consists of analysing the relations which structure co-ordination within the industry. Are these based upon occasional *compromises* (e.g. issue-by-issue trade-offs closely related to short-term market conditions), or do they possess more regularity due to the importance of explicit and institutionalized intra-industry *conventions*?

Finally, on the basis of stages 1 and 2, the couple *co-operation–coercion* enables research to interpret the asymmetries of power within the industry. Ultimately, does its regulation depend upon *co-operation* between protagonists of relatively equal politico-economic power? Or, on the contrary, is the industry's regulation the result of *coercion* of the dominated by the dominant?[1]

Before proceeding to show how we conceptualize IRs as part of industry-specific Institutional Orders, it should be added that Figure 1.1 as a whole, and its top part in particular, also seeks to capture how we conceptualize the way trans-industry trends and norms take effect within specific industries. As Théret underlines, an institutionalist approach to this question implicitly takes inspiration from Marcel Mauss because it leads research to consider the empirical reality studied 'not only as social facts but also as total social facts, i.e. facts within which social totality is always present' (2001: 130). For this reason, we consider that each IR of every industry is located within an overarching meta-order which, in turn, is composed of three interrelated meta-orders concerning law, politics and economics. More precisely, these orders not only structure the IR but are also shaped themselves by interactions with the multiplicity of IRs within a society. In the chapters which follow, each IR of the industry under study will be shown to contain relevant parts of meta-orders (the top part of the diagram) which then play out in the relations summarized in the bottom part of the diagram.

As will be seen throughout the book, one of the principle advantages of conceptualizing IRs in this way concerns taking into account how the geographical scales which structure meta-orders differ widely from industry to industry, from one period to another and even between the IRs of the same industry. In general terms, four scales of regulation effect these relationships: the sub-state, the state, the supranational (e.g. the European Union) and the global. This means that actors within industries engage in multi-scaled political work in order to take advantage of the opportunities, or avoid the obstacles, present at each scale of regulation. Over time, the cumulative effect of this political work means that some IRs are still essentially regulated nationally, whereas others have come to be dominated by sub-state, supranational or global scaling. Put simply, within the same industry, each IR tends to be defined at a territorial scale that differs from the three others.

This situation creates a considerable challenge for research. The response most commonly used in political science – 'multi-level governance' (Hooghe and Marks, 2001) – leads one to consider that all the actors in an industry are subject to the same constraints and opportunities institutionalized by its dominant 'level' of regulation. Our own response to the challenge of rescaling is instead to embrace the differentiation between territorial scales found within each industry and how they produce competing 'sub-orders' (Carter and Smith, 2008). This approach is particularly advantageous because it encourages deeper investigation into the degree to which each industry has or has not been globalized. The question one is then able to answer is, whether, in each IR, apparent displacements of regulatory decision-making towards 'superior' levels has genuinely occurred and is complete and, if so, has it then contaminated the industry's other IRs? If these processes have taken place, then one can conclude that a homogenization of the IRs has taken place and that, as a result, this can be qualified as globalization. If this is not the case, however, globalization needs defining instead as a political enterprise designed to attempt to cause change in the scaling of different parts of an industry's regulation.

1.1.2. Institutional Orders

As per the terms used in this book, an industry can be said to have been institutionalized as a relatively autonomous entity only when it has given rise to its own durable set of the four IRs: its Institutional Order (IO). Crucially, these IRs are linked through a set of relationships which, as Figure 1.2 attempts to visualize, constitute the industry's 'centre' wherein debates and decisions about certain industry-wide issues are shaped and take place (e.g. professional identities or the meaning attached to products).

It follows that each industry contains internal diversity which can be studied by discovering how each firm is involved in and effected by each of the four IRs. In some cases, representatives of firms cause difference within one IR by referring, either implicitly or explicitly, to practices and processes which make up the IRs of associated and/or competing industries. For example, we show in Chapter 3 how producers of orgin-labelled wine have regulated their industry's Commercial and Purchase IRs through certification schemes. This choice, and the conception of economic activity which underpins it, can be understood only by the comparisons producers constantly make between 'their' part of the industry and another centred upon unlabelled 'table' wine.

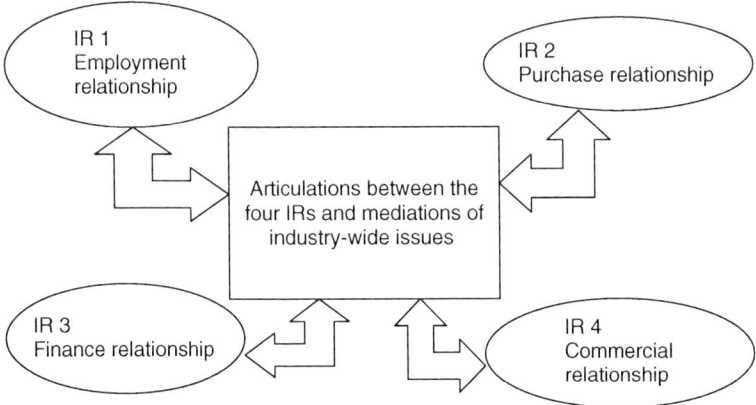

Figure 1.2 An industry as an *Institutional Order* of four *Institutionalized Relationships*

A second advantage of conducting analysis in terms of IOs is to rebalance the generation of knowledge about the institutions which shape industrial activity. If institutionalist approaches to economics have already identified and demonstrated the importance of such social relationships, they rarely provide balanced accounts of their whole range of effects upon specific industries. For these reasons, we question the part of Hall and Soskice's 'varieties of capitalism' model which accords a great deal of importance to change and stasis in what we call Employment and Finance IRs (2001). In so doing, for example, they rightly highlight the importance of national patterns of wage-bargaining and social protection or of the liberalization of capital markets. However, they pay almost no attention to a Purchase IR which they reduce to inter-firm relations. Moreover, Hall and Soskice totally overlook the producer–distributor relationship at the heart of each industry's Commercial IR. As nearly all the chapters in this book underline, over the last 20 years, the Purchase and Commercial IRs are frequently where the most political work, and the most reinstitutionalization, have been taking place within industries.

Finally, from the point of view of the 'political work' which we place at the centre of our approach, analysis in terms of IRs also provides a means of going beyond a sterile opposition between the 'sectoral analysis' practised by industrial economists and statisticians (Arena *et al.*, 1990) and the analysis of politico-administrative sectors undertaken by political scientists (Muller, 1995). Rather than continuing to consider that each 'sector of production' is linked to several 'politico-administrative sectors', we consider instead that each industry possesses both functional and political dimensions which simultaneously play out within and across the four IRs.

As we hypothesized above, roles of the different actors concerned are partly distributed as a function of the power relations that exist between dominant and other firms (Fligstein, 1996). Defining spaces of co-operation and coercion in this way allows one to study the varying capacity of actors to tell clients, suppliers, employees and financiers what an industry is and what they should expect from it. The heart of this sectoral arrangement, what Fligstein calls a 'field', is itself linked both structurally and functionally to more specific regulations which can and should be analysed within each of the four IRs. Indeed, the latter vary in their degree of specificity: they are specific when the rules of an industry apply only to it (e.g. certification and labelling laws); they are generic when these rules also apply to other industries (e.g. competition policy). Similarly, political work can also take the form of demanding more specific rules by extracting the industry from more general ones (through negotiating exemptions) or, conversely, of obtaining a despecification of rules by submitting one's industry to the conditions set out in general law. Within each IR, different protagonists will interact around issues that are likely to be framed along these lines.

This means that within each IR the terms through which industrial issues are defined, debated and institutionalized are distinct. Economically this distinctiveness and its effects can be studied within firms and by examining their interactions. Politically it can be analysed by unpacking the rules and strategies of legitimization mobilized by each actor. In other words, work carried out within vineyards and garages, the wine market or that of car servicing, or the relations between such actors and their respective suppliers, is not framed directly at the scale of the industry as a whole but IR by IR. However, conceptualized as a dynamic configuration of four IRs, an industry as a whole nevertheless engenders its overall effects and identity (its 'industry-ness') in the way private, collective and public actors attempt to attain coherence between the IRs during the course of the competition and co-operation they constantly engage in.

Finally, compared to approaches such as the 'Variety of capitalisms' model (Hall and Soskice, 2001) which tend strongly to consider that key forms of industrial regulation are located at the scale of the nation state, our approach provides a means of grasping the regulation of industries from an angle that embraces its increasingly 'multi-territorial' character (Carter and Smith, 2008). More precisely, there is no reason to consider that one IR is regulated at the same geographical scale as the other three. For example, just because a certain type of 'globalization' influences an industry through its Finance IR, one cannot simply assume that this scale or location is mirrored in its Commercial, Purchase or Employment IRs. Indeed, as several of the chapters in this book underline, it is quite possible that attempts to deinstitutionalize or reinstitutionalize these other IRs might take place within national or intranational sites of negotiation.

1.1.3. *Trans-industry regulation*

From a similar perspective, our approach transforms the issue of sectors and their importance for the regulation of productive activities (as defined by economists such as Boyer) into a question to be researched rather than a theoretical postulate. Indeed, implicitly, Figures 1.1 and 1.2 hypothesize that the articulation between the four IRs occurs at the level of an industry as a whole. However, in some cases empirical evidence could also be marshalled to show that these four relationships are not necessarily articulated at the meso-level. Instead, one needs to extend the approach beyond sectoral regulation in order to encompass inter- and trans-industry regulation.

In response to this analytical challenge, our claim is that it is only by defining and setting out the four IRs of each industry that one can study in depth the particular forms of disjunction between different levels of regulation that occur therein. For instance, the Employment IR which partially structures the way garages operate is not specific to the car industry but concerns all small and medium-sized industries. Similarly, the Finance IR and the ownership issues it entails often also take a transectoral form. Nonetheless, this does not mean that one cannot grasp car retailing as an industry because a specific set of institutions still refracts how the Employment IR in this industry effects the relations between competing suppliers (car manufacturers) on the one hand, and between suppliers and their clients on the other. Thus by considering that each IR is not necessarily structured solely in a sectoral manner at the level of an industry, but that nevertheless the articulation between these IRs certainly is, one can problematize the frontiers of an industry and their durability as an empirical question that is conducive to systematic study.

In turn, this area of investigation is strongly linked to that of the relationship that an industry develops and maintains with other industries and, more generally, with macro-economic and political phenomena. As our diagrams suggest, we set out to treat industrial issues as 'total social facts' which can be studied only by identifying the mechanisms through which this totality is made to fit together. This means that macro phenomena, such as exchange rate fluctuations or WTO-provoked trade barrier removal, can rarely be treated as the direct cause of industrial change. Rather, collective action (which takes the form of either economic transactions or political work, see *infra*.) is always the mediation through which specific translations of macro influences take place. In order to conduct research into this process of translation, IRs need to be understood as structuring these mediations and the way macro-economic, political or legal issues are diffracted. Political work here concerns the efforts made to define issues as industry-specific, or not, in order to obtain either their extraction from, or their submission to, trans-industry pressures.

Research into this issue area – and more generally into the dual economic and political nature of the forms of industrial organization we seek to study – brings us back to the problematics of institutionalization. In order to transform the latter into operationalizable questions for empirical research, it is important first to accept that the dynamics of any configuration of industrial organization can be studied through investigating the links between processes of institutionalization and deinstitutionalization. The dialectic between these processes structures each IR and causes either their reproduction or their change. According to the way each IR or the linkages between them are redefined, a restructuring of an industry can take place which can even result in 'decoupling' it from its sector because the latter is no longer central for the firms within it. Be they predominately deinstitutionalizing or reinstitutionalizing, the dynamics of reproducing or changing the link between an industry and its sector entails political work. What needs underlining here is that there are two reasons why one cannot consider there is a world of firms that are structured by technological, productive or economic 'necessities' on the one hand (to be studied by economists) and a world of public intervention and legislation on the other (the subject of political scientists). Instead the politics of industry has two interdependent parts that should be of major interest to both disciplines:

1. Well before public action intervenes, relations between the actors of an industry are fundamentally political because of the unequal access to processes where 'problems' and cognitive frameworks are defined, processes which in turn shape the 'functional' issues that each IR regulates.
2. When one does analyse public action within specific industries, one soon discovers it involves reasoning, anticipation and transactional issues which all contain powering. Indeed, as we set out below, the definition of such issues is always a political process.

1.2. The regulation of industries as political work

Within French political sociology, the term 'political work' was coined around 15 years ago (Briquet, 1994; Lagroye, 1994). However, thus far it has been used only metaphorically and never to study the politics of industry. When transposing 'political work' to this field of research, one must first widen the spectrum of actors studied because here 'political' is not an adjective that applies only to practitioners who are elected to or work for public bodies. Instead, as we have underlined elsewhere (Jullien and Smith, 2008a: 6), moving away from restrictive definitions of politics leads one to conceptualizing a range of actors within industry as political for two reasons:

1. both upstream and downstream of formal political decisions exist actors (private companies, trades unions, bureaucracies, consumers associations, etc.) which are all engaged in a political struggle made up of both power relations and systems of justification and/or legitimation.
2. in parallel with this interactive game, each of these actors is led to position itself publicly and organise forms of internal deliberation through which it can set and strive for objectives that are considered both realistic and legitimate.

Consequently, we seek here to conceptualize political work around two phenomena which, in practice, are inextricably linked. This work is political first because it entails a series of practices undertaken in order to develop and manage interdependencies between private, collective and public actors (Section 1.2.1). Such work is also political because it involves debates over the values used to set goals for and justify collective and public action within any industry (Section 1.2.2).

1.2.1. Interdependence, competition and co-operation

At least within the regulation of industries, political work is seldom solitary. On the contrary, both upstream and downstream of formal decisions (e.g. seeking a derogation from the EU's competition policy), political work takes place through and across a range of configurations of actors who compete to construct alliances – *political enterprises* – that are capable of winning the negotiations they are involved in. Turning to Figure 1.3, it must be stressed that 'interdependence' rarely means harmonious co-ordination. Instead, it entails a range of relations which can range from violent conflict to seamless co-operation. In order to grasp the activity that lies at the heart of attempts to construct such alliances at local, national, European and global levels, one must first distinguish between two types of interdependence that every industry contains.

The first concerns the *industrial communities* which most often constitute the daily negotiating sites within which the collective and public dimensions of an industry's regulation occur. Made up of representatives of public bodies, interest groups, trades unions and large companies, many of these communities of actors have been studied in great depth by specialists of public policy-making (Marsh and Rhodes, 1992). The

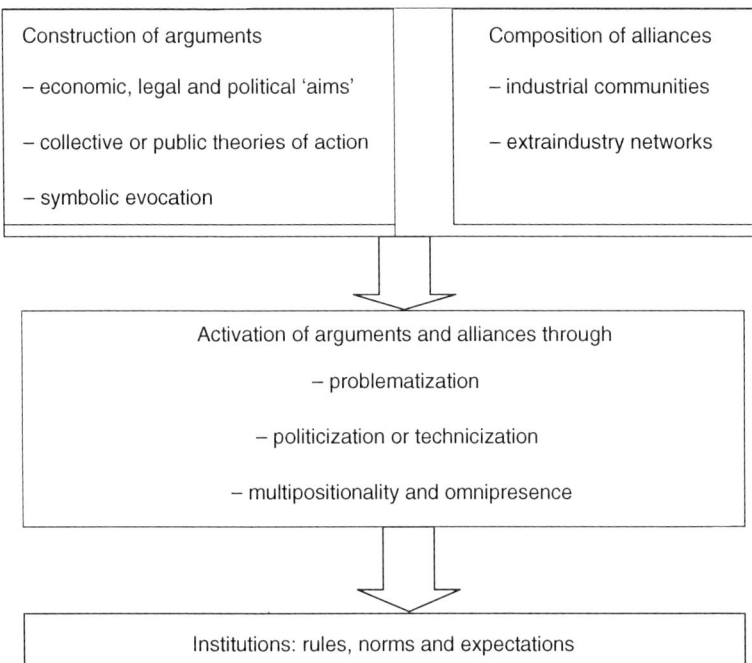

Figure 1.3 A framework for the analysis of political work within the regulation of industries

only amendment we make to such uses of the concept of policy communities is to underline that one cannot be certain that either public policy-making or public authorities lie at the centre of industrial communities. By avoiding such a starting point, research is better positioned to progressively discover the substantive issues, the membership and the hierarchy of each community through examining how each of an industry's IRs are regulated, as well as how all four of the latter are made to fit together.

The second type of interdependence found within the regulation of any industry is generally less constant than that of sectoral communities but every bit is important. It concerns controversies which extend beyond the frontiers of one single industry, such as employment rights and tax policies. Being able to act outside one's own industry by mobilizing *extraindustry networks* constitutes a major political resource for private, collective and public actors. Indeed, the 'multipositionality' of actors obtained through their accumulation of professional or public offices merits much detailed analysis because the regulation of contemporary industries is generally multi-site (regional 'interprofessions', national professions, States, the EU, WTO, etc.). The polycentric nature of industrial regulation thus heightens the competitive advantages of developing a capacity to intervene simultaneously in several sites with the ambition of becoming 'omnipresent'.

In summary, we consider that the competitive and reticular dimension of political work within industries is ubiquitous because it is present at the scale of local, national, European and global regulation. Of course, the constraints and opportunities which set limits upon the construction of alliances vary from one industry and one scale of politics to another. However, the need to seek and shore up these alliances always involves identifiable processes which research can compare between industries, temporally and geographically.

1.2.2. The political construction of industrial goals: Judgement, rationalization, legitimization

The interdependencies, and therefore the power relations, found within the configurations of actors who regulate industries clearly constitute an essential part of their political content. However, detailed study of political work in industry cannot restrict itself to this question. In order to bring about change within any of the four IRs which structure its regulation, latent relational resources need to be activated by converting them in a manner that is considered 'legitimate' (Lagroye, 2003a and b). It then follows that forms of argumentation which look to define an industrial issue as justifying collective or public action take on their importance. From an analytical point of view, this has two consequences.

The first is the necessity of taking seriously the public and private discourses of professional and public actors as an integral component of the interdependencies and competitions outlined above. Discourse is obviously a key means through which actors seek to change or to consolidate an IR. A cursory examination of the specialized press of any industry is enough to uncover the range of political uses made of the diagnoses of its disfunctionings and of the antidotes proposed in order to 'solve' them. Overflowing with diagnoses, aims and action theories that are often presented as simple 'legal' or 'economic' 'facts', these analyses also invoke values and symbols which all feed into the political content of the discourse that circulates within an industry (Muller, 1995). Indeed, if the political content of discourse is often dissimulated or downplayed, it can also enable certain actors to present themselves 'above' an industry's power relations. In so doing they seek to situate their argumentation outside direct confrontations with their respective opponents which might entail excessive political risk.

The second consequence of a perspective on political work centred upon the discourse of actors within an industry is that it clearly takes analysis away from the reasoning and concepts of 'rational choice' theory. As institutionalist or 'convention'-based approaches to economics have highlighted, controversies within industries are never simply about neutral calculations and evaluations of 'efficiency' (Kandil, 1998). On the contrary, debates of this nature are invariably marked by confrontations over the very ends of collective and public action, as well as over the 'best' forms of collective and public organization for defining and implementing them. Indeed, research needs to grasp the 'rationality', the logic of action and the reflexivity of each of the actors involved in the regulation of an industry, as well as the uncertainties and the dilemmas that the industry as a whole contains. In short, how and why each actor defines and gives meaning to their actions are precisely what make them political.

In summary, political work within any industry entails

- attempting to influence the regulation of the industry as a whole, and therefore each of the four IRs it contains, by formulating team- and alliance-building strategies which contain intra-organizational meaning;
- seeking to make this meaning shared in a durable way by investing in inter-organizational relations which construct not only interdependencies that are favourable, but also winning political enterprises.

Defined in this way, political work can and should be conceived of as THE cause of the regulation of industries.

2. Political work as a framework for causal analysis

In order to validate our overarching claim that political work is the cause of the regulation of industries, it is important to undertake in-depth study of two processes during which the reticular composition of alliances and the political construction of 'economic reality' take place: the transformation of industrial issues into collective and public 'problems' (Section 2.1) and their politicization (Section 2.2). Through structuring empirical analysis of the regulation of industries, analysis of this two-sided process enables research to develop precise explanations of what structures and orientates the political work they engender.

2.1. The problematization of 'challenges' for the regulation of industry

Contrary to functionalist theory, 'industrial difficulties' do not arise spontaneously from social conflict or technological innovation and then automatically or mechanically become objects of collective or public intervention. In reality, an industrial difficulty engenders such action only through undergoing a process of *problematization*. In order to study this process, it is useful to distinguish between different stages of a form of political work which defines, institutionalizes and legitimizes industrial controversies.

On a day-to-day basis, companies work within sets of 'conditions' which include transport costs, health and safety law, employment and tax law, and so on. As long as representatives of these companies do not seek to change these conditions they remain 'flat' and unproblematized (Kingdon, 1984). From the perspective of analysis in terms of IRs, in such circumstances production, finance, purchasing and commerce are subjects which actors within companies engage with by adopting a logic of action that is essentially mono-organizational and market transaction–centred. However, as soon as such actors seek to modify their conditions, they attempt to transform them into 'problems' of three types:

1. *Collective problems* emerge whenever their definition is shared by an inter-organizational grouping of actors who can claim to be representative of their industry and/or their profession. Indeed, much of the regulation of industry revolves around struggles to define problems and strategies of collective action.
2. *Public problems* develop when the process of definition widens to include politicians and civil servants, who, at least in theory, are supposed to work for the public interest (Padioleau, 1982: 25). Indeed, the formulation of public problems constitutes an indispensable step in both agenda setting (Rochefort and Cobb, 1994) and the formulation of policy instruments (Lascoumes and Le Galès, 2007).
3. Finally, as we will set out in more detail below, public problems can also become *politicized problems*.

2.2. Politicization and depoliticization as strategies of legitimation

Be they collective or public, the problems which structure the organization and the regulation of an industry are never intrinsically 'political' or 'technical'. Rather either of these labels is attached to them over the course of the social interactions which give rise to their definition and regulation (Dubois and Dulong, 1999; Lagroye, 2003a). Politicization is thus a form of political work that needs to be studied from an angle that is simultaneously constructivist and relational.

A constructivist perspective is necessary because one of the fundamental aims of research into the politics of industry must be to understand the registers of legitimization and the types of dramatization used to define an issue as 'political'. Here politicization occurs when actors explicitly employ values either to transform the meaning of an issue or in order to transfer its treatment to another site of negotiation. In addition to discourse, publicization and mediatization can also be used to attain such ends. In certain cases the aim may be 'to inscribe a problem on the list of issues treated by politicians', thereby 'enrolling' them (Lagroye, 2003b: 367). In others, the aim is more generally to enable actors to 'go beyond the limits set by the sectorization' of political spaces (Lagroye, 2003b: 356).

Importantly, when studying politicization it is also just as necessary to study its apparent opposite: depoliticization. Often also called 'technicization', depoliticization is a type of political work which downplays values in favour of arguments based upon 'expertise' and 'efficiency' (Radaelli, 1999). In such instances, the actors involved in the regulation of industries frequently seek to categorize an issue as a-political in order to 'differentiate' its treatment (Arnaud and Guionnet, 2005: 18) and thereby reduce the uncertainty that surrounds the decision-making processes. Although superficially this may appear paradoxical, from an analytical point of view it is therefore vitally important to consider that strategies of legitimization based upon depoliticization are highly political.

Our constructivist definition of politicization is also relational in order to take into account the entire spectrum of actors who participate in this process. If researchers, particularly political scientists, are often tempted to think that certain actors, notably politicians, are always better positioned than others to be the 'entrepreneurs of politicization' (Arnaud and Guionnet, 2005: 17), empirical research invariably uncovers a wider range of protagonists. Indeed, it is important to underline that politicization does not take place outside the web of interdependencies which lie at the heart of the organization and regulation of an industry. On the contrary, politicization is a tool of political work which is generally deliberately deployed in order to modify the state of such dependence. Indeed, politicization is frequently employed either as a means of anchoring actors within a pre-existing sector or for providing a means for extracting themselves from the commercial and political

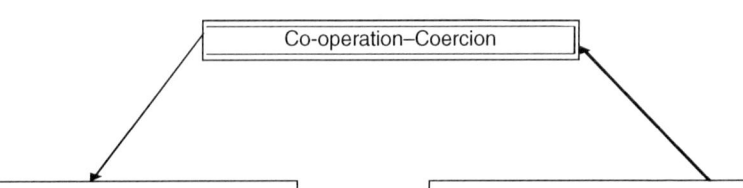

Figure 1.4 Political work and the 6 'Cs'

limits of containing one's activity within such a purely sectoral space of mediation.

In summary, political work is not only omnipresent in the regulation of industries but is its very cause. Indeed, defined in the way we have suggested, political work provides a concept upon which is built a framework for analysing politics as a highly structured configuration of processes, relations, representations and expectations which is endogenous to each industry, rather than as a random range of 'exogenous factors' which somehow make up its 'context' or 'environment'.

Moreover, it is highly important to underline that political work does not intervene solely at the moment of an industry's initial problematization. On the contrary, political work is an ongoing process at the heart of the reproduction of each industry's IRs. Figure 1.4 seeks to clarify this process by returning to the 6 'Cs' introduced in Section 1.1. Here we highlight how the political power in, and hierarchy of, an industry that plays out around the co-operation–coercion dialectic generally impacts first upon the compromise–convention dialectic before giving rise to conflicts or co-ordinations. Political work therefore goes on not only within each couple of 'Cs', but also between each of them.

3. Applying the analytical grid: A presentation of the chapters that follow

The remainder of this book applies this analytical framework to the politics of six different industries: automobile distribution, wine, pharmaceuticals, defence, fisheries and foie gras. This range of case studies has been chosen and developed for three reasons.

First, each chapter empirically illustrates *The Politics of Industry* approach using a common set of concepts, vocabulary and questions. In particular, in each case a concerted attempt is made to identify the causes of change or its absence through presenting research findings on the political work undertaken within and between the four IRs of all of the industries concerned. As will be shown, in the 1990s the Commercial IR of all six industries was considerably destabilized. However, intense political work has most often been concentrated in one or more of the other IRs. In short, our cases provide a cross-section of these concentrations of political investment which test our approach against the different angles from which regulatory change can come.

Second, each chapter seeks to validate the two claims made about globalization set out at the beginning of this introduction:

1. This phenomenon effects industries and political systems in very different ways. Consequently, globalization is more a vector of the renewal of diversity than a force for generalized convergence.
2. Analysis in terms of 'path dependency' and 'institutional constraints' provides insufficient explanation of this trend.

Third, our selection of case studies will show instead that political work is the cause of both the reproduction and the change of each industry's IO. In so doing, and in every case except that of defence, it will be shown that different parts of the politics of each industry now possess decision-making arenas which have been institutionalized beyond the boundaries of the state (e.g. the EU, the WTO). Nonetheless, this does not necessarily mean that the state has become 'hollow' (Rhodes, 1996) or meaningless to the actors involved in the regulation of industry. On the contrary, states, and in some cases sub-states, remain pertinent, albeit often partial, components of each industry's institutional order. In short, our range of case studies enables us to apply our analytical approach to the multi-arena configurations of actors, rules and processes which today structure the regulation of virtually every industry (Carter and Smith, 2008).

Centred upon the European car-retailing industry, Chapter 2 retraces the political work that has been carried out within its institutional order over the last 15 years. In so doing, Bernard Jullien shows that political work is much more than just the lobbying deployed by large companies in order to obtain the regulations or policy measures which best suits them. Whilst this lobbying has indeed taken place, thus constituting one aspect of political work, the case of the car industry underlines that the negotiations undertaken within the EU's decision-making arenas also have a wider catalytic effect upon the strategy-making of all the actors involved in this industry. Indeed, this type of strategy-making is ultimately the part of political work through which the preferences and the power relations within this industry have been redefined. In more concrete terms, the key issue which emerges from this case study is how car makers have re-established their symbolic power within the car industry both by anticipating regulatory change and, subsequently, by adapting to its effects. Through applying the book's analytical framework, the chapter highlights the characteristics of the initial institutional order of this industry, the sustainability of the alternative configurations that have been proposed, and the political and economic consequences of the points of view that have emerged from each of the categories of stakeholders concerned.

Chapter 3 is devoted to the European wine industry. Like car retailing, this industry has experienced massive change over the last 20 years, change that many commentators have not hesitated to ascribe to 'globalization'. By this they generally mean that international trade in this product has increased partly as a response to reductions in tariffs and partly because multinational companies have become involved in the financing, production and selling of wines from 'the New World'. Without denying the importance of these developments, Andy Smith's account of change in the French wine industry differs from this standard narrative in three main ways. Starting from a finding that in France reinstitutionalization of the Finance and Employment IRs has occurred only at the level of the firm, his chapter first shows that causes of change in this industry's institutional order instead have their roots in political work carried out within and between its Purchase and Commercial IRs. The chapter's second point of difference with mainstream analyses of change in the wine sector concerns the linkage between these two IRs. Significant destabilization of the Commercial IR did indeed constitute the initial cause of wider change. However, it has not prompted sustained political work by collective or public actors. Instead these protagonists have concentrated their activities upon the certification rules which heavily structure the industry's organization through its Purchase IR. The chapter's third and final point of difference with standard accounts of a globalized wine industry highlights the political weakness of French merchants and public authority as compared to the strength of growers. This strength continues to be based upon the latter's omnipresence within all the four IRs which structure this industry, as well as their long-standing commitment to reproducing the policy instruments which, at least through the 1990s and by structuring the Purchase IR, provided them with high degrees of commercial and political certainty. More generally, Smith argues that the political backing given to these policy instruments also explains why the EU has yet to institutionalize a common European wine policy designed to promote innovation and market shaping rather than the protection of territorialized rents.

As Chapter 4 recounts, the institutional order of the world's pharmaceutical industry can be considered to be both highly globalized, because it contains very large multinational companies, and nationally differentiated, because of the importance of each state's regulatory and health care systems. Additionally, as Matthieu Montalban recounts, for decades this industry's Commercial IR has been based on a political compromise between two partially contradictory objectives: public health care and the competitiveness (or profitability) of operators who have undertaken intense political work in order to protect their interests. However, Montalban's chapter underlines that more recently the industry's Financial IR has been reinstitutionalized because of the increased role given to shareholder value management and the stock market. More fundamentally still, transformations in US stock market regulations have influenced the strategies of pharmaceutical companies and the political work undertaken by their respective agents. Having first presented the role played by these US regulations, change in the Financial IR and political work carried out to modify the strategies of firms, the chapter then shows how a number of European pharmaceutical companies have attempted to import some of the US regulations by undertaking a type of political work designed to increase profitability and defend competitiveness. However, the chapter also stresses that, particularly for financial analysts, the traditional representation of 'good' pharmaceutical companies has been eroded for several reasons. Consequently, today the historical compromise between health care and profitability has largely been transformed. This is the result of a process of deinstitutionalization/reinstitutionalization of the Commercial IR which has placed the pharmaceutical industry as a whole, and its dominant firms in particular, in a state of crisis.

Centred upon defence, Chapter 5 also examines the institutional order of an industry for which political work undertaken within the US has had wider ramifications. More precisely, in setting out the politico-economic history of the US defence industry since the Second World War, Sylvain Moura shows how the political work carried out by its stakeholders has influenced its regulation through their attempts to change its rules. Through examining the linkage between the Commercial and the Finance IR, the central claim made in this chapter is that the post–Cold War era has not fundamentally changed the manner through which this industry is regulated, and this despite the range of reforms introduced in the 1990s to bring about such change. Consequently, globalization in the US defence industry of today is not very different from what it was 20 years ago: export markets are still highly important to the industry but its regulation remains essentially domestic. Moura attributes this absence of change to political work undertaken within firms, the army and governmental organizations. Representatives of these bodies have used the following two arguments in order to reinforce protectionism and enhance US export capacity. First, these actors have consistently played up the idea that a race for military technology exists in order to consolidate the industry's Commercial IR. Second, they have stressed a 'need' to increase shareholder value as a means of stabilizing its Finance IR and, thereby, protect US defence firms from the uncertainties of a potentially volatile stock market.

Chapter 6 illustrates how changes in global discourses on regulation affect the political work of actors within sub-state territories in the regulation of local industry and vice versa. Exploring changes in international and EU understandings on how to regulate the supply of fisheries in a global context of diminishing fish resources, Caitríona Carter examines how actors within the Scottish fisheries industry have 'worked' to maintain and update their industry in the face of declining fish stocks. Identifying a Scottish industrial configuration with a specific set of IRs, Carter shows how, since the establishment of the EU's Common Fisheries Policy (CFP) in 1983, actors within the industry have made a constant and increasing investment in the Purchase IR. Given that fisheries is a 'common resource', the political work of catchers, and to a lesser extent processors, has been directed towards their supply of fish, regulated by the EU instruments of Total Allowable Catches (TACs) and Quotas. Significantly, political work over this supply has not been static, but has responded to shifts in international thinking, underpinned by a constant tension between conservation of planetary resources and the survival of local communities. More precisely, changed political work is identified whereby negotiations to 'increase' the supply (short-term) are being replaced by ones to 'maintain' a supply (medium-long term). Carter shows that whereas for many years the Purchase IR was thus an important driver of regulation and actor coalitions, recently new political work is occurring within the Commercial IR which centres on the re-programming of markets to sell 'sustainable fish'. This in turn has encouraged partnerships across the industry to co-ordinate their strategies in decision-making arenas of the EU. Overall, the chapter demonstrates the importance of sub-state territories not only as venues for global and EU regulation, but also as coalitions of actors who seek to influence regulation on wider stages.

The impact of sub-state territory upon the regulation of an industry is also highlighted in Chapter 7 in a case study of the foie gras industry. As Bernard Jullien and Andy Smith recount, over the last 15 years this industry has been completely transformed and is now dominated by firms from Southwest France. This development has involved change in the daily industrial and commercial practices of producers (duck rearers and finishers), processors and distributors which is most often attributed to three technological innovations (in breeding, rearing and feeding). However, this changed 'productive system' has also been stimulated and structured by the emergence of a new normative and cognitive framework – and thence an IO – for this industry. Whereas before 1990 this framework was purely national and contained few formal rules, the industry now features EU legislation regarding geographical labelling (Protected Geographical Indications, PGIs) that has had an impact upon all parts of the productive system. In constraining industrial and commercial practices, this legislation is politically controversial for at least three reasons. First, it not only divides actors within the industry itself but also gives rise to interdependencies and alliances. Second, as a derogation from EU competition law, it reflects and refracts ideological and political cleavages which lie at the heart of European integration. Third, stigmatized as 'protectionist' by the US and Australian governments, the EU's system of PGIs is currently the subject of a WTO dispute. In focusing upon the problematization and politicization of these issues, Jullien and Smith explain the recent politics of foie gras in two stages. Sparked by changes in the Purchase IR, and heavily influenced by the EU's regulation on PGIs, the first saw the institutional order displaced from one based on relatively autonomous artisans to a Taylorized order of intensified production. Five to ten years later, however, this order has been subject to deinstitutionalization and reinstitutionalization, this time caused by change that occurred first in the Commercial IR.

Finally, the book's conclusion compares and contrasts our six case studies in an effort to highlight and interpret the contributors' collective findings about the politics of industry and the role globalization has played therein. More generally, we revisit our analytical approach in order to highlight its advantages and limits as a means of providing 'signposts' for future discussions and research. Indeed, this book as a whole can, and we think should, be seen as a systematic proposition for studying industries from a viewpoint that is quite different from that generally adopted in the existing literature. Firm believers in the cumulative ethic of social science, we welcome responses which engage critically with what is proposed here and look forward to the exchanges, dialogues and opportunities for improvement this would engender.

2
European Automobile Distribution: Globalization and Incomplete Liberalization

Bernard Jullien

Introduction

The issue of globalization has a certain immediacy for actors in industries such as pharmaceuticals or defence where it has had a direct impact on both strategic and operational issues. Generally, however, industrial actors are caught up in changes which observers or analysts attribute to an expansion of political and economic space whilst they themselves – be they the regulators or the regulated – instead perceive this change occurring at the different levels at which mediation and problem-solving actually take place. Indeed, even when the economic and strategic questions posed are globalized, or are in the process of being so, such processes are hard to grasp using the category of globalization. *A fortiori*, an examination of industries which spontaneously manifest resistance to the application of the concept, without being exempt from its forces, allows us to better understand how the dialectics of globalization takes shape. The fact that globalization is not experienced directly in such industries reveals the existence of mediations between meta-tendencies and the realities of each industry's dynamics. Consequently, we hypothesize here that particularly within such industries, globalization is a political enterprise that generates competitive reactions.

It is from this perspective that we propose to examine the overall group of activities classified as automobile distribution. While it is intrinsically linked to an industry often considered emblematic of globalization – car manufacturing- the retailing and servicing of automobiles constitutes a separate, albeit fragmented, industry. Its structure may initially appear quite similar from one country to another but further examination reveals significant differences. However, in Europe in particular, the pressure for integration and harmonization has become very strong and is closely linked to the European Union's (EU)[1] political project to globalize this industry, a project within which the 'legislative intention' has primarily been to both achieve a single market for goods and services and remove barriers to entry for non-EU competitors. From the perspective of a single market for services, the associated objective is to encourage the development of international operators in an industry that has been dominated by small artisanal firms. In short, the objective here has been to encourage the emergence of larger firms which would be in a position to rationalize and modernize the sector by developing a unified strategy for the whole market of automobile distribution.

In order to analyse the emergence, adoption and implementation of this political project, this chapter applies the *Politics of Industry* approach to identify how the interaction of the four Institutionalized Relationships (IRs) structures production and competition in the European car distribution industry. Based upon several years of empirical research, first this application of our framework will be used to show how an initial Institutional Order (IO) was built, then reinforced around the concessions the EU won from various national actors (Section 1). Subsequently, we will see how, for endogenous reasons, the industry has been restructured since the middle of the 1990s. In particular, I have attempted to unpack the recent political enterprise led by agents of DG Competition to 'liberalize' this industry and its impact on the industry's dynamics (Section 2). Finally, I have used these analyses to develop more general conclusions concerning the mechanisms that underpin such dynamics and the consequences structural characteristics of the EU has had upon the way in which globalization manifests itself in the case of car distribution in Europe.

1. The automobile retail and service industry: Institutionalization by its actors legitimized by European authorities

Before examining the recent attempts to change it, the structure of the industry (Section 1.1) and the role played by EU rules (Section 1.2) will be analysed. In so doing, our framework will be used to illustrate how an exemption regime for the car industry as a whole made the Purchase IR the cornerstone of this industry, and then to present the political tools it spawned for the regulation of automobile markets.

1.1. Domination in the Institutional Order

In order to apply our framework, let us first conceptualize car retailing and servicing as an industry. Within it, manufacturers' retail networks coexist with a large number of professionals who either operate independently or are part of specialized networks involved in the business of automobile servicing, repair and the sale of second-hand cars. These two sub-sectors are interlinked and the industry is defined in such a way as to include both. Secondly, it should be noted that the most pertinent point of entry for any discussion concerning automobile distribution is the very specific Purchase IR which regulates links between a multiplicity of distributors and repair specialists to a relatively small set of automobile manufacturers. Here there is clearly a situation of very strong asymmetry in favour of the manufacturers, and a closer look at the characteristics of the traditional structure of this sector highlights some of the problems this has tended to cause (Figure 2.1) (Jullien, 2003a).

Different regions of the world have each developed their own specific pieces of legislation that allow manufacturers to control the distribution landscape, as well as its day-to-day operations and the profitability of its members, without needing to invest heavily. In reality, this asymmetry has allowed manufacturers to delegate a great deal to their distributors. This in fact has entailed a compromise in which the requirement that dealership networks submit to the whims of manufacturers in relation to the sale of new vehicles (NVs) was partially counterbalanced by the relative lack of interest of manufacturers in used-car sales and after-sales

Relationships between 6 'Cs'	Stakeholders	Businesses
Conflict–Co-ordination	Car Dealers vs Carmakers Independent repairers vs Carmakers	Dealers/Subdealers/Independent repairers
Compromise–Convention	Selectivity and exclusivity for retailing of new cars admitted Retail networks highly controlled but relatively autonomous for used vehicles and after-sales questions Value and risk sharing very unequal	Limited competition Respective roles of competitors hierarchized and well defined Independent repairers dependent upon car dealers Spare parts markets controlled by dealers Consumers segmented by the age of the vehicles owned
Cooperation–Coercion	Carmakers dominate	Car dealers dominate independent repairers

Figure 2.1 The Purchase IR in the traditional configuration of the automobile distribution industry

service, activities which were left to the dealers (Jullien, 2001). The Purchase IR was also of key importance for independent operators because of the intellectual property rights relating to the 'original spare parts' they were obliged to buy from the manufacturers' networks at high prices. This guaranteed that manufacturers would continue to profit from a significant proportion of the price charged by independent operators to clients who had, in fact, either chosen to abandon or who had never been clients of the manufacturers' networks (Jullien, 2002, 2004). This situation thus clearly constituted an instituted supply relationship for distribution actors in relation to automobile services purchased upstream in the value chain. The duality of this relationship has had two striking effects.

i) The relationship first established actors upstream of distribution and servicing, including of course automobile manufacturers, as dominant over the multiple small firms that made up the majority of the industry.
ii) Consequently, a 'conception of control' (Fligstein, 2001) emerged and a distribution of roles according to which those actors closest to those who dominated – in this case, the networks of automobile manufacturers – were positioned above those whose 'independence' moved them to the margins of the system. Network members carried out all automobile distribution and repair tasks and, for each, were supported in technical and marketing terms by their manufacturers. The independent operators, on the other hand, concentrated upon automobile repair, used-car sales or the distribution of spare parts. To do so, however, they were never entirely free of all links to the manufacturers and their networks.

As Figure 2.2 shows, the other three IRs aligned themselves with the overriding logic of the Purchase relationship. Thus the Commercial IR was instituted as a relationship between households who bought automobiles and networks of dealers, in the sense that it was envisaged and presented in this way although this was only part of the market reality. In fact, the Commercial IR linked suppliers not only with clients who sought to buy an NV but also encompassed those in need of repair services and second-hand vehicles. NV purchasers who keep their cars for a number of years were in the market for servicing and repairs and these markets were even more important to purchasers of second-hand cars. However, this major segment of industrial activity and its commercial significance were economically and politically marginalized.

	IR1 Employment IR	
	Between stakeholders	Between businesses
Conflict–Co-ordination	Small business owners vs Sales force, managers and qualified workers	Struggle to employ and keep the best sales people and mechanics
Compromise–Convention	Qualification, know-how, product-based co-ordination	Top-down hierarchy: manufacturer-owned outlets, dealerships, agents, garages
Cooperation–Coercition	Legitimate domination of the small business owner Desire to open own business	Labour protection – Collective bargaining agreements vs Delegation and advancement from independence
	IR3 Finance-control IR	
	Between stakeholders	Between businesses
Conflict–Co-ordination	Families and banks who are captives of the manufacturers vs Small business owners	Access to finance = access to retail locations
Compromise–Convention	Cash Goodwill of manufacturers, suppliers and sales force	Successful businesses vs Those in difficulty Reputation, external signs
Cooperation–Coercion	Manipulation of margins, open book vs Independence	Hierarchy based on inventory and the capacity to offer credit
	IR4 Commercial IR	
	Between stakeholders	Between businesses
Conflict–Co-ordination	Automobile sellers vs Buyers Repair specialists vs Users	Those who sell and others Those who are honest and/or long established and the others
Compromise–Convention	Representing the make Service relationship, information asymmetries, trust (or mistrust)	Makes, products Reputation, brand recognition, length of market presence Competence, honesty
Cooperation–Coercion	Client as purchaser in the symbolic system vs Client as user in the everyday system	Hierarchy based on the level of proximity and/or distance from the NV sale

Figure 2.2 Dominated IRs in the traditional configuration of the automobile services sector

In practice, the activities involved have remained small-scale and far removed from the managerial norms and marketing techniques that have been adopted in other service activities. In this context, many clients were aware that the dealership networks were targeted mainly – if not entirely – at NV purchasers. Consumers who were not NV buyers did not use these networks and those who did initially frequent them as purchasers tended to stop doing so as their cars aged and they themselves became transformed from purchasers into users (Jullien, 2003). In addition, policy-makers considered that the particular nature of the automobile requires that its retailers be obliged to deliver 'associated services' (Telser, 1960) covering product information, servicing, repair and guarantee of spare parts.

The small scale of firms involved in the industry outside of the manufacturers' dealership networks has had clear implications for both management practices and workforce relationships, thereby further enhancing the manufacturer-dominant IO and 'conception of control' within the competitive landscape. The latter was made up of a myriad of small firms, among whom the 'least small' were those dealers who represented makes of car and sold their respective vehicles. These firms were dominated contractually and effectively by the manufacturers (IR 2). They, in turn, dominated the other group of representatives of makes comprised of agents. Agents were contractually linked to dealers and were responsible for selling a certain number of vehicles for them and for the service and repair of vehicles of their make within the dealer's territory. Dealers also dominated independent repair outlets who needed to source spare parts from them. The landscape was thus clearly structured with a functional and symbolic distribution of roles. Within this economic and social structure, vehicles moved from one category of operators to another as they aged and moved down the social pyramid via the used-car market.

Figure 2.2 outlines in more detail the dual nature of each of the other IRs and allows us to refine analysis of the industry's traditional conception of control. It specifies the institutional complementarities (Amable, 2003) and highlights the institutional coherence of the differentiated forms of access to resources. We can thus identify the 'dominant values' of the industry which were associated with an ideal version of the good professional who has succeeded in the sector. At the other extreme of the social hierarchy, among those actors who were dominated, we can also see the counter-example that typifies the rejection of a set of values which serve to underline its inferiority. In essence, the system was based on the Purchase IR because it was structured around the interests of manufacturers who – both individually and collectively – sought to co-ordinate their downstream value chains. In this respect, it is worth noting that the sector was always presented as that of 'vehicle' distribution, that this structured the dominant conception of control and then influenced the other IRs. Access to key resources, for example, was easier to obtain for operators who were close to manufacturers and less favourable for those who did not sell NVs or spare parts. In the same way, the most highly regarded professional path was one whereby an apprentice qualified as a craftsperson and then went on to set up their own business and become a franchised agent of a dealership.

As an agent, they might succeed in achieving a high-enough level of sales to be given the opportunity to open their own dealership. Their name was thus associated with a given automobile make in their locality. At the other extreme, of course, losing a dealership was seen as synonymous with professional decline. Success in the world of car distribution was thus long defined by the level of 'servitude' of each member to the interests of the dominant group made up of manufacturers. Above all, becoming the exclusive representative of a make for a particular territory was the way to generate wealth throughout the long years of the growth of automobile ownership. This status also afforded a certain amount of power over the attributed territory to the head of a network of agents with the exclusive right to supply spare parts to all repair operators.

Participants in this system who were most removed from the heart of the dominant logic and who had little chance of improving their relative position created a form of 'counter culture' (Jullien, 2007). Together they developed a symbolic representation of car dealers that highlighted the exorbitant prices they charged to support the 'useless luxury of their show rooms' and the 'fat salaries' of their sales forces. Implicitly they made reference to the period of black markets during and after the last war and the images that persisted of profiteering from 'the misery of poor, honest people' (Loubet, 1995). Those excluded from the system, both professionals and clients, recognized this representation as pertinent. Clients saw the alternative proposed as an opportunity to possess a car and have it serviced without having to frequent 'that world'. For professionals working in servicing, what was attractive was the idea of keeping contact with the manufacturers' networks to a minimum and spending more time concentrating on their clients' vehicles than on the outward appearance of their garages and the illusion of a quality of service.

This counterculture was not entirely absent amongst agents (also known as the secondary network) and it could also be found to some degree in the workshops of dealers and among dealers themselves. It was mobilized to complain about marketing and the requirements of manufacturers and their 'lack of economic and commercial realism'. To an extent, the porosity of the two worlds guaranteed that the established order would persist with its clear allocation of roles and values. It reflected the differentiation of access to the automobile that existed but neither clients nor professionals were so far removed from other groups that they were not aware of each other. Fordist income distributions and

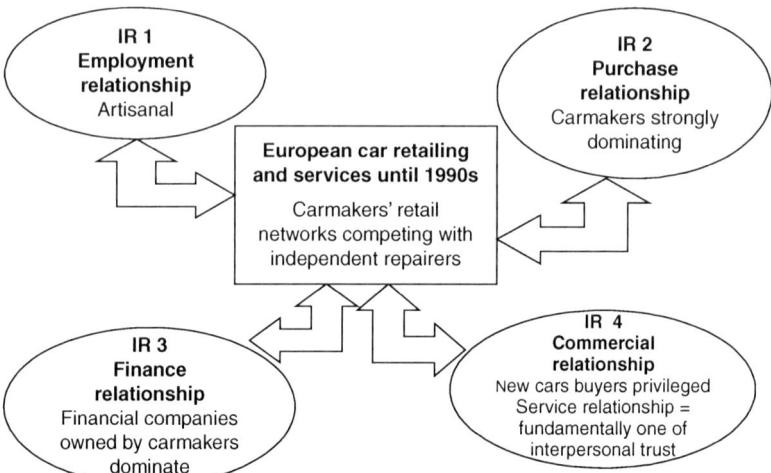

Figure 2.3 The European automobile distribution and services industry in the early 1990s

their dynamics (Lipietz, 1995) meant that households could imagine one day becoming an NV purchaser. The expansion of the automobile market and the arrival of foreign manufacturers linked to the Common Market in the 1960s and 1970s meant that professionals had a range of possibilities to become agents or dealers within a manufacturer's network. In the early 1990s the industry was thus structured as outlined in Figure 2.3.

1.2. 'Exemption' as legal validation of the domination of manufacturers through the Purchase IR

The structure of the industry as it was presented in the preceding section can be explained in part by the legal framework that applied to it. On the other hand, it could be argued that the specific laws for this industry served both to legally endorse the dominant position of manufacturers and to protect the weaker parties from potential abuse. In reality, from the perspective of economic law, the manner in which the distribution of new cars and spare parts was organized corresponded to what are known as 'vertical restraints'. This means that the manufacturer operated a form of quasi-integration of downstream activities within which it was possible to restrict access to downstream activities to operators of its choosing without needing to make the investments that would normally be necessary. For operators who were not chosen by the manufacturer this meant that the manufacturer could refuse to sell to them for the purposes of resale and that this practice was not considered illegal. For this to be legally possible in the EU, the manufacturer needed to insert its distribution into a franchising regime that was covered by a specific Community regulation. In the case of automobile distribution, however, the whole car sector was granted a specific 'block exemption'.

It is worth considering how and why such a specific block exemption was adopted and considered legitimate in the EU until the end of the 1990s. There is an interesting contrast between the attitude of the EEC in the 1960s when the block exemption was granted and that which prevailed at the beginning of the 1990s when the question was re-examined. From the perspective of DG Competition, the special treatment afforded to the sector of automobile distribution with regard to EU competition law was initially seen as legitimate, and almost normal. It gradually became a problem for both the sector itself as well as the automobile industry overall and its access to global competition. Before explaining this development as part of the overall evolution of the industry, I will first examine how competition policy was initially problematized and how this intervened in the industry's operations. This will allow us to understand how the block exemption subsequently came to cause tensions that were linked to this interaction between legislation and industry, and to wider political and ideological developments that were taking place during the same time period.

Until the end of the 1990s, car manufacturers obtained permission from the Commission to organize the distribution of their vehicles and spare parts in a unique way. This meant they could continue to benefit from 'vertically restrictive practices' by obtaining a specific derogation from competition policy as defined in Article 81 of the Treaty of Rome. More precisely the entire industry was accorded a 'block exemption' that applied to all producers and distributors and that was, in fact, both selective and exclusive.

It was mainly 'selectivity' that interested manufacturers as it allowed them

- to refuse to sell to any distributor that they had not chosen;
- to ensure that their sales outlets conformed to a certain number of norms considered essential to represent the make and, above all, to oblige their dealers to sell their entire range, to maintain guaranteed levels of inventory for spare parts and to offer service and repair activities.

Meanwhile, however, 'exclusivity' also allowed manufacturers to require dealers to dedicate their outlets to their make and, in return, manufacturers offered a 'territory' over which the dealer had a monopoly, perhaps in association with a certain number of agents who were contractually tied to the dealer. Competition between brands was thus limited and, in theory, this ensured that market prices did not diverge from 'catalogue prices'. The aim was to protect the specific investments made by dealers to meet the requirements of their manufacturers.

These principles of selective and, to a lesser degree, exclusive distribution emerged initially in the 1910s in the United States and were transferred to other markets in a fairly homogenous way. In the postwar years, Europe experienced the rapid market expansion of a smaller number of makes of car and, in turn, adopted these principles. European competition policy in this area was thus essentially one of accepting the status quo. To justify doing so within an acceptable doctrine, reference was made to an abundant economic literature from America that had been attempting to show that restrictive vertical practices in car distribution systems were coherent with principles of efficiency and thus legitimized the institutionalization of the Purchase IR described in Figure 2.1 (Jullien, 2005a). As Ramirez has shown, however, European debate on this question between 1962 and 1990 was not purely concerned with competition policy. Rather the automobile sector, along with many others, was dealt with in Europe in a way that served the development of an industrial policy that promoted the strategic interests of 'national champions' (Ramirez, 2006). From this point of view, certain structural traits of the European IO allow one to understand why 'vertical restraints' were seen as more vital for European manufacturers than for those from elsewhere. They also enable one to grasp how this question was linked to that of the common market (and subsequently the single market), on the one hand, and to the rising power of Japanese manufacturers in Europe, on the other.

In the 1960s, there were significant structural differences between the American market with its three manufacturers and the European market, in which over 12 manufacturers were present. In the latter continent, each of the manufacturers and their dealers were in a more fragile situation. In addition, in the 1960 and 1970s, European manufacturers sought to expand beyond the policy of single models to become generalist suppliers as General Motors had done in the United States in the 1920s. Both these factors enhanced the perceived need of manufacturers to benefit from selective and exclusive distribution. One important advantage of this form of distribution was that the sector was spared the negative consequences of a price war. Another was the support it afforded manufacturers in the management of their product policy. As manufacturers increasingly added to their ranges and renewed them more frequently, they were faced with higher levels of uncertainty with regard to the future revenues with which they would have to meet the heavy investment levels necessary to design and manufacture new models. Selective and exclusive distribution allowed manufacturers to impose or 'push' their products onto the network, even when sufficient levels of demand had not yet been expressed by the final consumer. European manufacturers saw the adoption of this economic model as vital[2]. The economics of diversification and innovation in the automobile industry were such that an exclusive and selective distribution network was considered to be required which would not be in a position to refuse to sell models in the range that were poor performers. This, of course, was no guarantee for manufacturers against poor market performance for certain models, but it reduced uncertainty and allowed them to even out the peaks and troughs of their performance cycle. From the perspective of dealers, it was mostly true that their status as 'shock absorbers' for variations in demand was not advantageous. However, in Europe the level of sales for each dealer was relatively low so they preferred to have exclusivity for their territory. Anxious to ensure that firms such as Fiat, Renault, Volkswagen, Volvo and BLMC managed to become generalist suppliers, and to avoid handing the European market over to American manufacturers, the European Commission's DG Competition accepted these arguments for the block exemption.

While this was the overriding thrust of the decision, there were other contextual elements in Europe in the 1960s that made automobile distribution a particularly noteworthy industry. Having signed the Treaty of Rome, attention in Europe was focused on the potentially devastating effects of opening borders and allowing inter-make competition in each of the markets within which national champions dominated. The period during which the opening of markets was being prepared for was one in which intense negotiations in relation to the automobile industry and the strategic and operational activities of manufacturers simultaneously contributed to defining the political and economic conditions for the emergence of the common market. In this context, the question of selective and exclusive distribution was seen as slowing down market liberalization because a key element to gaining access to new markets was the difficult and costly development of an exclusive network. This afforded pre-EEC markets a certain inertia and was, in fact, reassuring to both manufacturers and dealers. In addition, traditional forms of distribution structure meant that price wars were avoided and manufacturers and dealers continued to enjoy good margins. From this point of view, manufacturers were very anxious not to have to harmonize prices between different national contexts. Being in a position in which they could oblige dealers of their make of car to buy only directly from them was a guarantee that dealers would not be in a position to re-import vehicles from other parts of Europe where prices were lower. T. Pardi has shown that this element of negotiations was particularly significant in the British case, where consensus to defend this model remained in place only as long as there was a national champion whose interests were being defended (Pardi, 2006).

In 1985 and, to a lesser degree, in 1995, concerns were raised about protecting the European automobile industry against the growing power of Japanese manufacturers that had already made a significant impact in the United States. More precisely, a combination of import quotas and the necessity to have a selective and exclusive dealer network served to restrict the penetration of European markets by Toyota, Nissan, Honda and Mazda. It was clearly difficult for these companies to attract distributors and to impose conditions on their activities when they knew they would not be able to achieve a market share of more than 1 or 2%. As there were no cars from these makes already in circulation, potential dealers would also have very limited after-sales service. The profile of dealers who did take up this challenge thus tended to be that of independent multi-make repair shops that also happened to sell some Japanese cars. The only other solution would have been to allow the dealers for established makes to become multi-make. Dealers for manufacturers such as Volkswagen, Peugeot or Fiat could thus have been persuaded to add a new, relatively marginal activity to their business by distributing Japanese makes in addition to their main make. The 1985 EU regulation, however, limited this possibility by requiring dealers to dedicate themselves to a single car manufacturer. Thus, the situation in Europe was unlike that of the United States, where there were no quotas and where dealers of American makes were also able to represent Japanese makes at the same time. In Europe, the dealer network for Japanese manufacturers therefore grew slowly and, even after the disappearance of quotas, remained relatively limited in its penetration until 2000 (Jullien, 2007).

Overall, research on the evolution of the block exemption over time shows that the construction of the common market in the automobile sector was partly facilitated by efforts made to permit a cartel to dominate supply and to assert collective control over prices. This was the political and economic landscape in which the block exemption was allowed to persist. In addition, up until the 1990s, the very 'pragmatic' approach adopted to competition policy in general reflected a European standpoint, demanded with some success by numerous institutional and industrial actors, in which a European industrial policy played a structural role (Ramirez, 2006). In this context, the car manufacturers managed to avoid problematization of the issue of car distribution taking place: this industry did not become visible on its own and its law was fundamentally defined only in reference to industrial questions which were framed in such a way as to consider that cars were a major productive industry for the EU's member states (and, for the largest of these in particular, who, it should be added, all happened to be countries where manufacturing of cars took place). Small wonder then that the issue of car distribution and services at this time was never politicized. Instead, it was framed as a technical annex of the problem of industrial policy.

The system of legitimization on which the rules dictated by the EC were based around the Purchase IR shows how the overall regulatory, fiscal and administrative edifice consecrated or enhanced the power of manufacturers through an industry-specific process of co-defined public action. It is as if it had been decided that automobile manufacturers were best positioned to define themselves a framework in order to guarantee their own development along with protecting the interests of their clients. Thus, when one examines the economic and contractual relationships linking manufacturers to their distributors in the framework that dominated until the 2000s, it is clear that they were profoundly asymmetrical and that they ensured that the distributors were given a submissive role. The Purchase IR was a reflection of the ways in which the manufacturers managed to have their commercial work done by the group of legally independent firms who made up their distribution network. Legal support for this position was thus a form of upstream recognition of the omnipresence and omnipotence of manufacturers that became even more evident downstream. The law and the position it afforded to exclusivity and the requirements that manufacturers could impose on their representatives completed the tool kit of economic pressure available to manufacturers. In addition, by recognizing the existence of a 'natural link' between sales and after-sales service, the law positioned the contractual framework designed by the manufacturer in the name of the general interest (e.g. road safety) and made it appear as the only viable alternative. Subsequently, as long as the relationship lasted, it generated a 'convention of effort' (Salais, 1994) between firms that regulated the subordination of distributors. However, for reasons related both to the evolution of the automobile distribution industry and to the institutional, political and general economic context, the manner in which the supply relationship was treated changed quite radically after 1995. In Europe, this led to a questioning of the legal situation that supported the order I have just described, as well as challenges to the IO itself, that is the very economic and political organization of the industry.

2. The European Union and automobile distribution: Industry reforms perceived as arms against globalization

Challenges to this industry's IO began with market disruption during the 1990s. Difficulties faced by car manufacturers increasingly undermined the foundations of this order and generated the strategic prevarications of different actors, which typifies the phenomenon of de-institutionalization. Described more fully elsewhere (Jullien, 2002, 2006b), this process is briefly presented in Section 2.1 to explain the context within which, over the last 15 years, the EU has chosen to revise its regulatory approach to the industry. Over this period, issues have been reproblematized and a very different political treatment of the industry to what had previously been the case has emerged (Section 2.2).

2.1. De-institutionalization of the traditional order

What is notable about change as regards the traditional order is the relative marginalization of the manufacturers and their networks within the industry. Indeed, the major strategic innovations occurred outside their sphere of influence because they were unleashed by newcomers in search of market share. In this context, the innovations subsequently introduced by the manufacturers were essentially counteroffensive moves.

To understand what went on, it is important to grasp that the order explained above involved a general phenomenon of 'cross subsidization' of vehicle sales by after-sales services. This conformed to the manufacturers' desire to 'push metal' and was a fundamental feature of dealerships which were heavily dependent on after-sales service and sales of spare parts to guarantee their survival. This provided the framework within which the evolutions of the last 20 years need to be placed. In essence, it was this 'deformation' of the structure of prices that created the market opportunity for new entrants. New 'fast fitters' appeared offering alternatives to automobile users who considered themselves badly treated by the dealership networks of manufacturers.

Instead, these newcomers offered competitive pricing that avoided the need to sell NVs. From the point of view of manufacturers and their networks a growing proportion of household spending on automobiles and a growing number of households thus exited the market. They generally acquired older used cars and went to independent operators, specialists and auto centres for after-sales services, thus escaping from the practices whereby NV buyers were being subsidized by other users.

Although it is difficult to evaluate the full extent of this phenomenon, it is possible to say that the tendency became more marked for a number of reasons.

- The relative prices of NVs tended to increase more as exacerbated levels of competition led to a race for differentiation and diversification which could not have been achieved at constant costs.
- Income inequalities have tended to increase, further limiting access to NVs to a shrinking number of households.
- The choice of used cars on offer has grown and their quality has improved as NV buyers sell their vehicles more quickly and as the vehicles themselves increase in reliability and are heavily guaranteed.
- The alternatives to what was on offer from manufacturers in terms of spare parts and after-sales services, as well as credit and guarantees, have become structured and more professional.

In short, this has been the general trend underlying the major initiatives for change. Overall, the increasing difficulty that manufacturers have faced to sell NVs has led to a more complex range of products in terms of the variety on offer and the speed of introduction of new models. In addition, the shrinking of the 'business to consumers' (B2C) client base and the growing importance of the 'business to business' (B2B) sales has put pressure on profit margins and led to price cuts and promotions at all levels of the network. As a result, after-sales service and spare parts have become increasingly important to save the dealer networks and to generate opportunities for profits for the manufacturers' groups themselves.

During the same time period, the manufacturers' dealership networks have tended to lose market share to new entrants in market segments for profitable automobile parts that had to be replaced regularly with relatively simple operations. In reaction, the manufacturers sought to develop competitive offers by creating their own 'rapid service' centres and a second range of spare parts for older models of their vehicles. They also took steps to 'consolidate' their networks to control them better and attempt to take advantage of economies of scale. They developed labels for used-car sales and tried to develop packages that included new-car sales and servicing, extended guarantees, a guaranteed repurchase price, financing and often insurance. Clearly, from the point of view of the manufacturer, these moves were an attempt to avoid becoming marginalized and to maintain access for themselves and their networks to a significant part of consumer spending on automobiles.

Analysing this change through the *Politics of Industry* framework highlights significant transformations in the fundamental IR; the Purchase IR (Figure 2.4). In effect, the manufacturers' reign over the entire industry has been undermined by the growth of alternative suppliers. Through their presence alone, as well as through the innovations they offered, the growing list of alternative suppliers reinforced all suppliers of services that were competitive with those offered by the dealership networks of manufacturers. Manufacturers reacted by strongly reinforcing their control over their networks and by expanding this control to cover all their activities. The areas of used-car sales and after-sales service, for example, had tended to be relatively broadly delegated downstream and these activities gradually became regulated by labels, standards and norms. As a result, it became very difficult for dealership networks to take advantage of the opportunities that were now available from the new alternative suppliers. At the same time, 'independent suppliers' became less independent as they became members of franchised networks that offered clients and professionals alternatives to the solutions on offer from manufacturers.

This de-institutionalization of the industry's fundamental IR led to a gradual questioning of the manner in which the other IRs were defined (Figure 2.5). In addition, some of these relationships were also undergoing their own evolutions. The increasing amount of electronics inNVs, for example, had an impact on the structure of qualifications for labour involved in after-sales servicing. It also altered the types of breakdown and the nature of demand for after-sales service. Nonetheless, it is primarily the interplay of the offensive moves of new entrants and the counteroffensive reactions of the manufacturers which explains the de-institutionalization/re-institutionalization dynamics in the Purchase IR that have had an impact on the three other IRs.

The Employment IR in many distribution firms was altered, for example, through the introduction of the classical workforce model, adopted by franchise operations such as Midas and Speedy and other car centres, in contrast to the craft-industry model that had previously dominated

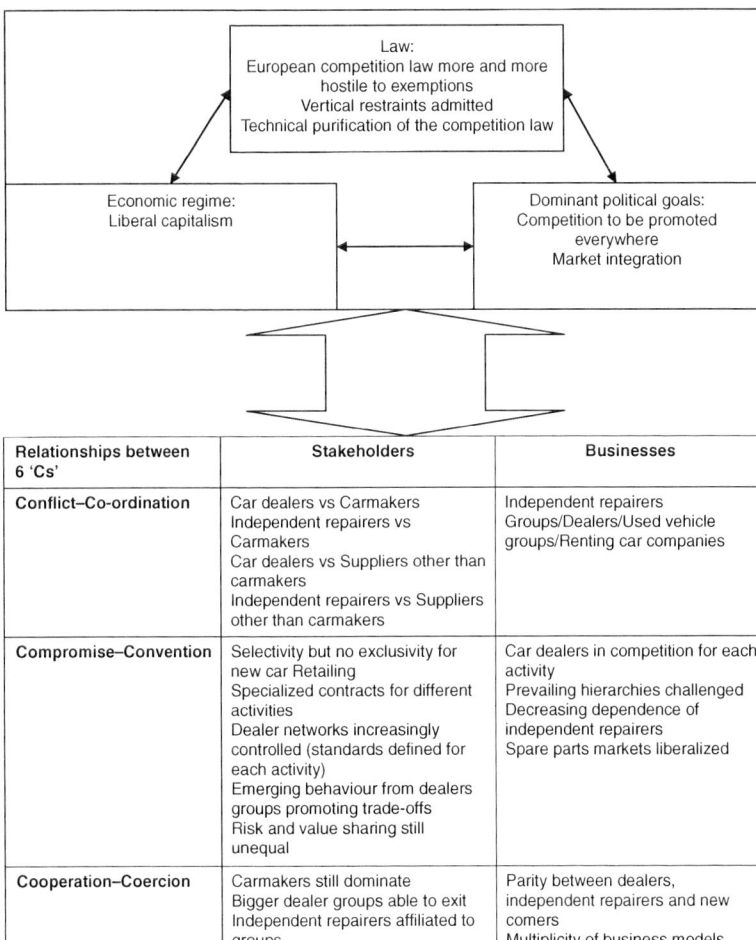

Figure 2.4 The new Purchase IR

the industry. Such companies also limited the autonomy of their personnel at all levels by creating profit centres for each site in which standardized norms were to be applied and by requiring all workers to respect standard processes and time for all work undertaken. They engaged in significant training both in reaction to the new types of vehicles and in order to ensure a level of discipline in the workplace that would guarantee homogeneity from one site to another. These new

	New IR1 or Vectors for change in IR1 Employment IR	
	Between stakeholders	Between businesses
Conflict–Co-ordination	Boss of distribution groups or manager of franchises vs Salaried workers	Struggle to employ or keep the best employees
Compromise–Convention	Dequalification – requalification Codifying of sales (scoring multiples, procedures): triangulation of the work relationship	Employment market very active and competitive with employees evaluating alternatives Turnover – labour shortage
Cooperation–Coercion	Reduced hope of owning own business Growing gap with rest of the world of work	Crisis in the two pre-existing employment models
	New IR3 or Vectors for change in IR3 Financial IR	
	Between stakeholders	Between businesses
Conflict–Co-ordination	Families, banks, manufacturer's credit arm vs Heads of groups and franchises	Race for consolidation and to recruit franchisees
Compromise–Convention	Improved control of margins Increased financing requirements (inventory, adherence to norms, property costs) Problem with financing M&A activities Cost of equipment and cautiousness of bankers	Weak profitability as both a stimulus for regrouping and a strategic problem Financial hierarchy of makes and franchises Arbitrage behaviour
Cooperation–Coercion	Manipulation of margins and maintenance at the limits of survival vs Faculty to exit	Threat of expulsion vs Hope of gains
	New IR4 or Vectors for change in IR4 Commercial IR	
	Between stakeholders	Between businesses
Conflict–Co-ordination	Multiple professionals with different levels of polyvalence vs Buyers and users with increasingly different behaviours	Bundlers – Unbundlers Manufacturers – Independants Contesting the monopoly of the client interface in B to B (rentals) and in B to C (second-hand cars)
Compromise–Convention	Rebalancing of the figures of the buyer and the user 'Marketization' of after-sales service Growth in the power of B2B Segmentation and development of product ranges	Makes, products Reputation, brand recognition, length of market presence Competence, honesty
Cooperation–Coercion	Clients of different types more capable of choosing and differentiating their usage system	Ongoing challenges of manufacturers and their makes vs reaffirmed centralization

Figure 2.5 De-institutionalization of the other three IRs

practices were the origin of the first move to destabilize the traditional IO during the 1980s and were gradually adopted by the manufacturers' dealership networks who applied them to a much broader array of services. The outcome was a vast Taylorization movement characterized by a centralisation of the definition of work content. Given the complex nature of the activity and, in particular, the multiple sites to be integrated by each operator, it is not hard to understand why these moves were not entirely successful. They did, however, manage to undermine the traditional relationship with the workforce as it became both less probable and less desirable to envisage becoming one's own boss (one of the major pillars of the craft-industry model). With salaries, hours and career paths not keeping up with practices in other sectors, the industry's attractiveness suffered and a significant gap emerged between the number of employees trained in these skills and the overall number of employees in the workforce. Employees tended to leave the industry when opportunities arose elsewhere and, therefore, competent personnel became scarce leading to a significant turnover rate.

The Financial IR has also significantly changed, in particular in more recent times. The business relationship that had been traditionally paternalistic and linked to family capitalism became one of investors who were less interested in the longevity of a garage or a dealership than in the relative profitability of each activity in each outlet. The normalization of reporting processes introduced by specialized franchises and adopted by dealerships facilitated this management logic. The technical changes required relatively heavy investments for independent operators and bankers became cautious and began to apply norms and scoring techniques that implemented the same type of logic. Finally, and above all else, automobile manufacturers promoted a huge consolidation movement in the 1990s that led to a fundamental change in the nature of their network participants. From this period on, more and more distribution groups have become multi-make and have specifically focused on the profitability of their businesses and those they wish to acquire. Nonetheless, at this time, the profitability in question was relatively low and was generally determined by the manufacturer's good will and willingness to manipulate profit margins. Modifying the balance of power would involve these groups exercising their power to renounce a contract they did not consider sufficiently profitable. Whilst this potential threat has continued to exist, it has rarely been carried out. The balance of power thus still remains largely in the hands of manufacturers who are in a position to finance investments and acquisitions via their in-house financing arms and who still determine profitability – or its lack – in the distribution business.

Finally, the Commercial IR has been considerably altered because new entrants have defined themselves in terms of the service or repair operation to be carried out independent of the vehicle in question, the manner in which it was acquired (new or used) and the other repair work that needed to be done. The market had been one in which the purchase and servicing of a vehicle was a package, dominated by the purchase and, subsequently, by the seller. The new operators entered the industry with the promise of 'unbundling' these activities. This allowed them to present the services on which they intended to build their activity as a product and not as a service as they are traditionally treated. In effect, this attributed to the user a level of importance equal to that of the buyer in the industry's quality conventions (Eymard-Duvernay, 1989) and, more importantly, equal to that of the buyer of an NV. This development eventually led manufacturers to take the satisfaction levels of their after-sales service clients into consideration within the management of their distributorship networks.

Given the breadth of markets and the variety of services associated with the sale and use of vehicles, the dynamics unleashed by all these changes led to an intensification of the division of labour within and outside the network of dealerships of makes and a growing level of professionalism exhibited by each supplier across a large range of service offerings. It became difficult for clients to position the different players given the large number of competitors not only specializing in certain operations but also covering systematically a part of what was on offer from another specialist. For the segment of clients that was primarily interested in a simple and rapid service package – rather than the lowest prices – it was seen as worthwhile to 're-simplify' what was on offer by creating packages of different services. Manufacturers were the first to position their packages in this way as they could take advantage of the polyvalence of their network and hopefully stop clients abandoning them for competitive networks. They expanded their guarantees in a costly manner and went on to offer a guaranteed repurchase price and, finally, proposed clients that they only pay the cost of usage, depreciation and servicing.

Manufacturers were not the only ones to develop such packages and, as the company car became a growing element of remuneration, they also began to feel the pressure of competition from leasing firms and fleet management companies who offered to choose on behalf of businesses among the very complex range of service suppliers that had emerged from the intensification of the division of labour. At the same time, air traffic growth and the growing number of urban dwellers who were choosing not to own a vehicle was leading to an increase in car rentals. Manufacturers found themselves selling ever greater proportions of their vehicles to these types of firms. Their networks were thus not only losing a significant volume of NV sales, but also their associated markets for servicing and repair as these purchasers played competitors off against one another to obtain the best prices for changing tyres, windscreens and other such common purchases. In relation to this attack on the NV business, the manufacturers did their utmost to develop credible alternatives. To do so, both manufacturers and their networks developed significantly different pricing policies for the same vehicles. In so doing, they added to the overall confusion in the market place as they gave out numerous, different and partly contradictory messages.

2.2. Recent renegotiations of the EU's 'block exemption'

The EU, and the European Commission's DG Competition in particular, initially began to change its approach to automobile distribution with the adoption of the regulation 1475/1995 (see Figure 2.6). Over the past ten years, however, there has been an even more clearly pronounced change in direction in relation to the previous compromise in which it had been seen as politically and economically justified to structure this industry, both in fact and in law, in a way that served the interests of European manufacturers. A certain number of 'liberalisation' measures were introduced in 1995 that revealed the doubts that were emerging in relation to the appropriateness of the derogation afforded to

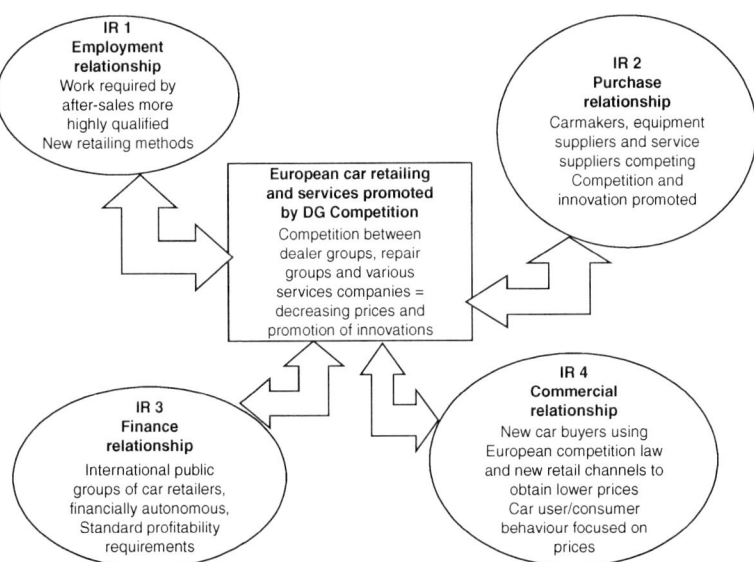

Figure 2.6 European car retailing and services promoted by DG Competition

the activities of car distribution and after-sales service and repair. These measures consisted of

i) reinforcing the ability of certain operators (brokers) to take advantage of the differences that persisted in pre-tax prices of automobiles from one European country to another in order to offer lower prices to consumers;
ii) favouring the development of multi-make dealerships by limiting the ability of manufacturers to block them;
iii) allowing repair outlets to purchase spare parts from suppliers other than manufacturers.

With the same intention in mind, the block exemption was not renewed for ten years, but only for seven, sending a clear signal to manufacturers that their behaviour was being watched and could lead DG Competition to revise its position. Given the context of a single market and a common currency, the ongoing significant price differences between member states in relation to the same version of the same model (which exceeded 30% in certain cases) led to the establishment of a permanent observation system which noted the persistence of these price discrepancies.

The then Commissioner for Competition, Mario Monti, led the renegotiation between 1999 and 2001 and it was his DG that defined the regulation 1400/2002, which has taken effect since October 2003. In this section, I will begin by recalling how he evaluated the regulation 1475/1995 and its effects and how this led to the evolution of the regulatory framework for automobile distribution (Section 2.2.1). This analysis is based on the 'Monti Report' of 2000, the current regulation and the arguments and explicative notes that appeared following its adoption. I will then set out the positioning of the different actors in the industry prior to and subsequent to the publication of the new regulation (Section 2.2.2). Finally, I will deal with how its impact has recently been evaluated and how this may evolve in relation to both future regulation and current practices in the industry (Section 2.2.3).

2.2.1. From the Monti report to regulation 1400/2002

Between 1999 and 2000, DG Competition sought to evaluate the effects of the regulation then in place and to verify that the conditions under which the sector proposed its products and services could be considered to be 'in the overall interest of the consumer'. A certain number of reports were commissioned and several phases of discussion were organized between industry actors and states. On the basis of these measures, the Monti report was produced and it was followed by another round of discussion that gave rise to the 1400/2002 regulation.

Commissioner Monti was initially quite narrowly focused on the issue of the price of new cars which were supposed to converge given the free movement of goods and the single currency. Even with directly comparable prices, however, price differences persisted from one member state to another. The manufacturers insisted that they maintained such differences to compensate for differences in taxation which precluded price homogeneity. They found it more difficult to admit that they had implicitly or explicitly decided to avoid additional competition between countries for the same make of car to add to the already-high levels of competition between makes in each country. In essence, price differences were the result of relatively classic practices of price discrimination whereby manufacturers do not charge the same price for their products in a market where their brands are preferred by consumers as they do in markets where it is their competitors' products that are preferred. Even if this allowed some actors – brokers – to develop a lucrative business and to increase pressure for convergence, this effect remained relatively marginal. The level of the price difference between markets did not appear large enough to create enough cross-border traffic to provide the incentive for automobile manufacturers to homogenize their pricing practices. However, the consumers who suffered the most from these practices were the British, who suffered from a dual disadvantage of their geographical position as an island and the fact that cars on British roads had to be altered for driving on the left. Hence, the ideological push to end the block exemption between 2000 and 2002 was heavily supported by the British government.

Commissioner Monti concluded that the EU should not just facilitate the work of brokers but permit distributors to position themselves as more independent of manufacturers so that the internationalization of vehicle distribution could also be accomplished by car dealer networks. The Commission thus adopted the notion of a 'multi-make dealership group with an international presence' as a form of efficiency to be promoted. It was also concluded that the regulation 1475/1995 had defined a specific status of distributor without which no manufacturer could legally assure the sale and after-sales service of its vehicles. According to Monti, this limited the potential for innovation of manufacturers, be they European or not, and of other current or future distribution actors. As the analysis of the reports commissioned progressed, Monti became more attentive to the arguments of the independent repair sector and of certain suppliers who were worried about the restrictions on competition in the area of after-sales service. They were particularly worried that the significant technical developments of the automobile product, such as those linked to electronics, were leading to an increase in these restrictions. Similarly, a report commissioned from an English consultancy firm, Autopolis, submitted to the Commission in 2000 was centred upon what had traditionally been called the 'natural link' between new-car sales and after-sales service. It clearly highlighted the existence of cross-subsidies, which meant that after-sales service activities in the dealer networks of manufacturers were subsidizing the sale of NVs. As they were thus benefiting from a form of rent, manufacturers had not offered and were not going to offer to their networks the same advantageous conditions that existed for vehicle sales (Jullien, 2002).

These elements were used by legislators to develop the major innovations introduced in the regulation 1400/2002. In comparison to that of 1475/1995, three significant developments were introduced.

i) Selectivity and exclusivity were no longer both possible and manufacturers had to decide to choose either of them. Given the relative importance of both options in the manufacturers' priorities, this was the equivalent of doing away with territorial exclusivity.
ii) The 'localisation clause' that permitted dealership contracts to refer to one or several explicitly designated distribution sites was abolished. Thus, all operators who were given the right to distribute the vehicles of a make could, in theory, decide to open or close sites as desired, even at a distance from the initial site.
iii) It broke the 'natural link' between sales and after-sales service and considered that the right to distribute the vehicles of a make and that of being an 'authorised repairer' with the right to carry out operations under guarantee should be negotiated and contractualized separately. It thus became possible to be a sales outlet without being involved in repair activities and vice versa.

The common aim here was, at least in theory, to introduce some freedom into a system that was considered sewn up by the manufacturers and closed to a degree that the routines in place had become part and parcel of previous regulations. Concretely, under the new regime it became possible for Internet businesses and mass retailers to consider moving into the area of new-car sales. Without having to become involved in after-sales services and without having a contractual obligation to a territory, it is now, at least on paper, feasible for groups such as Carrefour, Corte Inglese or eBay, having signed at least one dealership contract with each branded manufacturer, to be present in the market without having to ask anything else of manufacturers beyond the delivery of their vehicles. This should, in the eyes of the legislators, encourage innovation, and the principal result should be greater competition between brands, easier international penetration and price homogenization with greater efficiency overall to the benefit of the consumer. Monti is quoted as saying in relation to the regulatory innovations that they had placed the consumer 'in the driver's seat' of the European car distribution system.

From a different perspective, in relation to spare parts and after-sales service, the new regulation tried to ensure that the consumer would benefit from continued and, if possible, enhanced competition which the technological evolutions of car products was threatening to reduce.

i) In relation to spare parts, the Commission considered that the monopoly of manufacturers on 'original spare parts' was no longer justified. To a very large degree, these spare parts were not only manufactured but also designed by original equipment manufacturers (OEMs). A significant gap thus existed between the market shares of 'manufacturers' channels' for spare parts in comparison to their role in the manufacturing of the parts for the original vehicle. On the other hand, OEMs of the majority of spare parts for the original sale of vehicles had only relatively small shares in the market for spare parts. The monopoly in question was imperfect as a large part of the market for manufacturers' spare parts was in competition with 'matching quality' parts. Nonetheless, it led to a structural tendency with regard to prices for spare parts that was upward moving and that was visible in the healthy margins that they offered both manufacturers and their dealer networks. By permitting OEMs to develop their own distribution channels for 'original spare parts' and by encouraging dealer networks to distance themselves from the manufacturers' dominance in this market, the Commission wished to increase competition and make prices fall.

ii) In relation to servicing and repair of vehicles, the Commission was open to the arguments of actors from the independent distribution networks. They insisted that electronics had grown to represent an important part of work upon recent generations of vehicles and that manufacturers were voluntarily marking it impossible or difficult to access the entire range of technical information necessary to ensure that all these electronic elements were correctly managed when a car was being repaired. While it was not possible to standardize them or to demand that they be made available for free, the regulation 1400/2002 required manufacturers to offer access to all necessary technical information and codes needed 'at a reasonable price' to independent repairers in order to allow them to compete with the manufacturers' networks.

The strategic intention of all of these measures was clear. In the vocabulary of *The Politics of Industry* approach, they were intended to 'deinstitutionalize' the Purchase IR in order to encourage all firms operating in the industry to build their automobile product and service ranges using a more varied set of sources. For the dealership network of the car-makes, the objective was clearly to encourage larger dealerships to become more strategically autonomous because

- they would no longer be tied to one manufacturer but to several;
- they could source spare parts, used cars and credit from alternative sources;
- they could choose to opt for certain contracts and not others in their dealings with manufacturers.

For 'independents', what was being sought was a broadening of their opportunities by restraining those that had been previously been restricted to manufacturers. In relation to independent repair specialists, the objective was not only to ensure their survival but to encourage their development so that consumers could continue to have a choice and that the manufacturers' networks would be encouraged to improve the quality–price relationship of their service offering. If successful, this regulation was destined to create a more fragmented power base of actors dedicated to reducing prices and increasing the quality of the overall range of automobile services, and to replace the existing IO that had been built around the interests of manufacturers and their need to push new cars towards consumers who no longer tended to buy them in sufficient quantities.

2.2.2. The behaviour of manufacturers before and after this legislation

Throughout the process of renegotiation of the block exemption, as well as after the Council's decision, the attitude of manufacturers has been ambiguous. This has largely been because the majority of these actors had themselves become involved in a fundamental restructuring of their own distribution networks since the mid-1990s (Jullien, 2004, 2006). We will come back to some of the reasons that led to this restructuring but, at this point, I simply outline the main factors that led to their decision to rationalize their distribution channels during this period.

i) the desire to adapt their commercial practices to a product range that was increasingly varied and more frequently renewed (Behr, 2004; Ballot, Segrestin, Weil, 2006);
ii) the quest for reduced costs;
iii) the need to homogenize and control more closely the quality of the service levels of their dealers as they carried out the entire range of activities required by the manufacturers.

This rationalization consisted of a 'consolidation' of distribution channels which involved

- a reduction in the number of sales outlets and an increase in the number of vehicles sold per contract;
- a reduction in the number of operators and an increase in the number of contracts per operator.

This process mostly involved the creation of regional platforms made up of several sales outlets for the same make or for makes of the same group and who shared a certain number of functions. It also involved the manufacturers taking back in hand all of those functions that the network carried out and that were to be subject to the imposition of more precise and demanding standards to ensure the quality level of service delivery and outcome (Jullien, 2000).

Such moves on their part appear to indicate that the manufacturers themselves were unsure of the efficiency of an industry which they were, if not responsible for organizing, at least allowed to organize as they preferred. They themselves were, in fact, pushing for the development of distribution groups of a larger size. They were also introducing growing levels of conflict into the relationship with their networks as many existing distributors were destined to disappear and those who remained were going to have to accept greater levels of control.

This means that the Commission's intentions to reform the sector appeared in a context where the actors themselves had already begun a process of strategic reflection for unrelated reasons. Hence, the information asymmetry between the regulator and the principal industry actors was particularly strong. This also explains why, both before and after the regulation, the manufacturers appear to have negated, whether consciously or not, all potential threats posed to them by DG Competition. This can be seen by recalling the major innovations of regulation 1400/2002.

i) The fact that distribution was no longer exclusive but only selective has mainly served the interests of manufacturers. They have been able to use this change to threaten their dealers with loss of market share if they do not improve their performance in comparison to neighbouring dealers. As they continued to remunerate dealers based on their performance as measured by the potential of a catchment area, the overall effect was only marginal. The manufacturers knew this and their predictions have become reality. In addition, when the manufacturers wished to oust a dealer to transfer the zone to another dealer, they were able to do so without ending the contract. The difficulties that the dealer experienced when in competition with a more effective dealer were sufficient to give rise to the desired effect.

ii) For related reasons, the suppression of the localization clause has had no effect as there was virtually no dealer that used this clause. This is because margins on new-car sales are very low and dealers often forego them in order to make sales with discounts. Dealers avoid losses through the bonuses they receive based on reaching the objectives that the manufacturer has set. In such a system, no distributor would open an outlet in a zone where it would be impossible to access these bonuses.

iii) Similarly, given the structure of profitability of a car dealership, no dealer could cover all fixed charges without after-sales service and spare parts. Manufacturers have consciously reinforced this phenomenon since 2000 by limiting margins on new-car sales to discourage non-sought-after new entrants. Thus, in 2003, when they were obliged to rewrite their contracts in order to propose three options instead of only one, no dealer chose an alternative to the original contract covering the three major activities. In addition, the manufacturers used the opportunity that arose to rewrite the contracts to make their standards more exacting, thus piggybacking on the regulation to promote their own strategies of consolidation.

Clearly, both in advance of and since the regulation, the manufacturers appear to have benefited from the means necessary to maintain and renew their central role vis-à-vis their distribution networks. From this perspective, Monti and his DG neglected taking into consideration the crucial fact that the manufacturers had tight control over margins of dealerships through remuneration systems which have not evolved and which have neutralized the effect of the major regulatory moves introduced.

In relation to spare parts and after-sales service, the same conclusion is also valid.

i) The question of spare parts is similar to that of new-car sales. Car distributors are also distributors of spare parts because, in their respective territories, they are responsible for the supply of spare parts to both authorized and other repairers to repair vehicles of their make-owner. Manufacturers set them revenue objectives that give them access to bonuses. Using or distributing competitive parts in this context is feasible only if dealers can at least earn as much profit by selling the alternative spare parts. If the dealer has accepted a spare parts contract with the manufacturer, this will not be the case. If the spare parts contract is not accepted, the dealer has little chance of being offered the others and it would subsequently be difficult to find a partner who would be in a position to offer them a high-enough service level to meet the expectations that repairers have for the representative of a make-owner. The distributors of makes have an important advantage over multi-make wholesalers because they cover the entire range. As they realized this, manufacturers were anxious to remain the most important partner to independents. To do so, they restructured their product policy and their logistics. They also managed to convince OEMs – for whom they were relatively powerful negotiators given the size of their purchases for car manufacturing – that it would be advantageous if the majority of the spare parts activity continued to pass through their networks.

ii) As regards the sharing of technical information, the principles are less important than the real-world conditions under which the legislation is applied. From this point of view, the majority of manufacturers obeyed the law and developed systems that theoretically allowed repairers access to the technical information they needed at a reasonable price. These prices, however, become relatively high for an independent repair specialist who must purchase them for each make-owner. However, they are relatively low for independent repair outlets that have numerous outlets or for training institutions and organizations that edit technical documents or supply the diagnostic equipment. Prices are defined for independent repairers and stipulate that this price is only for private enterprises that use the information and do not disseminate it. A first level of ambiguity lies here. Automobile professionals know from experience that such information is useful only if it can be translated into solutions to real problems. This gives rise to a more nuanced difficulty. It is not enough to have access to technical information. Instead, it is necessary to ensure that the manufacturers provide information of an operational type.

In summary, the whole range of the legislator's intentions were problematized around a vision of the automobile industry that was a poor representation of reality and that thus had little chance of changing it as intended. The manufacturers' capacity to organize themselves around, rather than submit to, the changes in the industry's regulatory framework does not appear to have been taken into account sufficiently. Indeed, in its scenario of the industry's future, the Commission makes reference to actors such as mass retailers, large multi-make dealerships and OEMs wishing to confront car manufacturers head-on, but whose existence is entirely fictitious. The real actors in the marketplace have not, in fact, sought to take advantage of the opportunities that the Commission was seeking to offer them. In its representation of the industry, the Commission presents the manufacturers as the dominant actors in a marketplace in which the law has allowed them to engage in rent-seeking behaviour. In doing so, it appears to have actually encouraged them to develop this role even further. Already, before this legislation was decided and introduced, and particularly since then, the manufacturers had begun a fundamental restructuring of their dealership networks that has renewed their dominant role over the entire range of trades involved in automobile distribution and servicing (Jullien, 2006).

2.2.3. Evaluation of the regulation's impact and future scenario

The regulation 1400/2002 was, like its predecessor, adopted for seven years. The process of evaluating its impact and new negotiations over the shape of future legislation began in the summer of 2006 with the publication of a report commissioned from the English consultancy firm, London Economics (2006). The report and the subsequent commentary by the new Competition Commissioner Nelly Kroes offer insights into the way in which actors from the Commission interact with industrial dynamics (Jullien, 2006), and on the possible outcomes that may emerge for the industry in which we are interested (Jullien, 2007).

The report from London Economics could only bear witness to the elements outlined in the previous section. Automobile manufacturers had indeed strengthened their positions in relation to each of the areas that had been exempted: the sale of NVs, the sale of spare parts and after-sale service activities.

i) In relation to the sale of new cars, none of the initiatives had been genuinely implemented. The landscape had not changed. Vehicles continued to be distributed in Europe by single-make sites that, as in the past, proposed the range of possible automobile trades accorded to the dealership network. Nevertheless, the point was made that there are now more large dealership groups than hitherto and that a growing number are multi-make. The Commission takes credit for this development and highlights the fact that this has facilitated the penetration of European markets by dealers representing Japanese and Korean manufacturers – thus increasing competition.
ii) In relation to the second and third areas, the units of measurement adopted by London Economics indicate that the market shares of manufacturers for spare parts has risen significantly and that the dealership networks continue to source the overwhelming majority of their spare parts from manufacturers. The report does underline the emergence, in Germany and France in particular, of alternative distribution networks to those of the manufacturers who appear more capable than before of supplying repairers with the necessary spare parts and services to deal with technological change. Nonetheless, the report accepts that these emerging alternative suppliers have not stopped manufacturers reversing the trend noted in the 1980s and 1990s when they were losing market share in spare parts.

In addition to these points, the report also shows, as does our own research, how this single EU regulation has been readily adapted to the very strong structural and organizational differences that persist in the industry from one national configuration to another.

However, in both the report submitted by London Economics and the commentary of the Commission on the report, it is quite striking that the obvious contradiction between what was desired and what actually happened has not given rise to a negative evaluation of regulation 1400/2002. On the contrary, by changing the arguments used, DG Competition prides itself in the ongoing developments for which it takes credit. The argument from this perspective is as follows: previously, the manufacturers and their dealer networks dominated the sector for the wrong reason and, henceforth, now that the regulatory barriers to entry have been removed, this dominance exists for the right reasons. The Competition Commissioner has explained explicitly that the role of DG Competition is neither to offer artificial life support to firms that are technologically and economically unviable, nor to guarantee an equitable power balance in the contractual relationships between the different industry actors. In essence, the Commission accepts that the strongest actor is such by virtue of its 'competence' and 'efficiency'. Consequently, the fact that it uses this position to eliminate some actors from the market and impose on others contracts that deprive them of all strategic autonomy is seen as the functioning of the normal 'market' mechanism in a modern economy. From a theoretical perspective, this corresponds to a classic opposition in Industrial Organization between two points of view. One is a structuralist viewpoint that considers competition can only exist when there are competitors; the other is that of the Chicago school, which says that if no competitors exist when nothing is stopping them from being there, this is because there should not be any. Today's Commission thus appears to accuse its predecessor of having developed the first approach when the second is more appropriate. For Nelly Kroes, the Commission is not supposed to have preferences with regard to this industry – nor in others – and its role is simply to ensure that what should occur actually does so.

What this reveals above all is the development of a doctrine in relation to competition that is less and less 'pragmatic' and thus less likely to integrate different types of requirements and priorities (Ramirez, 2006, 2007, 2008). Adopting this approach in this case has given rise to the paradox I have outlined whereby the politico-legal domination of the manufacturers has been reinforced. The politically fragile DG Competition has subsequently turned out to be concerned primarily with protecting itself from attacks on its own legitimacy and from a reduction in its powers and sphere of influence. Moreover, this weakness renders it structurally incapable of self-criticism. The evaluations of its own actions are thus systematically self-congratulatory. A final revelation from this case study is that the regulator is incapable of developing sufficient expertise on the industries concerned by its decisions to avoid becoming overwhelmed by them. The new doctrine that appears to be emerging within the Commission can thus be interpreted as a form of rationalization of – or even a certain level of pride in – its own powerlessness.

In 2007, this unequal struggle between the manufacturers and the Commission led to a form of consensus concerning the idea that the law is not, in fact, very important. Thus, unlike what had been seen in regulations 1475/1995 and 1400/2002, the manufacturers are no longer necessarily convinced that they need to benefit from a block exemption in order to continue to carry out their role as organizational architects of the automobile service sector. The franchising solution that they may be required to apply no longer poses any significant problems for them. A clause-by-clause comparison of the types of contract they currently have (block exemption rules, BER) and those they may be obliged to offer (franchising rules) highlight two main elements:

i) A franchise in the car industry is used to allow a manufacturer to control the conditions under which its products are distributed and/or repaired. As a result, the franchisor has a lot of room to manoeuvre and is mainly limited in what can be imposed by its ability to attract franchisees willing to sign up, rather than by the legal protection afforded to franchisees.
ii) As both parties are entirely free to choose to enter into the contract or not, the legislator does not see it as necessary to protect the interests of the weaker party against those of the franchisor.

In short, the regulatory framework of franchising appears more favourable to car manufacturers than the current block-exemption-based regulatory framework (see Figure 2.7).

In this scenario, because the law no longer has much to say, issues concerning distribution and servicing of automobiles will, more than ever before, be determined by the power-based relationships between manufacturers as franchisors and dealers, who in turn will have become managers of a portfolio of franchisees. From a French perspective, where even the largest emerging dealer groups are still dwarfed by manufacturers in terms of their size, the outcome is not hard to predict. All that remains uncertain in such a context is whether dealers will manage to come together in a structured fashion to negotiate collectively with regard to each clause in the franchise contracts that the manufacturers will propose. This potential for rebalancing the unequal distribution of power appears highly unlikely, however, given both the individualistic tendencies that dealer groups exhibit and the clearly divergent interests that certain groups have vis-à-vis others. From the perspective of the United Kingdom, the Netherlands, Belgium or Austria – countries without car manufacturers – things appear different. In these countries,

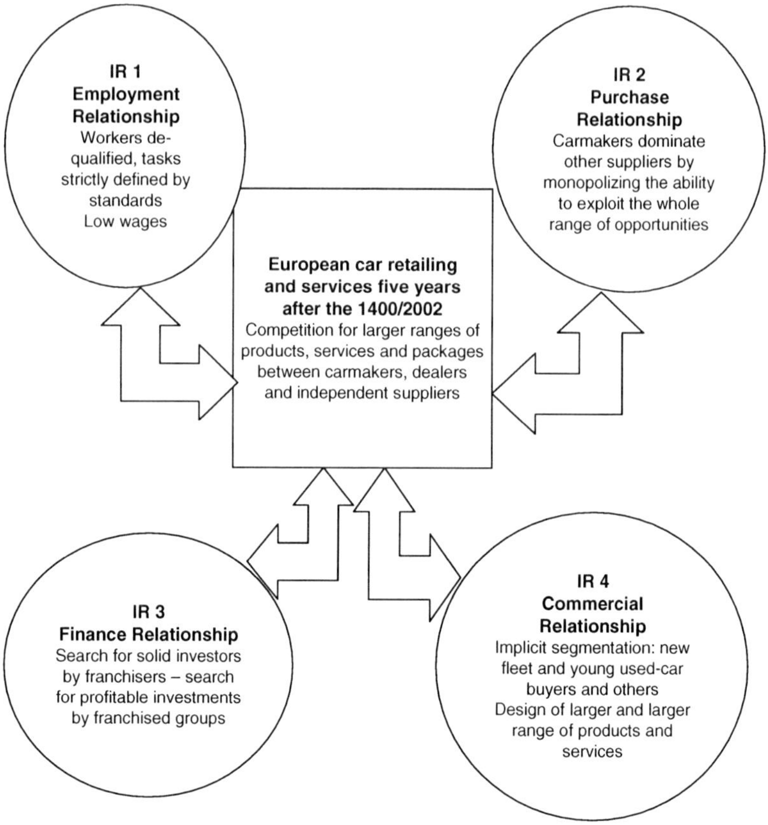

Figure 2.7 European car retailing and services five years after the new BER

dealer groups have emerged already who are capable of managing portfolios of franchises and of operating trade-offs between them based on their respective profitability levels. The franchises that manufacturers will be proposing in the future will not be easily imposed on these groups. Each manufacturer will have to build its own terms, defend them and adapt them in the light of the competing proposals of other manufacturers, operators and the dealer groups themselves.

Conclusion

With respect to the questions asked in the introduction, the examination of our industry allows us to outline how industrial actors and public policy-makers responsible for regulating an industry interact during a phase of de-institutionalization/re-institutionalization. As we have seen, globalization has not had many direct impacts upon this process. However, through providing legitimizing impetus for the increased intervention of EU competition policy, globalization has been used as part of a liberalizing political project (Hay, 2006) which has had a number of indirect impacts which I synthesize below. More precisely, by applying the *Politics of Industry* approach, this chapter has generated four sets of insights upon this indirect relationship between globalization and change in Europe's automobile distribution industry.

i) Competition policy is obliged, whether or not its decision-makers so wish, to take into consideration problems not related to competition. This is particularly true when it has to judge whether exemptions are feasible for an entire sector. DG Competition has thus been called upon to seek compromises between the perspective that is dictated by its mandate and the – equally legitimate – perspectives of other actors and policy-makers. In reality, competition policy (or what is presented as such) is also liable to play roles other than that of promoting competition or economic efficiency even when it needs to integrate these aspects into specific arguments. This has not improved debate in terms of either clarity or democratic efficiency. At least in the past, however, the effectiveness of public action has been improved whenever DG Competition has acted in a manner that has been economically and politically 'pragmatic' (i.e. concerned with industrial organization and not just competition).

ii) Even when DG Competition has imposed a common regulatory framework on all member states, there is no guarantee that the outcome will be a harmonization of the industry that corresponds to the discovery of an efficient and 'liberalized' model. In relation to automobile distribution, this is because the European regulatory mechanism is incomplete and covers just one of the IRs – the Purchase IR – and this only partially. The supply of automobile-related services requires the simultaneous regulation of both the overall competitive arena and the three other IRs. As these other relationships are not highly subject to European regulation, they are essentially instituted at national (Employment, Commercial) or global (Financial) levels. Consequently, the European automobile services sector operates as a grouping of national industries rather than as a European industry.

iii) When DG Competition has limited itself to the mandate of regulating competition in an industry, its vision of the latter has been very limited and relatively unrealistic. In part, this is because its approach is cognitively incomplete. Competition policy conceived in this way involves imposing a 'sectorised' and static perspective on productive practices and strategic behaviours. Firms, however, adopt new practices which adapt to the mobility in activity required by new competitive orders. It is hardly surprising that the outcome of this asymmetry is that the impact of regulatory changes does not confirm to the 'legislator's intentions'. To use a military metaphor, it is as if DG Competition were playing 'a war of position' against industrial operators, whereas the latter are playing 'a war of movement'. What is clear is that representatives of DG Competition believe they are regulating 'markets', whereas the competitive arenas in question are not in fact structured by market characteristics.

iv) Nonetheless, and despite these fundamental inadequacies, European regulatory activity in a sector such as automobile distribution has had a major impact. It has operated as a catalysing force on the strategic activity of actors between 2000 and 2007. Threatened with imposed changes that the Commission was announcing as major, the principal groups of actors have engaged in political work and strategic initiatives, both in advance of and subsequent to the introduction of EU regulations. These initiatives themselves have operated as powerful forces for change and tended to be discussed and negotiated in the field rather than within DG Competition in Brussels. By lacking representation in the areas where change has actually been occurring, the Commission has in fact been left out of much of the process of change.

# 3
Globalization Within the European Wine Industry: Commercial Challenges but Producer Domination

Andy Smith

Introduction

Since 2000, a widespread consensus amongst practitioners and commentators has emerged that the European wine industry is 'in crisis'. Public demonstrations, blockades and acts of industrial sabotage have grabbed the newspaper headlines whilst collective and public actors have accumulated diagnoses and proposals for reform (Berthomeau, 2001; César, 2002; EC, 2006; Wine & Spirits Intelligence Service Ltd, 2002). Many of these social mobilizations and analyses ascribe surpluses and price falls to an allegedly unregulated form of 'globalization' which, through encouraging new entrants in the form of New World wines, has led not only to market disruption but also to a change in the product itself. In short, globalization is perceived as a threat to European methods of growing grapes, transforming them into wine, selling this product and, more fundamentally, to the professional identity of all those involved in these processes.

In proposing an alternative explanation for the relationship between globalization and wine which places political work at the centre of analysis, this chapter first adapts the interdisciplinary analytical framework presented in this book's introduction to the study of the European wine industry (Section 1). Once 'vinified', this framework is then applied in order to identify the sites within which political work has been invested since the beginning of the 1990s[1] (Sections 2–4). Precise causal hypotheses are developed in the next section. At this stage, I simply wish to underline three general claims made throughout the text.

1. The cause of change or its absence in this industry is the 'political work' engaged in by private, collective and public actors operating within and across global, European, national and regional negotiating arenas.
2. Identifying where and over what issues political work has taken place within the European wine industry provides a means of grasping its particular relationship between economics and politics.
3. Studying the instrumentalization of references to territory in and around this relationship sharpens a focus on political work as a means of understanding the causality of change in the regulation of an industry or the resistance it inspires (Carter and Smith, 2008).

1. Studying the politics of the European wine industry

I first identify the spaces where mediation over the regulation of the European wine industry is played out (Section 1.1). Only once this disciplined description is in place can one then begin to analyse the 'political work' which has brought about and given life to the institutions that structure these spaces (Section 1.2), before developing causal hypotheses regarding the type of work (and 'workers') this has encompassed over the last 15–20 years (Section 1.3).

1.1. Wine's Institutionalized Relationships and spaces of mediation

The four Institutionalized Relationships (IRs) which together make up this industry first concern the interdependencies and areas of conflict which actors within a territorialized productive system (growers, co-operatives, merchants) have developed with four sets of 'partners'. In the Bordeaux region, for example, the Employment IR directly concerns relations between growers and their workforce on the one hand and merchants and their employees on the other. The Financial IR is played out around the financing of both growers and merchants by banks and other sources of finance. The Purchase IR is essentially a set of rules that regulate relations between growers and merchants by defining how and where grapes should be grown, turned into wine and sold to wholesalers. Finally, the Commercial IR concerns relations between wholesale sellers of wine and retailers. Although each of these IRs is clearly different from the others, within all of them institutionalized norms set limits upon actor behaviour. These norms have frequently been transformed into formalized rules through the intervention of collective and public actors. For example, certification systems determine the right of a wine to bear a geographical designation, for example 'Bordeaux' or 'Bourgogne' (thus affecting the Purchase IR), whilst labelling laws dictate how this designation can be displayed on bottles sold in retail outlets (a serious constraint within the Commercial IR). In this way, each IR thus also needs to be seen as one of four sets of rules, many of which can be enforced by collective or public actors (Figure 3.1).

In short, I conceptualize the wine industry as a whole as an institutionalized configuration of actors, practices and representations which, through its IRs and the articulations which exist between them, simultaneously structures market transactions as well as collective and public action. At this stage, I wish to simply underline three advantages of conceptualizing the European wine industry in this way.

The first is that it allows one to show that institutions are not 'outside' the wine market but are rather an integral part of it. Consequently, it will be argued here that institutions – defined as systems of rules (Stanziani, 2003, 2005; Thelen and Steinmo, 1992) – constantly provide the framework within which market competition in the wine industry takes place. As Swidler (1986) has so cogently underlined, institutions are not only constraints upon market competition, but also provide the very conditions under which such competition can durably take place.

A second advantage of examining the organization of the wine industry in this manner is to highlight that institutions and public policies have not been imposed upon growers and merchants by the EU and

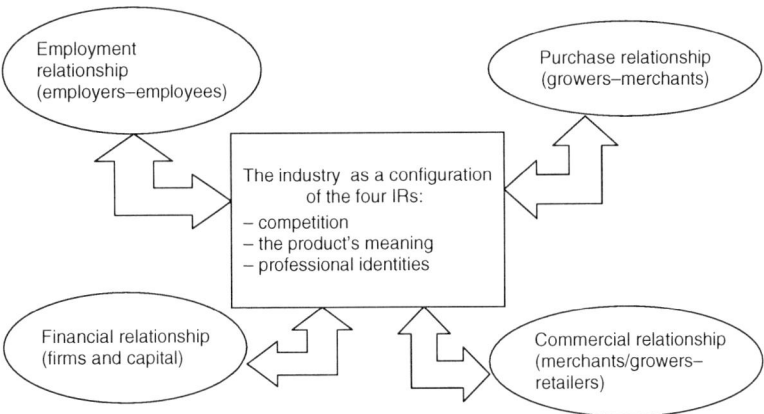

Figure 3.1 The European wine industry as an Institutional Order of four Institutionalized Relationships

national politicians and civil servants. In reality, the vast majority of rules in the wine industry were initially proposed by grower and merchant representatives before being 'co-produced' into binding legislation. Moreover, these rules are generally implemented with considerable involvement by practitioner representatives.

A third and final advantage of conceptualizing the European wine industry in this way concerns the question of institutional change. In this industry it is particularly important to reject simplistic and culturalist analyses of 'old world immobilism' in favour of careful analysis of the successive attempts that have been made over the last 15 years to transform the IRs of this industry. Simply noting that today's wine institutions in Europe are remarkably similar to those of yesteryear utterly fails to examine why, despite a constant flow of propositions and debate, policy change has taken place at a relatively leisurely speed. As will be shown below, in this industry, causes of change or stasis are neither 'cultural' nor 'economic'. In both cases they are fundamentally political.

1.2. Political work within European wine industry

The politics of any industry takes concrete form through two phenomena: alliance-building and argumentation. The building and the maintenance of alliances within the wine industry is political because this is how interdependence is engaged with, be it co-operative or competitive. Discourse construction, delivery and dramatization are political because, during the definition and defence of the interests and goals of intra- and inter-organizational action, values are at issue (Kandil, 1998). The politics of wine thus encompasses the range of activities which alliance-building and argumentation entail, as well as the linkages made between them. From the point of view of empirical research, the construction and activation of alliances and arguments can be discerned through examining two processes which occur within each of the four IRs: the problematization of issues and their politicization.

The concept of problematization enables one to capture how the difficulties actors face within the wine industry have not spontaneously become issues that are accorded the attention and action of collective or public actors. Rather collective or public 'problems' have arisen only as a result of work carried out by certain actors to convert the difficulties experienced within isolated private firms into problems that a sufficient number of actors have been convinced into believing are shared (Rochefort and Cobb, 1994). Such problems are accorded one or both of the following types of legitimacy.

The first of these types is given to collective problems which stabilize when a problem's definition is accepted as mirroring that of an interest group. In the European wine industry, such groups have at least four spatial manifestations: the guild representing a geographical wine area (the terroir of an Appellation d'origine contrôlé – AOC – or a 'vin de pays'); regional 'interprofessions'; national committees of regional bodies (e.g. the French national committee of AOCs: le CNAOC); and EU level confederations of national grower and merchant organizations.

The second type of legitimacy is given to a 'shared' problem in the wine industry, which is 'public'. Public problems occur when their definitions are validated by politicians or civil servants, that is by actors who ostensibly work to further the public interest (Padioleau, 1982). In France, for example, members of parliament from wine-producing areas ('les deputes du vin') were traditionally vectors for the transformation of collective problems into public ones. Since the 1950s, however, such a process has been more likely to take place through civil servants working in the Ministry of Agriculture or the Institut National des Appellations d'Origine (INAO).

Be they collective or public, institutionalized problems set the framework and agenda within which discussions over the regulation of an industry take place. Consequently, these problems also set limits upon the content of policy instruments that are devised, adopted and implemented within the industry, often putting in place institutionalized norms, processes, expectations and 'path dependencies' (Lascoumes and Le Galès, 2007). Indeed, in the wine industry, the link between problems and instruments is a constant object for political work both for advocates of change and for those who seek to resist it. For example, in certain areas where the 'quality' of wine is defined as a problem, instruments have been established in order to regulate grape-growing and wine-making practices more strictly.

Research into problematization is essential but insufficient because although political work is always their cause, the problems which structure the organization and the regulation of an industry are never automatically 'political' or 'technical'. Instead these terms are category-forming labels which are attached to problems over the course of negotiations about the definition of issues and instruments that could be devised to alleviate or solve them (Dubois and Dulong, 1999; Lagroye, 2003a & b). Politicization thus needs studying from an angle that highlights the use of categorization during the building of arguments employed during intra- and inter-IR negotiations. In addition, one needs to closely, and simultaneously, examine the relational activity involved in presenting and dramatizing these arguments.

In the wine industry, a particularly clear example of this political work concerns the spatial and certifying categories such as AOCs which have been used to differentiate products, create collective brands and segment markets. At both national and local levels, the construction of these categories in the first half of the 20th century was the result of a long and often stormy debate between proponents of this form of interventionism and their more liberal opponents. One of the reasons the former won this debate is because they successfully politicized a linkage between territory (terroir) and wine quality that was couched in the language of values and symbols (Capus, 1947). The second reason this politicization was effective is that proponents of AOCs forged effective alliances for the delivery and dramatization of their line of argumentation. Indeed, this example provides a clear illustration of a political enterprise which took its membership not only from wine growers but also from within the French administration, parliament and judiciary.

In summary, within the European wine industry, problematization and politicization are the processes that make up the political work through which its four IRs have been built, challenged and continuously reconstituted. At any point in time, the industry as a whole is a configuration of these four IRs that has emerged as a cumulative result of this political work.

1.3. Causal claims

Largely inspired by a combination of (usually implicit) neoclassical economics and rational choice theory, the orthodox narrative[2] of Europe's wine crisis attributes the growth of wine surpluses and falls in prices to the following chain of 'facts':

1. Since the 1960s, consumption of wine has fallen within producer countries, thereby increasing the importance of export markets both within and without the EU.
2. Since considerably reducing production levels in the 1980s, EU production rates have remained relatively constant overall but have increased in certain regions.
3. Since the mid-1990s, competition for export markets with wines from outside the EU has increased dramatically. Benefiting from lowered tariffs and lower overheads, economies of scale, less restrictive

rules and greater marketing budgets, New World wines have replaced EU wines in many export markets.
4. Faced with all these changes, EU and Member States public authorities have 'stood by while Rome burns'. More precisely, they have systematically been accused by growers and merchants of developing public policies which, instead of enhancing their competitiveness and chances of survival, are actually harmful to their short- and long-term interests.

Rather than engaging directly with the normative dimension of this orthodox narrative, the remainder of this chapter takes issue with a number of its analytical premises, propositions and conclusions. More precisely, although the 'facts' presented in points 1–3 are not disputed, each of these, point 4 and the theory of action behind them contain a number of major flaws which lead the narrative as a whole to overlook or oversimplify the politics of the European wine industry. Instead, it will be shown that even if debates within at least three of its IRs have undergone substantial change since the beginning of the 1990s, the pressure for change has distinct and identifiable origins which are not shared by all three. More precisely, three claims will be made.

First, I argue that the re-institutionalization of two IRs – Employment and Finance – has occurred principally at the level of the firm without entailing collective or public action (Section 2). Instead the causes of this change lie in a politics that has essentially taken place within the Commercial (Section 3) and Purchase (Section 4) IRs.

Second, I claim that within and between these two IRs the cause of change is more complex than it first appears. I argue that the initial cause of change lies within substantial upheavals in the Commercial IR. However, this deinstitutionalization has provoked relatively little political work from either collective or public actors. Instead, their diagnoses and proposals for change have been concentrated upon the Purchase IR. Not only has this IR proved difficult to reinstitutionalize, its political saturation (i.e. the tendency for many issues to be politicized) has also meant that the industry as a whole has undergone relatively little displacement.

Third, it will be argued that the relative neglect of the Commercial IR in favour of the Purchase IR has been caused by the continuing power of growers as opposed to merchants or representatives of public authority. In explaining this asymmetry, the electoral strength of growers should not be ignored. However, its fundamental cause is the enduring omnipresence of growers across all four IRs, their capacity to mobilize territory as a powerful legitimizing strategy, the relative political weakness of merchants and the passive connivance of civil servants and politicians.

2. Objects of change but not its cause: Employment and finance

Changes in employment conditions and capitalization are often presented as classic signs of globalization. On the one hand, the institutions which regulate labour are seen as weakening in the name of 'flexibility' and increased productivity. On the other, the liberalization of the international movement of capital is identified as the cause of mergers undertaken in the name of vertical and horizontal integration. In the case of the European wine industry since the late 1980s, firms and collective and public debates within both the Employment and the Finance IR have certainly been effected by trends of this nature. However, neither have they thus far undergone significant reinstitutionalization nor, consequently, have they brought about a shift in the industry as a whole. This is because although labour and finance issues clearly effect firms, they have seldom been problematized or politicized.

Historically, labour relations have of course played a major role in the evolution of Europe's wine industry. Since the end of feudalism, in all wine-producing regions property ownership has obviously undergone significant change. In more recent years, mechanization, the enlargement of farms and the concentration of wine merchants have all contributed to this process. Notwithstanding the importance of these trends, however, for growers most change in this issue area took place well before the 1990s. Between 1990 and 2003, it is important to note that while the total area of vines in the EU fell by 0.7% per year, the average (wine) farm size only rose from 7.6 to 9.2 hectares (EC, 2006: 111–112). Most European wine grapes therefore continue to be produced by thousands of relatively small holdings, each employing few salaried workers. Unfortunately much less systematic knowledge is available about Europe's wine merchants (Réjalot, 2003). Indeed, a recent 160-page report by the European Commission (2006) on the 'economy' of the wine sector contains virtually no information about them. As I show below, concentration of these firms has been the global trend but in Europe the fragmentation of this part of the industry is still a principal feature. In short, for both merchants and growers, over the last 20 years labour relations have not re-emerged as objects of collective or public action. Consequently, the Employment IR's debates and rules have been marked by continuity and remarkably little overlap with the other three IRs which structure this industry.

In the case of the Finance IR, debates have undergone considerably more change yet its rules have again remained remarkably stable. More precisely, although the definition of the problem of finance has changed within a number of large and medium-sized firms, this issue has not led to widespread agenda setting or the transformation of rules, policy instruments and processes.

An initial means of examining this question is through presenting the three types of firms, each with their own form of finance, which have come to structure the world wine industry since the mid-1980s: multi-beverage multinationals, large specialized wine-making companies and small or medium-sized independent firms. Over the last 20 years, four multi-beverage multinationals have emerged: Diageo, LVMH, Allied Domecq and Pernod Ricard. Products of intense merger activity in the 1980s which initially entailed beers and spirits, all these groups have steadily increased their involvement in the production and selling of wine (Table 3.1).

Table 3.1 Multi-beverage multinationals involved in the world wine industry (2005)

Company	Wines and spirits (meuros)	Wine sales only	Examples of wine brands
Diageo	10.737	492	Barton & Guestier, Piat d'Or, Moët & Chandon (Fr), Tanqueray, Beaulieu Vineyard (US)
Pernod Ricard	6443	755	Alexis L, Fontenoy (Fr), Palacio de la Vega (Sp), Jacob's Creek, Wyndham estate (Aust), Montana (NZ), Campo Viejo (Sp)
LVMH	2994	993	Cheval Blanc, Château d'Yquem, Veuve Cliquot (Fr), Newton (US), Cloudy Bay (NZ)

Sources: Company web sites and Pomarici (2005).

Table 3.2 The world's top five specialized wine companies in 2005

Company	Wine sales (meuros)	Examples of brands
E & J Gallo (US)	985	Gallo, Carlo Rossi, Bartles & James
Constellation Brands (US & Aust)	950	Opus One, Robert Mondavi Coastal
Fosters wine estates (Aust)	na	Penfolds, Yellow Glen
Castel Frères (Fr)	689	Blaissac, Villa Veroni
Val d'Orbieu (Fr)	na	Cordier, Listel, Vins de Pays d'Oc

Sources: Pomarici (2005) and the companies' Internet sites.

Around 20 companies specialized in wine make up the second category of firms in this industry. Within this category, five companies are particularly large (Table 3.2).

The third and final type of firm within the world wine industry is made up of a range of small and medium-sized firms. Whilst most growers of grapes in New World countries tend strongly to sell their product to one of the above-mentioned companies to be vinified and marketed, many European growers continue to make and sell their own wine. Others sell their wine in bottles through wholesaling merchants. Others still send their grapes or their wine in bulk to co-operatives and merchants to be vinified and sold. This variety of practices mirrors the fragmentation of the wholesale or merchant dimension of the European industry. In certain regions, merchants have experienced mergers and acquisitions which have led to the enlargement of the capacity of each individual firm (Albert and Martin, 2001; Jesus Oliveira Coelho and Rastoin, 2001). For example, in the Bordelais, a number of 'family' firms have been bought out by large commercial groups (e.g. De Luze, Calvet, Eschenauer, Cruse, Ginestet), as shown in Table 3.3.

There is thus no doubting that over the last 20 years the financing of wine firms has undergone significant change throughout the world. For many European growers and merchants, new sources of finance have been deemed necessary in order to expand, modernize equipment and improve the productivity of their businesses. In some regions (e.g. the Médoc), refinancing has entailed changes in ownership with outsiders such as insurance companies buying wine Châteaux as investments. In others, for example the Midi (Torrès, 2005), wine companies from outside the vignoble, and in particular from the New World, have attempted to obtain a foothold. Meanwhile, European wine companies have frequently financed the expansion of New World wines and their respective

Table 3.3 Ownership of the largest wine merchants in the Bordelais

Company	Owner	Brands
Castel	Pierre Castel	Baron-de-Lestac, Blaissac, Malesan
Johanès Boubée	Carrefour	Grand Moment
Grands vins de Gironde	JJ. Mortier et cie	Vins de châteaux
CVBG	Thiénot	Dourthe, Kressman
Les caves de Landiras	Grands chais de France	Louis Eschenhauer
Baron Philippe de Rothschild	Philippine de Rothschild	Mouton Cadet, Cuvée Barons et Baronnes
Cordier-Mestrezat	Val d'Orbieu	Cordier Prestige, L'exception Cordier
Ginestet	Taillan	Ginestet, Villa Burdigala, Mascaron
Yvon Mau	Freixenet	Yvecourt, Premius

Sources: Réjalot (2003, annexe 1) and Internet sites of the companies concerned.[3]

productive systems. However, notwithstanding these intra-firm trends, little change in the IR that governs the financing of wine companies has occurred. Of course, representatives of some of these firms, and the larger ones in particular, have supported trans-industry political enterprises which have sought to liberalize the movement of capital. For example, groups such as Pernod Ricard have been consistent supporters of both the completion of the EU's single market and the establishment of the WTO. However, our research unearthed no evidence to show that within the wine industry itself the issue of liberalizing the movement of capital has been transformed durably into a collective or public problem. Just as importantly, the pressure to merge and/or vertically integrate that wine wholesaling companies have recently experienced has not engendered change in the way the profession of wine merchant is represented at regional, national and European levels. In the Bordelais, for example, owners and managers from the same handful of companies as in the 1970s continue to invest in collective action at this level whilst representatives of even some of the larger firms continue to freeride on this activity. Moreover, one of the conditions of representing the interests of merchants as a group continues to be the avoidance of any collective action which might question or challenge the way individual firms finance and run their respective businesses.

In summary, within the European wine industry the issue of finance has certainly undergone considerable modification over the last 15–20 years. However, just as with the Employment IR, such change has occurred essentially at the level of individual companies. Within these spaces, power relations have played a significant role. However, despite isolated and regionalized cases of politicization (Torrès, 2005), the involvement of collective and public actors in these IRs has been remarkably muted. This observation strongly supports our contention that, at least over the last two decades, political work within this industry has been undertaken elsewhere.

3. The initial site of political work: A problematized but non-politicized Commercial IR

In the wine industry, the Commercial IR concerns the relationship between retailers and wholesalers (not only merchants but also producers who sell their own wine). In Europe, this IR is incarnated, on the one hand, by relations between growers and merchants and their respective buyers (supermarkets, off-licence chains, etc.) and, on the other hand, by relations between official representatives of each of these professions (Figure 3.2).

On the surface, debates within this space of mediation have recently been dominated by issues that include the quality of wine, pricing, labelling, marketing and distribution. Behind these terms lie deeper divisions over the meaning prescribed to wine and battles over how its contemporary consumption has been problematized and politicized (Section 3.1). Just as revealingly, and despite the importance of distribution and retailing, much less political work has been devoted to these activities (Section 3.2).

3.1. The political conversion of changing patterns of consumption

Consumption patterns for wine have changed massively since the 1960s. First, in producer countries, much less wine per capita is being consumed. Second, this product is increasingly drunk in many countries where little or no wine is produced (e.g. the UK). Third, there has been a general shift away from 'table wines' without regional identification (Vin de table: VdT) towards what the EU labels as regionally specific and 'quality' wines (Vins de qualité produits dans les regions déterminées: VQPRD). Fourth, since the mid-1990s, the EU has experienced a sharp rise in imports of 'New World' wines which have successfully competed with Europe's own wines (see Tables 3.4–3.7).

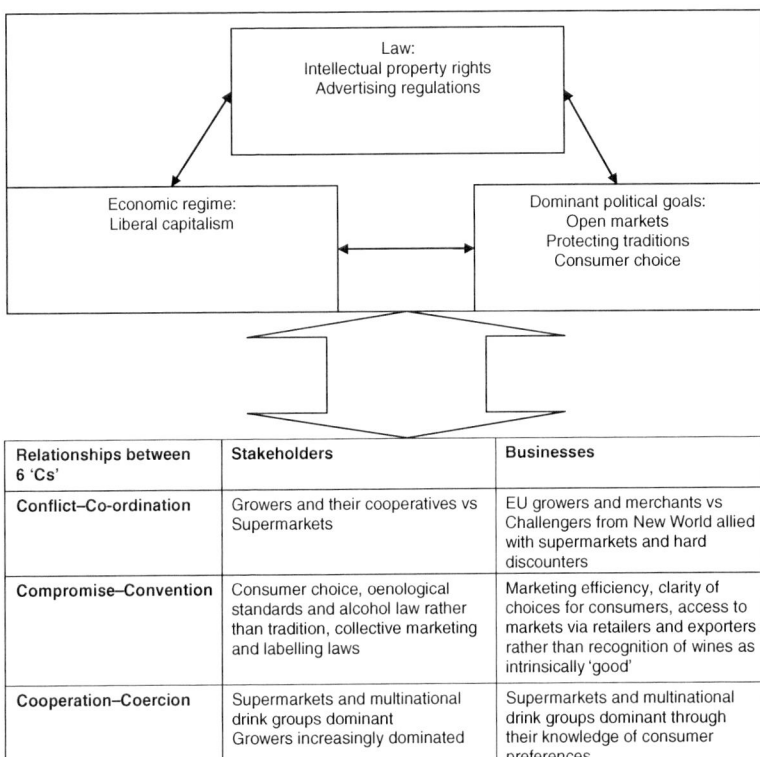

Figure 3.2 The commercial IR in today's European wine industry

Table 3.4 Principal countries of wine consumption (1000 tonnes)

	Average for 1992/94	Average for 2000/02	Evolution (%)
France	5249	4426	−16
Italy	4262	3937	−8
USA	1896	2719	+43
Spain	2247	2317	+3
Germany	1922	2101	+9
Argentina	1591	1231	−23
China	524	1128	+115
UK	710	978	+38
Russia	648	607	−7
Australia	455	603	+32
South Africa	672	585	−13
Portugal	525	496	−6

Source: CE, 2006: p. 21.

Table 3.5 Principal wine-buying countries (1000 tonnes)

	Average for 1991/93	Average for 2001/03	Change (%)
Germany	1000	1180	+18
UK	650	1050	+61
USA	250	550	+120
France	580	490	−16
Russia	250	320	+28
The Netherlands	220	280	+27
Belgium	220	260	+18
Canada	150	240	+60
Denmark	120	200	+67

Source: CE, 2006: 27.

Table 3.6 International trade of wine in the European Union (in 1000 hl)

	1991	1993	1995	1997	1999	2001	2004
Imports	2315	2667	4648	5562	6485	8823	11,657
Exports	9584	12,167	9876	12,250	11,589	12,328	13,944
Difference	7269	9499	5228	6688	5104	3505	2287

Source: Eur 15: CE, 2006, annexe 10.

Table 3.7 International trade of wine in the European Union (in millions of euros [constants 1995])

	1991	1993	1995	1997	1999	2001	2004
Imports	291	375	541	994	1404	2004	2091
Exports	2150	2204	2255	3122	3540	3617	3790
Difference	1859	1829	1714	2128	2136	1613	1699

The combined effect of these four trends has clearly had a major impact upon most European wine producers and merchants. At the level of the firm, new markets have had to be sought and competed in whilst either developing new products (e.g. AOC wine in the Midi) or striving to retain market access and prices for older ones (e.g. generic Bordeaux's). However, within different spatial configurations of the industry – regional vignobles, national wine sectors or that of the European Union – it is striking to note how vaguely this challenge to the

Commercial IR has been problematized around two issues: wine quality and collective marketing.

Still omnipresent in the discourse of today's representatives of the wine sector, a concern for improving the quality of wines produced in Europe has been a collective and public problem since at least the early 1970s. As we shall see in Section 4, the most powerful and durable effect of a discourse on wine quality has been to reorientate policy objectives and instruments whose target has essentially been the grape-growing and wine-making practices of individual growers, merchants and co-operatives. This manner of defining the problem of European wine has been consistently framed by a range of producer-led political enterprises situated within each vignoble, aggregated using national representative bodies and defended in Brussels through the wine committee of the Europe's principal agricultural interest group: COPA-COGECA. According to these political enterprises, the solution to market disruption caused by new patterns of consumption is to weed out 'poor quality wine' using a combination of incentives (subsidies for grubbing out vines and for modernizing wine-making equipment) and disincentives (plantation rights, maximum yields).

Notwithstanding the impact such policy instruments have had upon the quantity and content of wine produced in Europe, in problematizing the Commercial IR in this way actors deliberately or unconsciously have sidestepped a dilemma around which it has proved much more difficult to develop political enterprises: should one make a wine and expect the consumer to buy it? Or should one analyse a market, decide what the consumer wants and then alter one's product to fit that demand? Whilst certain actors, particularly growers, resist the second commercial strategy using highly symbolic language about their product ('standardization', 'Parkerisation', etc.), others see a 'demand-led' strategy as preferable or even inevitable. In both cases the imprecision of terms such as wine quality and demand (be it current or future) is caused by the social representations and values used to construct these terms.

This fundamental uncertainty over what the consumer wants is reflected in a second aspect of the politics of wine addressed in our study: collective marketing in general and advertising in particular. Although a consensus between European growers and merchants has emerged about the need to increase marketing budgets in order to compete with new entrants from the New World, debate and cleavages emerge about how and why this money should be spent. Individual wine firms have always

Table 3.8 Advertising investment in the French wine industry in 2002

	Amount (millions of euros)	Share (%)
Firms with branded table wines	2.8	8.2
Firms with branded AOC wines	12.8	37.1
Interprofessions with table wines	1.5	4.3
Interprofessions with AOC wines	15.3	44.1
Firms that use postal and internet selling	2	5.7
TOTAL	34.6	100

Source: ONIVINS Infos n° 109, December 2003, p. 10.

marketed their own products and of course continue to do so. Instead, the change that has gone on in the Commercial IR over the last 15 years concerns marketing that is collective. A fraction of this is EU sponsored, a little is national but most is regional (Table 3.8).

Although these figures have increased significantly in percentage terms, much is made within the industry about the gap between such budgets and that enjoyed by large Australian or American brands (here the case of Pernod Ricard's Australian brand Jacob's Creek is often cited because it sells more than 65 millions bottles a year. Its success is attributed to the policy of this firm that refuses to allow the price of a kilo of grapes to be more than 10% of the price of a bottle of the finished product (Réjalot, 2003: 113). In Smith, de Maillard and Costa (2007, chapter 6), we focused upon the most powerful levy-funded interprofessional body in France (and perhaps in Europe if not the world): the Conseil interprofessionnel des vins de Bordeaux (CIVB). Over the last 20 years, this organization has vastly increased its advertising budget and range of actions. Moreover, it has attempted to transform Bordeaux into a 'brand' through obliging firms in the region to harmonize parts of their labels. However, advertising strategies are highly controversial and are currently being revised, whilst branding Bordeaux has not attracted widespread support from either within the industry or public authorities.

Overall then, since 1990 some reproblematization of the Commercial IR has taken place over the issues of wine quality and collective marketing but this has generally been incomplete. Importantly, retailers are still considered to be outside the sector, not an integral part of it. In other words, they are the targets and/or the recipients of actions, not actors whom growers and merchants have sought to involve in reframing and reinstitutionalizing the Commercial IR.

3.2. Retailing as a non-problematized and depoliticized issue

Indeed, if the relationship between producers and merchants from the wine industry on the one hand and retailers on the other has not been the object of sustained problematization, the political work that has been carried out contains even fewer attempts to politicize this issue area. Instead, most, if not all, of our interviewees from the industry adopt an attitude of 'resigned acceptance' as regards three issues over which retailers are directly implicated: the importation of New World wines, the power of supermarket chains and the labelling of European wines.

As we saw before, the rise in New World imports is clearly linked to the lowering of tariffs imposed by the 1995 GATT agreement. These tariff reductions have sparked some protests in regions such as the Midi. Mostly, however, there is ambiguity on this point. In the Bordelais, for example, producers and merchants may be suffering from increased competition from New World wines in markets such as the UK. However, the GATT agreement has also enabled them to penetrate lucrative new markets in Asia. More generally, our interviews suggest that most merchants and growers have come to consider that EU policy-makers simply cannot 'swim against the tide of increasingly open markets'. In short, once a highly politicized issue, today imports of wine are generally framed as an institutionalized part of the European wine industry's Commercial IR.

If international trade is now conceptualized as being 'beyond the reach of politics', the same can certainly be said about the power of supermarkets within the retailing of wine. As with other agricultural products, wine producers occasionally publicly protest about the pricing strategies adopted by these retailers. For example, growers in Bordeaux have complained about their wine being sold for as low as 1 euro a bottle. However, little collective and no public action has been undertaken to discourage supermarkets from lowering their prices. Just as importantly, no such action has been taken to encourage these retailers to maintain the diversity of the wines that they stock and thus provide an access to markets. Instead, as Marette and Raynaud (2003) have underlined, the subject of supermarket power has occasionally been politicized around issues of their geographical implantation or price margins (marges arrières). However,

Table 3.9 Trends in types of wine retailing in France (%)

	2002	2004	2006
Hyper and supermarkets	62	62.1	63.5
Hard discount	16.6	19.2	20.9
Specialized shops	19	16.7	14.3
Grocery shops	2.4	2	1.3

Source: VINIFLOR stats 2007.

the power of these companies is generally considered an a-political issue (Table 3.9).

The third and final issue debated within the Commercial IR but that has rarely given rise to a politicized framing within this space of mediation concerns the labelling of European wine. The categories used to present wine from this continent (AOCs, vins de pays) are frequently criticized as 'too complicated' by representatives from the New World. More precisely, these categories impose on producers and merchants precise rules about what can and cannot feature on a wine's label. Representatives of supermarket chains often support the New World view on this issue and justify their choice to import wines from outside Europe because this supply is 'simpler' and 'what the consumer wants'. From the point of view of our analysis of political work in the European industry the issue of labelling is highly revealing because very few actors publicly defend the European way of presenting wine. However, within the industry itself, the labelling and certification schemes it reflects give rise to constant and often heated debate. This contrast between an absence of politicization but ongoing struggles to problematize highlights a fundamental trait of the European wine industry: its categorization of wine is not framed as an issue to be dealt within the Commercial IR, but rather as a problem that needs to be tackled within the Purchase IR.

In summary, far from being an issue just for private operators, the European wine industry's Commercial IR has sporadically yet surely become a significant subject of debate for collective actors. Nevertheless, within European, national or regional arenas, the framing of this problem is far from stabilized, and has rarely given rise to sustained political work and seldom to the emergence of durable political enterprises. Finally, the absence of retailers and public authorities from negotiations over this issue area provides further indication of the continued political importance attached to the Purchase IR.

4. A politically saturated Purchase IR: The weight of grower influence

In the European wine industry, the Purchase IR essentially concerns relations between growers and merchants and their respective representatives. In this industry, this IR is strongly marked by the sedimentation of policy instruments that have been put in place since the end of the 19th century (Figure 3.3).

Having first outlined the extent and the nature of the political work undertaken within this IR (Section 4.1), this section then proceeds to show how and why the actors who dominate the regulation of this space also dominate the European wine industry as a whole (Section 4.2).

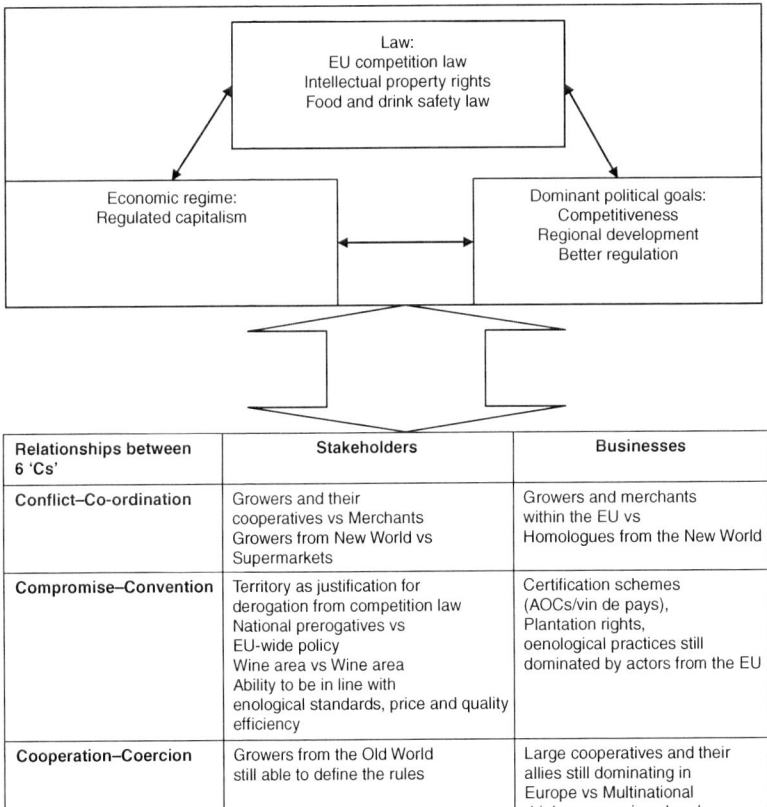

Relationships between 6 'Cs'	Stakeholders	Businesses
Conflict–Co-ordination	Growers and their cooperatives vs Merchants Growers from New World vs Supermarkets	Growers and merchants within the EU vs Homologues from the New World
Compromise–Convention	Territory as justification for derogation from competition law National prerogatives vs EU-wide policy Wine area vs Wine area Ability to be in line with enological standards, price and quality efficiency	Certification schemes (AOCs/vin de pays), Plantation rights, oenological practices still dominated by actors from the EU
Cooperation–Coercion	Growers from the Old World still able to define the rules	Large cooperatives and their allies still dominating in Europe vs Multinational drinks companies elsewhere

Figure 3.3 The Purchase IR in today's European wine industry

4.1. The omnipresence of politically worked policy instruments

All the four IRs which make up this industry are marked by rules, norms and expectations that have been institutionalized over time. However, those which structure the European wine industry's Purchase IR are not only particularly abundant but most often take the form of two types of legally enforceable policy instrument. The first endeavours to regulate the quantity of wine produced whereas the second seeks to orientate its 'quality'. In briefly describing these instruments, the intensity of the political work undertaken to develop and maintain them will be underlined.

Within the EU, three instruments have been developed to set limits upon the quantity of wine which is produced and allowed to enter the marketplace. The first is a system of plantation rights. Introduced in 1976 and set for the EU as a whole, these rights to grow wine-producing grapes operate through national quotas which are subsequently regionalized and managed by national administrations. Introduced at a time of massive wine surpluses, these rights correspond to a problematization of Europe's wine industry as being in a state of structural overproduction. Advocated by not only the European Commission but also the French government, plantation rights were thus seen as a means of limiting and orienting production. Since then this problematization has not been frontally challenged. However, through adroit use of decision-making processes within the European Council of Ministers, plantation rights have not been consistently applied with great rigour. Indeed, these rights actually increased between 1999 and 2007. In short, within the EU and national arenas, this instrument attracts political work from growers that consistently has inflationary results. Generally this work has not been politicized at the scale of the EU. However, within national decision-making arenas representatives of some regions regularly and publicly denounce the favouring of other wine regions. For example, in France growers from the Midi frequently consider they have lost out to producers of Bordeaux wines.

The second policy instrument used to limit the quantity of European wine is a system of subsidies for grubbing out vines (primes d'arrachage). Again, this instrument was introduced across the EU in 1976 in order to curb production and reduce that of table wine in particular. For example, it was used massively in the 1980s in regions such as the Midi (Genieys, 1998; Laporte and Touzard, 1998). More precisely, table wine without geographical designation was identified by many actors, and those from the European Commission in particular, as the segment of

EU production that was causing surpluses and reducing prices. Although their initial introduction sparked considerable and politicized opposition, increases in subsidies to grub out vines have since been sought after by the representatives of numerous wine regions and their allies within national governments. In 2006, the Commission proposed to reinvigorate this policy in order to cut back production (EC, 2006), a change ultimately supported by the EU's Council of Ministers, albeit at reduced levels, in December 2007. Indeed, this instrument is so firmly ingrained within the Purchase IR that most actors within the industry do not even conceive of a reform of its regulation which would not include subsidies for vine destruction.

The third and final instrument used in Europe to control the quantity of wine on the market are distillation aids. These subsidies encourage merchants to remove unsold wine from the market by transforming it into a product that can be sold as raw material for the spirits industry. Distillation aids are supposed to be used only in periods of 'crisis'. However, since their introduction throughout the EU in the 1970s, their use has often been routinized at considerable cost to the EU budget. For this reason, officials from the European Commission are not consistent supporters of this instrument. However, growers, merchants and representatives of government in producer member states generally are and have frequently politicized the problem of distillation in order to defeat opponents within the EU's Council of Ministers (e.g. in December 2007).

Alongside these 'quantitative' policy measures, the Purchase IR of the European wine industry is also structured by two types of instrument designed to orientate the 'quality' of Europe's wines. The first of these concerns the definition of wine. Before the EU's Common Market Organization was first set up in 1970, the definition of this product had been the subject of considerable problematization and politicization focused upon the use of added sugar. Actors in certain producer member states (notably Germany) were in favour of this practice whereas their counterparts from other member states considered it abhorrent. Eventually a compromise was reached and a definition acceptable to all became institutionalized throughout the EU. More recently, however, the issue of definition has been the object of reproblematization and politicization because of the perceived threat of New World wines. Produced within states whose definition of wine imposes fewer or indeed no restrictions upon what winemakers can or cannot add during winemaking, these products have been seen by actors across Europe either as effective competitors whose definition of wine should be copied or as unprincipled traitors whose wines should be vilified or even outlawed.

The second policy instrument used in Europe in order to encourage and improve wine quality are systems of certification based upon geographical designations (AOC or Vin de pays). Encouraging the production of wine that is certified for both its origin and its quality has been seen as the antidote to the difficulties of the European wine industry since the beginning of the 20th century. Since then, the notion of origin has been institutionalized not only to provide geographical designations with legal protection, but also to regulate grape-growing and wine-making practices on the one hand and facilitate collective marketing on the other. In short, the link between certification, origin and quality has been problematized and institutionalized. However, since the early 1990s and again partly due to competition from less-regulated New World wines, this collective and public problem has become the object of considerable political work. For example, opponents of certification claim that standards of certification are not sufficiently restrictive and that implementation has been lax. Moreover, some of these actors underline that because AOC wines are regulated on a national basis, the European Commission has been left without any levers for influencing this (increasing) part of the European wine industry. In the case of wine, as in many others, the EU is not a neatly drawn multi-level polity within which the competencies of EU-wide, national and regional arenas are clearly and permanently defined (Carter and Smith, 2008). Instead, this industry is regulated through a multiplicity of decision-making mechanisms which, moreover, are constantly cleaved by a deep-set distinction between arrangements for table wine and those for wines with a geographical designation (De Maillard, 2001). In the case of the former, key arenas are composed of representatives of regions such as the Midi and Puglia, national ministries of agriculture, organizations such as the French VINIFLOR and the Commission's DG Agriculture. Meanwhile, the regulation of wines that have a geographical designation (AOCs in France, VQPRD in the terminology of the EU) is undertaken by representatives of regions such as Bordeaux and Bourgogne. Here DG agriculture is virtually absent, whereas national ministries are present but tend strongly to follow the orientations shaped by producer-dominated regulatory agencies such as the French INAO.

In summary, the five policy instruments described above together constitute a set of interlinked issue areas around which the regulation of this industry's Purchase IR has been shaped over time. As we have briefly seen, each instrument is currently dominated by the representatives of growers. In order to analyse this domination, however, one needs to grasp how the political work engaged in by these actors has enabled them to not only influence the rules and relations which structure the purchasing of wine but extend their power to encompass the regulation of the entire European wine industry.

4.2. The Purchase IR and domination within Europe's wine industry: The crucial significance of territory

Contrary to what many commentators believe, growers do not dominate the regulation of this industry because of their electoral strength or their capacity to disrupt public life through violent demonstrations. Rather their continuous political power stems from the durability of neo-corporatist political enterprises which continue to lock growers and public actors into a relation of interdependence on the one hand whilst locking out representatives of wine merchants, as well as dissident growers, on the other. Working from the citadel of their impregnable position in the Purchase IR, growers' representatives exert influence over the other three IRs and thereby over the four key traits of the industry as a whole: its production, its commercialization, the definition of its product and that of its professional identities. These actors have attained this position through ensuring that they are omnipresent inside the decision-making bodies located within and across the IRs. In order to understand how growers have obtained and maintained such access, however, a purely sectoral line of investigation is insufficient. Instead, it will be argued that political usages of references to territory cut across sectoral logics and, in so doing, provide a key for understanding grower strength, merchant weakness and public actor passivity. More precisely, as our work with Caitríona Carter has shown elsewhere, territory is not only a variable which actors take into account when defining policy orientations. It is the principal cause of the 'political assignment' of authority to make such decisions (Carter and Smith, 2008).

A first political usage of territory in the wine industry is to justify the protection of each wine region using the policy instruments presented in Section 4.1. This point can amply be illustrated using argumentation made publicly by the representatives of individual wine regions or national administrations. For instance, representatives of the Bourgogne wine interprofession highlight that their work to regulate their sector is carried out 'in the general interest'. More tellingly still, the European Commission has recently gone so far as to stress that 'in many regions the value of wine production represents more than 30% of its total agricultural production' (CE, 2006: 11; see Table 3.10).

88 *Globalization Within the European Wine Industry*

Table 3.10   Europe's ten principal wine regions

	Area of vines (1000 ha)	Holdings with vines (1000)	Wine and regional agricultural production (%)
Castilla-La Mancha	538.4	62.8	–
Languedoc-Roussillon	286.4	27.0	44.8
Aquitaine	154.6	16.0	36.1
Puglia	110.8	69.5	9.2
Sicily	106.6	54.6	8.2
Norte	98.9	97.4	20.0
Provence Alpes C. d'Azur	91.5	10.0	23.0
Veneto	87.5	54.5	16.3
Extremadura	82.9	9.9	–
Poitou-Charentes	81.1	10.7	4.8

Source: CE 2006: 118.

The Commission's report subsequently concludes by underlining the socially and environmentally 'problematic' effects that any widespread 'delocalization' of production would cause (2006: 144). This construction of current reality and of the future of the industry is a typical example of how and why the mobility of wine production between European regions is highly constrained. The definition of public problems and policy instruments tends strongly to lock in 'territorial rents' and thereby shore up the power of actors who already dominate each wine region. Moreover, through their multipositional presence in national and European decision-making arenas, representatives of these regions have a continuous impact upon the regulation of the European wine sector as a whole.

Ultimately then, the effect of territory upon the regulation of this industry concerns the arguments, symbols and techniques of dramatization used to advocate or resist change in the problematization of issues and the formulation of policy instruments. Consequently, and contrary to the postulates of rational choice theory, advocacy of change or its resistance cannot simply be explained in terms of 'economic' interests and studied as processes of conscious preference formation and strategy making. Of course, objective interests and tactical reasoning are an important part of any industry's regulation. However, their force or weakness depends upon how an interest is presented and alliances between actors take shape, endure or collapse. Here studying the political usage of territory again provides a salutary means of understanding such processes because territorial references are omnipresent in the problematization and politicization of issues and instruments. More precisely, European growers in particular have, thus far at least, succeeded in founding their legitimacy to represent wine regions and the sector as a whole by invoking what wine means not only for its producers and makers but for 'the general interest'. In so doing they have successfully updated symbols and cognitive frames in such a way as to present themselves as the modern defenders of a valued tradition, rather than as reactionary protectionists of territorial rents. In contrast, neither merchants nor representatives of public bodies have been able to mobilize references to territory in such a politically effective way. Merchants tend to present themselves instead as business people, an image which in much of Southern Europe does little to augment their legitimacy to intervene in the regulation of producer-dominated industries. Meanwhile, for their part public actors, such as national or Commission civil servants, either submit to grower-inspired politicizations of territory or engage in vague and symbol-less references to national or European interest. In summary, one can fully understand how representatives of producers have mobilized references to territory in order to shore up their position within the European wine industry's Institutional Order (IO) only by grasping the abdication of merchants, politicians and public officials within its arenas (Carter and Smith, 2008).

Conclusion

This chapter has uncovered three principal findings about the way the European wine industry has interpreted and reacted to globalization. First, it has underlined the fundamental importance of political work (or its absence) in each of the four IRs of the industry. The employment and finance IRs have not been problematized or politicized over the last 15–20 years. The Commercial IR has undergone some problematization but only at the level of collective problems. In contrast, massive quantities of political work have been devoted to the Purchase IR. Globalization is not therefore an anonymous and subjectless 'trend' that affects all parts of this industry simultaneously and in the same manner. Rather, it has been used to facilitate intra-firm change (employment and finance) or to marginally adjust collective marketing (commercial). However, as stasis in the Purchase IR underlines, globalization can also produce gridlock when producers are left to fight amongst themselves by the weak- or non-intervention of merchants and public actors. In short, globalization has been used within arguments for or against regulatory change. These

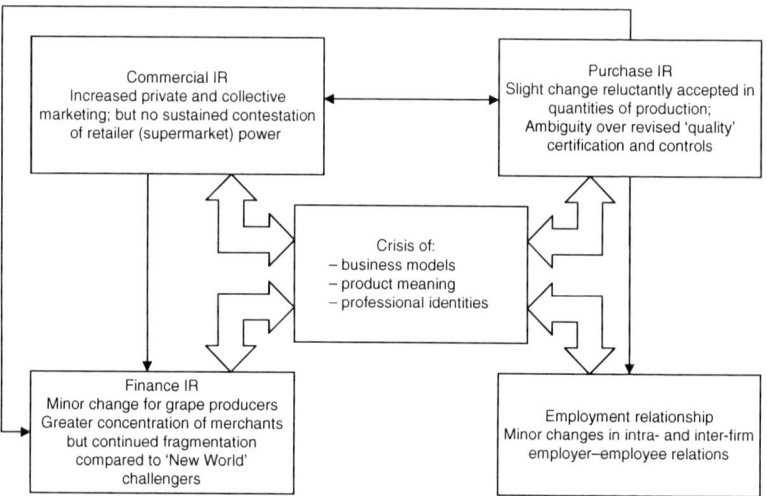

Figure 3.4 The European wine industry's destabilized Institutional Order

have been endogenized into, for example, the European wine industry through the differentiated political work conducted within and between each of its four IRs (Figure 3.4).

Second, within and around the Purchase IR, debates and negotiating outcomes have been strongly shaped by policy instruments from the past and descendants of the political enterprises which founded them. Growers traditionally dominated these enterprises and continue to do so, partly because of the political resources they have developed through constructing arguments and building alliances and partly because of the 'inappropriate' political work undertaken by merchants and dissident growers in order to change the regulation of the industry. As Section 4.2 has just underlined, growers have been particularly adroit in appropriating linkages between their policy objectives and references to territory which legitimize the equation of grower interests with those of the public interest. Overall, therefore, the case of the European wine industry validates our claim that studying the use of 'territory' during processes of institutionalization first enables research to reveal important linkages between industry-specific and trans-industry debates and negotiating arenas. Secondly, such a perspective also provides a means of sharpening the concept of political work so as to better grasp how, today, overlaps between differing scales of regulation (substate, state, EU, WTO, etc.) are the subject of continuous debate and powering within each industry. In this way, 'globalization' can be studied through the debates and alliance-building it prompts around the question of 'political assignment', rather than merely, and simplistically, be described as an anonymous and exogenous force which has given rise to 'multi-level governance' (Carter and Smith, 2008).

Finally, the chapter not only highlights how the public authorities of EU wine-producing states have blindly followed the same strategies of their respective growers, but also reveals how they have resisted the emergence of a common European wine policy which, conceivably, could have been legitimized as a vehicle for combating the negative effects attributed to 'globalization'. It would be excessive to lay the blame for this industry's current disarray entirely upon this non-policy. However, the latter certainly contributes to a pattern of regulation consistently marked by collective and public inaction over 'commercial' issues on the one hand and heavily path-dependent intervention over issues framed solely around the territorialized interests of growers on the other.

4
Shareholder Value, Political Work and Globalization in the Pharmaceutical Industry

Matthieu Montalban

Introduction

Globalization is a process which can have very different meanings which encompass

- the harmonization of rules between countries and the institutionalization of international rules;
- the increasing proportion of revenues and investments made in foreign markets by multinational corporations;
- the liberalization of financial markets and the increasing international mobility of financial capital;
- a growing number of non-domestic employees within private corporations, thus causing an international division of labour inside each company.

If all these processes have occurred in the pharmaceutical industry, in reality it has been both a national and a global industry for decades.

Health care systems and drug regulations remain national and their specificities shape the pharmaceutical industry of each country. All these regulations are social and political constructions which actors have developed over time. Public health care is of course a crucial political question which, in most developed countries, has engendered different forms of government intervention. Moreover, because of the growth of health care expenditures since the end of the Second World War, for many nations the pharmaceutical industry is also crucial as a source of wealth and innovation. Consequently, the relationship between public health care and the pharmaceutical industry is invariably a central issue for national political economies.

Over the same time span, most of the dominant pharmaceutical companies (commonly known as *Big Pharma*) have also become multinationals (e.g. US companies such as Pfizer or Merck & Co, and Swiss and German corporations such as Roche, Ciba Geigy or Hoechst). Moreover, many of the rules by which drugs are regulated in different countries have become very similar.

Nonetheless, the globalization of capitalism has accelerated during the last 20 years and effected this industry because of the liberalization of markets in general and financial markets in particular. Shareholder value management emerged in the US in the mid-1980s due to a growth of institutional investors in the ownership of publicly held corporations and the development of financial products with their own professional community (financial analysts, investment bankers, rating agencies, etc.) (Dobbin and Zorn, 2005; Fligstein, 1990, 2001; Froud *et al.*, 2006). This 'Anglo-saxon' and financial style of management is based on the objective of maximizing shareholder profits by adopting principles of corporate governance and refocusing on core businesses, through mergers and acquisitions, stock buy back, outsourcing and spin-off activities. As a result, managing in terms of shareholder value has generated a set of practices and customs that has become the norm for global capitalism, which defines 'institutional' shareholders as its most powerful agents. Indeed, many authors talk about the 'financialization' of capitalism (Dore, 2000; Froud *et al.*, 2006; Höpner, 2001; Krippner, 2005; Vitols, 2004). Whether one employs this term or not, when the general trends of globalization and financialization have been translated into political and economic processes, this has certainly challenged the influences which shape the social construction of the pharmaceutical market.

The pharmaceutical industry is sometimes analysed in terms of 'Sectoral systems of innovation' (McKelvey and Orsenigo, 2001), because the pharmaceutical industry not only has a highly innovative character but is also shaped by complex and complementary institutions. Because these include health care systems, patent systems, public research centres, public financing systems and drug regulation, a sectoral and institutionalist approach is necessary in order to grasp this sector's key relationship between innovation and competitiveness. More precisely, in this chapter I will use the *Politics of Industries* approach to explain the political and social construction of health care systems, intellectual property rights (IPR) and drug regulation as products of compromises between representatives of states, patients, health care professionals, insurers and the pharmaceutical companies. In particular, I will show that the specificities of the US pharmaceutical market, notably its domination by shareholder value management, have structured the global pharmaceutical industry. In turn this has pushed *Big Pharma* to engage in active political work to both protect their profits in the US and export some American regulatory instruments to other countries. In short, globalization in the pharmaceutical industry has taken place through the harmonization of rules towards a more 'American style' of regulation, the domination of US markets over the global pharmaceutical market and the hegemony of the norms associated with shareholder value.

In order to empirically document this claim, two questions will be addressed:

- How have globalization and shareholder value shaped the political compromise sustaining the pharmaceutical industry's Commercial Institutionalized Relationship (IR)?
- How has *Big Pharma* sought to reconcile constraints from the Commercial IR, in particular drug regulation, and those which pertain to the creation of shareholder value?

In order to answer these questions, the first section of the chapter analyses the institutionalization of this industry's Commercial IR between 1945 and the 1980s with a particular focus upon the specificities of the US market in the latter decade. The chapter's second section explains how the Financial IR, and shareholder value in particular, have constrained the strategies of pharmaceutical companies and, consequently, how the Financial IR has become complementary to the Commercial IR. The third section of the chapter shows how competition within US *Big Pharma* and shareholder value pushed the companies involved to undertake active political work in Europe, not only in countries such as France but also at the level of the European Union (EU), in order to shape the Commercial IR around a more 'American' and 'business friendly' type of regulation. Finally, the chapter's fourth section analyses the causes of recent crises within this sector linked to the de-institutionalization of its Commercial IR.

1. The specificities of the Commercial IR in the pharmaceutical industry: Political compromise and national differences

Modern health care systems were institutionalized through processes which involved the construction of compromises between pharmaceutical companies and states. Historically, two political discourses are opposed in the pharmaceutical industry: a 'good pharma' discourse, from the pharmaceutical industry itself, asserts that it promotes health care, whilst a 'bad pharma' discourse criticizes the monopoly power of pharmaceutical companies (Froud *et al.*, 2006). These discourses partly shape the compromise between the pharmaceutical companies, states and other stakeholders. 'Good pharma' discourse is frequently used by pharmaceutical companies to legitimize specific regulations of industry and thereby protect their profits and monopoly power. Meanwhile, 'bad pharma' discourse is used by activists, non-governmental organizations and essayists to criticize monopoly power and a highly profitable industry.

In each country, this industry's Commercial IR is based on a political compromise between two objectives: access to medicine for patients and profitability for the drug industry. The tension between these two objectives is mediated through a Commercial IR which brings together the interests and power of drug regulation officials, health care professionals, insurers and representatives of both the State and the patients. In so doing, medicines and IPR have been socialized in ways which structure the innovatory capacity and profits of pharmaceutical firms. The most important rules that structure the Commercial IR of the industry concern drug regulations, national health care systems and patents. All these rules are political compromises between the contradictory interests of stakeholders. I will first analyse the social and political construction of drug regulation; second, the role of health care systems in the regulation and competitiveness of industry; and third, the political construction of patents on drugs and their role in innovation and profitability of industry. To do so, I will underline the specificities of the US market and regulations.

1.1. Drug regulation: A political compromise

Drugs are dangerous products. Indeed, in Greek *Pharmakos* means both a drug and a poison. Moreover, most patients have no capacity to make their own diagnoses and therefore need medical expertise in order to judge a drug's efficiency. Consequently, if patients do not trust drugs, a market for them cannot exist. More precisely, patients, the pharmaceutical industry and health care professionals are dependant upon each other. Historically, sets of regulations have been institutionalized to solve the contradiction between dependencies and conflicts of interest. Indeed, the main consequence of State intervention in this industry has been the institutionalization of the regulation of drugs and of the State agencies of control. More fundamentally still, this is why the Commercial IR structures the pharmaceutical industry. It is also why substantial political work has been undertaken by representatives of firms in order to reconcile their interests with public health objectives. Cooperation and political work between drug manufacturers and State or agency officials is the means through which political compromise over public health/profitability has been reached. Indeed, the history of this industry is one of transformations that have depended upon changing power relationships and regulation.

The US government was a key pioneer in regulating drugs. In 1902, the Biologics Control Act was passed to ensure the purity and safety of serums, vaccines and similar products used to prevent or treat diseases in humans. Immediately prior to this legislation, the US Department of Agriculture (USDA) had investigated food adulteration and pressed for a national (i.e. 'federal') food and drug law. Indeed, former USDA officials also organized lobbying efforts to pass federal law legislation against the misbranding and adulteration of foods and drugs. Since the beginning of the 20th century, more than 100 food and drug bills have been introduced in Congress. Indeed, 1902 also saw Congress appropriating funds to establish food standards and to study the effects of chemicals on digestion and health. Shocking disclosures were made of the use of poisonous preservatives and dyes in foods and of the cure-all claims for worthless and dangerous patent medicines. The first Food and Drugs Act (1906) then prohibited interstate commerce in misbranded and adulterated foods, drinks and drugs and authorized the Department of Agriculture to seize unsafe substances and prosecute consumer fraud in order to prevent injury and death from poisons (Source: FDA website).

Notwithstanding the importance of this initial period, the real beginning of US drug regulation was in 1938. Following political work undertaken by scientists known as 'therapeutic reformers', the Food, Drug and Cosmetic Act was passed and then used to institutionalize a systematic control of drug safety by a Federal agency that had been created in 1930: the Food and Drug Administration (FDA) (Pignarre, 2003; FDA website). It also created the category of 'prescription drugs', which could obtain authorization only when their principal molecules had been tested by clinical trials.[1]

During the 1950s and 1960s, Senator Estes Kefauver undertook the first systematic piece of political work to denounce the monopoly power of pharmaceutical companies which, he claimed, was awarded to them by the US patent system and the cost of marketing a modern drug (Froud *et al.*, 2006). Arguing that most drugs were inactive and inefficient, Kefauver wanted stricter control of drugs through clinical trials made by a Federal agency which would compare them to placebos in order to both prove the drugs' safety and efficiency and at the same time constrain the use of patents and regulate prices. After some health incidents, in particular the Thalidomide scandal, where serious problems for babies and pregnant women had been caused, the Harris–Kefauver Act was finally passed in 1962. However, intense lobbying by pharmaceutical companies curtailed Kefauver's initial proposition to force them to prove the efficiency and safety of their drugs. On the basis of this legislation, since 1962 the FDA has been giving marketing authorization only if this has been proven and when the drug's benefits/risks ratio is considered sufficient (i.e. its therapeutic benefits are considered superior to its risk of secondary effects).

Regulation highly similar to this was adopted by most developed countries between the 1960s and the 1970s while international norms, known as 'the Helsinki convention', institutionalized 'good clinical trial' and 'good manufacturing' practices (Pignarre, 2003). All these regulations were compromises between states and pharmaceutical companies given that the latter wanted minimal control over their practices. However, these regulations also created barriers to entry that ensured domination of markets by incumbent firms. Today, all the developed countries have their own state agency which gives marketing authorizations if the benefits/risk ratio of the drug is sufficient. In practice, firms have to prove the efficiency of the drug versus a placebo, not versus a drug on the market (except in the case of very dangerous diseases).

In summary, we have seen that a drug is not something that is straightforward to define and that its definition is socially constructed. Ultimately, a drug is a therapeutic proposition which, when associated with a certain usage and dosage, is considered by the State to possess a sufficient benefits/risk ratio for health.[2] Three types of drugs now exist: *ethical drugs* (prescription and patented drugs), *generic drugs* (non-patented prescription drugs) and *Over The Counter drugs* (non-prescription drugs or OTC). Ethical drugs are the most profitable. However, the political construction of the pharmaceutical market is also linked to health care systems, which, in turn, also shape the demand for drugs.

1.2. National health care systems as socialized demand for pharmaceuticals

After the Second World War, many countries institutionalized their respective national health care systems. For example, in France, the *Sécurité Sociale* was created in 1945. However, this did not occur in the US because Medicare and Medicaid have been restricted to the old, the dependant and the poor. The US is also a unique case because the American health care insurance system is largely private. Most households (100 million Americans) subscribe to insurance contracts, such as Indemnity Plans or Managed Care Organizations and Health Maintenance Organizations (HMO). The system of managed care was institutionalized by President Nixon after the political work undertaken by the most important HMO, Kaiser Permanent. More than 47 million Americans have no health care insurance and therefore have to pay for drugs at very high unregulated prices.

If we except the US case, national public health care systems socialized health expenditures and the reimbursement of drugs (with some differences between states). Moreover, most of the drugs are prescribed by health care professionals. As a consequence, price plays a very small role as a mechanism for regulating a demand which has grown with the objective and perceived 'needs' of each country's population. To limit price rises, states have regulated them. This regulation has been the consequence of political work. For example, in France, pharmaceutical companies wanted limited price regulation when the *Sécurité Sociale* was first institutionalized (1945). But the State decided instead to regulate prices in order to avoid public deficits using the argument that because the *Sécurité Sociale* ensured there would be growth in the demand of each drug, pharmaceutical firms should accept price controls (Chauveau, 1999). By controlling prices, however, the profitability of pharmaceutical companies was lowered in France and other countries where similar measures were adopted.

Pricing mechanisms vary widely between countries. Prices are administered in some countries because their health care insurance systems disconnect drug demand from rises in incomes and the cost of living. Prices are also often negotiated between insurers/financiers and pharmaceutical companies. However, once again, the US is the only true exception because its drug prices are completely unregulated. Moreover, because of its strong growth in health expenditure, strict patent system and the market power of its pharmaceutical manufacturers, considerable inflation in drug prices has occurred. Today, the prices of new prescription drugs in the US are twice those of Europe. In addition, the consumer advertising of prescription drugs is also unregulated whereas this practice is forbidden in all other countries.

1.3. The patent system

Patents and IPR lead to monopoly rents. These rights are often analysed as a second-best compromise between providing companies with incentives to innovate and the need to publicize information (Arrow, 1962). Because of strong drug regulations, the time to market each new drug is long: between 10 and 12 years on average. Consequently, financial constraints and therefore barriers to market entry are very high for pharmaceutical companies. For this reason, through their respective interest groups (PhRMA in the US, EFPIA in Europe, LEEM/SNIP in France), pharmaceutical companies in all countries have defended strong patent systems. In order to do so they have generally combined a technicized discourse with appeals to political values: patents are a way to increase incentives to innovate and promote the progress of medicine and health care; patents also increase a drug's 'life' in an industry that is 'the most regulated in the world' where innovation is hampered by the need to test around 10,000 molecules to invent one drug.

Indeed, 'innovation' has always been used as an argument to promote a strong patent system which conciliates health care and the profitability of pharmaceutical companies. But patents on drugs are also political constructions: for example, drug patents have existed in France only since 1958, and this due to lengthy political work undertaken by French pharmaceutical firms to improve their capacity to compete against US, German and Swiss firms (Chauveau, 1999). In developing countries, patent systems sometimes do not exist or are limited. For example, the Indian Patent Act forbids patents on drugs but authorizes patents on their process of manufacturing (Launay *et al.*, 2004). However, developed countries with strong patent system have created a market for ethical drugs, that is those which are the most profitable.

The emergence of generic drugs in the 1960s provided an initial contestation of the patent system's legitimacy. However, even if the use of generic drugs is on the increase, as we shall see in the next section, during the 1980s and 1990s the patent system has continued to be protected due to political work undertaken by *Big Pharma* (Figure 4.1).

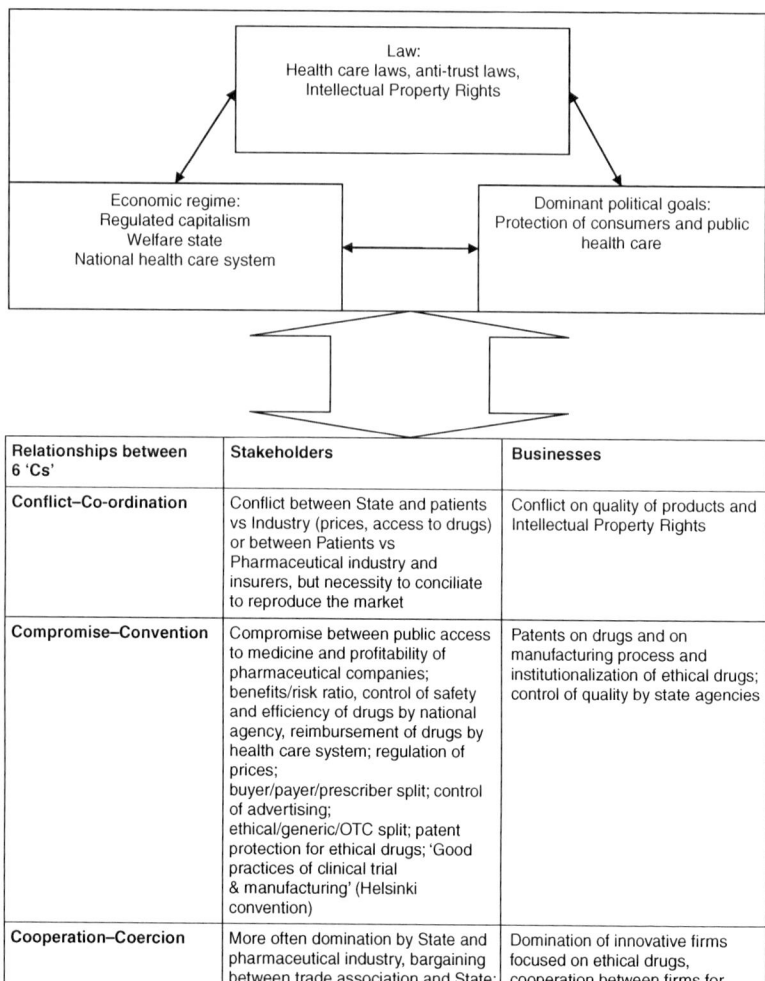

Figure 4.1 The pharmaceutical industry's modern Commercial IR in most developed countries

All the rules of the Commercial IR determine the rules of competition and barriers to entry which apply to incumbent and outsider firms, as well as conditioning their respective profitability and strategies. Through examining the US situation since 1985 the next section shows how shareholder value and the pressure to extract profits have both caused and been caused by political work which, in turn, has considerably modified the pharmaceutical industry's Commercial IR.

2. Globalization, shareholder value and struggles for corporate control: The articulation between the US Financial and Commercial IRs (1980–2000)

Globalization and financialization (defined as the hegemony of shareholder value) have increased competition for corporate control. In order to show the causes and effects of this trend, I will first analyse the transformation of the Financial IR through examining the financialization of *Big Pharma*. Second, I will show how the Financial IR has interacted with the Commercial IR, both through industrial strategies and through political work, in order to maintain shareholder value in the US. In particular, we will see that over the period 1980–2000 *Big Pharma* became increasingly dependant upon evaluations carried out by financial analysts and this for two reasons: company ownership structures and the specificity of innovation in the pharmaceutical industry.

2.1. Shareholder value management and IR hierarchy: Financialization in action

Big Pharma has become strongly controlled by institutional investors. However, the effects of this change have not been inevitable or automatic. Rather, dependence on this type of investor has increased largely because of the widespread adoption of shareholder value management.

2.1.1. The specificity of innovative activity in the pharmaceutical industry

Because of drug regulations, barriers to entry are very important: companies have to undertake extensive and expensive clinical trials in order to obtain their marketing authorizations. Split in three linear phases, these trials last an average of 12 years. Consequently, the cost of research and development (R&D) is very high. Moreover, the adoption of shareholder value management has introduced a logical contradiction between the long-term views of the innovation process and the short-term views of investors. Given that financial constraints are so strong, patent systems play a key role in protecting the profitability of drugs and ensuring the extraction of rents. Self-financing of R&D is generally preferred, not only to control innovation but also because the high profitability of *Big Pharma* has accorded them easy access to credit and financial markets. In contrast, access to external financing is much more difficult to obtain for less-dominant firms, and this because innovation is highly risky in this industry and barriers to entry are so high.

2.1.2. Ownership structures, financial evaluation and shareholder value

Ownership in the US is highly dispersed for several reasons, in particular the operation of a common law system which protects minority shareholders (Berle and Means, 1932; Jensen and Meckling, 1976; La Porta *et al.*, 1999). Nevertheless, ownership of pharmaceutical companies has increasingly become controlled by institutional investors, in particular pension or mutual funds. At the same time, the US and UK financial systems have also clearly become more market orientated and thus created a large space for changing corporate control. Finally, as mentioned earlier, since the late 1980s, shareholder value management has also become the dominant norm of corporate managers. Spawned by Jensen's agency theory (1988), this ideology transforms the manager into the agent of shareholders. Consequently, the sole objective of the firm becomes the maximization of shareholder revenues, that is stock price and dividends per share, by using stock buy back, mergers and acquisitions, divestitures, spinning off of non-core and non-profitable business, and outsourcing. Because of the possible problems of agency linked to asymmetric information between managers and shareholders, corporate governance and markets of corporate control are used as the key means with which to control managers. Corporate governance is the system of rules and practices that allows shareholders and other stakeholders to control managers. Modes of corporate governance are largely national and are the sedimented results of political compromises between stakeholders that have been institutionalized in law (Gourevitch and Shinn, 2005; La Porta *et al.*, 1999; Roe, 2001). Indeed, the more minority shareholders are protected by laws, as in the US, the more corporate governance is shareholder value oriented.

The US and UK pharmaceutical industries are both based upon the typical characteristics of this 'Anglo-saxon' model of ownership and corporate governance, that is the shareholder value model. Table 4.1 describes the ownership structure of the 43 most important pharmaceutical companies in the world. As it makes clear, institutional investors are hegemonic in the ownership of US and UK firms.

However, Table 4.1 also shows that institutional investors now hold important shares of ownership of European and Japanese pharmaceutical corporations, even if historical 'blockholders' such as families or banks are still important in these countries. Corporate governance modes also differ by country, partly due to differences in law.

Table 4.1 The hegemony of institutional investors in US and UK firms' ownership (May 2004)

Name	Ownership distribution by investors type in the top 50 shareholders in 2004 in %				
	Institutional investors	Industrial shareholders	Familial shareholders	Insiders	Bank
Abbott laboratories	86.4	0.0	0.0	9.4	4.2
Allergan Inc	90.6	0.0	0.0	0.0	9.4
Amgen Inc	97.4	0.0	0.0	0.0	2.6
AstraZeneca plc	95.0	3.3	0.0	0.0	1.7
Biogen-Idec	96.1	0.0	0.0	0.0	3.9
Bristol-Myers Squibb Co	98.1	0.0	0.0	0.0	1.9
Eli Lilly & Co	85.1	0.0	0.0	11.7	3.2
Forest Laboratories Inc	85.4	0.0	0.0	1.8	12.8
Genentech Corp	36.8	62.9	0.0	0.0	0.3
Genzyme	97.4	0.0	0.0	0.0	2.6
Glaxosmithkline plc	99.1	0.0	0.0	0.0	0.9
Johnson & Johnson Inc	94.6	0.0	0.0	0.0	5.4
King Pharmaceutical	98.3	0.0	0.0	0.0	1.7
Medimmune	98.8	0.0	0.0	0.0	1.2
Merck & Co Inc	98.1	0.0	0.0	0.0	1.9
Mylan Laboratories	92.0	0.0	0.0	5.9	2.1
Pfizer Inc	97.7	0.0	0.0	0.0	2.3
Schering-Plough Corp	96.7	0.0	0.0	0.0	3.3
Shire Pharmaceutical	94.1	0.0	0.0	0.0	5.9
Watson Pharmaceutical	91.1	0.0	0.0	7.2	1.7
Wyeth	96.7	0.0	0.0	0.0	3.3
Average anglo-saxons companies	91.7	3.2	0.0	1.7	3.4
AkzoNobel NV	100.0	0.0	0.0	0.0	0.0
Alcon	25.0	75.0	0.0	0.0	0.0
Altana AG	21.5	0.0	78.3	0.0	0.2

Table 4.1 (Continued)

Name	Ownership distribution by investors type in the top 50 shareholders in 2004 in %				
	Institutional investors	Industrial shareholders	Familial shareholders	Insiders	Bank
Boerhinger Ingelheim	0.0	0.0	100.0	0.0	0.0
Bayer AG	98.8	0.0	0.0	0.0	1.2
H Lundbeck	6.0	93.1	0.0	0.0	0.9
Merck KGaA	26.1	0.0	73.8	0.0	0.1
Novartis AG	62.0	34.6	0.0	0.0	3.4
Novo Nordisk	51.7	46.9	0.0	0.0	1.4
Roche Holding	1.7	39.2	58.9	0.0	0.2
Sanofi-Aventis SA	47.8	51.4	0.0	0.0	0.8
Schering AG	83.3	15.7	0.0	0.0	1.0
Serono SA	13.9	0.0	85.6	0.0	0.5
Solvay SA	27.0	0.0	72.9	0.0	0.1
UCB	29.4	0.0	69.6	0.0	1.0
Average european groups	39.6	23.7	35.9	0.0	0.7
Astellas Pharma Ltd	37.8	0.0	0.0	0.0	62.2
Daiichi-Sankyo Ltd	80.1	0.0	0.0	0.0	19.9
Eisai Ltd	72.8	6.2	0.0	0.0	21.0
Ono Pharmaceutical	74.0	16.2	9.4	0.0	0.4
Shionogi Ltd	62.4	0.0	0.0	0.0	37.6
Takeda Pharmaceutical Ltd	29.9	0.0	0.0	0.0	70.1
Tanabe Seyaku Ltd	91.5	0.0	0.0	0.0	8.5
Average japanese groups	64.1	3.2	1.3	0.0	31.4
Average total	67.9	10.8	13.3	0.6	7.4

Source: Thomson financials.

Nonetheless, even here a hybridization process has occurred within Japanese and European firms towards a much more 'Shareholder value orientated' mode of corporate governance. For example, many of these firms have imported rules such as the greater transparency of annual reports, growing numbers of independent directors on their boards, stock options and stock repurchasing (Montalban, 2007; Vitols; 2004). Moreover, increasing numbers of European firms are quoted on the New York Stock Exchange using American Depositary Receipts/shares (ADRs) (e.g. Novartis, Sanofi-Aventis, Serono, GlaxoSmithKline and AstraZeneca). These companies must therefore follow many US rules on corporate governance. Moreover, the high level of share repurchasing reveals that the stock market is not mainly a financing institution. Indeed, in this industry only biotech firms or start-ups use shares as external finance. Instead, for dominant companies stock markets function in the pharmaceutical industry as they do in the general rump of financial capitalism: as a means of organizing markets for corporate control (mergers and acquisitions) and structuring incentives for managers through stock option systems (Aglietta and Rébérioux, 2005; Carpenter *et al.*, 2003; Lazonick, 2005; Lazonick and O'Sullivan, 2000). The stock market has thus chiefly become a means of growing through mergers on the one hand and as a disciplinary institution which forces managers to maximize stock prices in order to avoid takeovers on the other. As a result, firms construct strategies in order to increase dividends, repurchase their own shares and maximize returns on equity.

Graph 4.1 underlines that for the 43 most important pharmaceutical companies in the world, shareholder value distribution (defined as the aggregate sum of dividends and stock repurchases) grew faster than capital expenditures between 1996 and 2005.

Consequently, pharmaceutical companies, especially those controlled by institutional investors, have had to maximize their stock price to avoid hostile takeovers. In so doing they have become increasingly dependant upon financial analysts. Like other financialized firms, pharmaceutical companies organize road shows and analysts meetings every three months to present their financial results. Moreover, every six months corporate managers organize 'R&D days' to present the development of 'pipelines' and the results of clinical trials (the pipeline is the portfolio of a molecule in clinical trials; blockbusters are ethical drugs that generate more than one billion dollars per year). This transparency makes it relatively easy to predict the profitability of a company over the next year. Financial analysts are specialized by sector and many therefore have excellent knowledge of the functioning of the

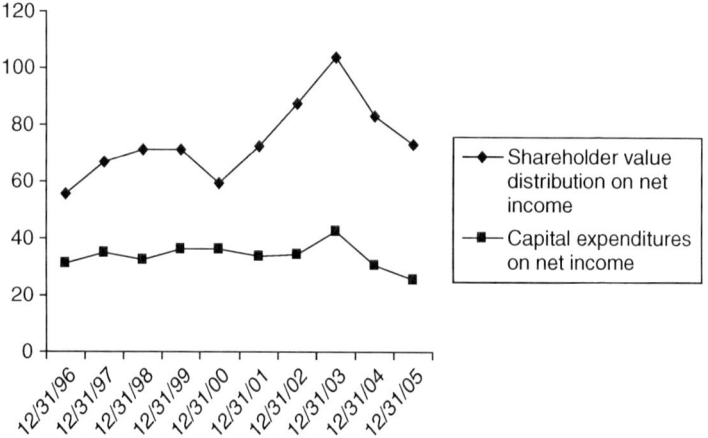

Graph 4.1 Shareholder value distribution and capital expenditure on net income of the 43 most important pharmaceutical companies in the world
Source: Thomson financials.

pharmaceutical industry. Because of this specialization, they prefer pure 'pharma' players and firms which have divested their non-core and non-profitable businesses (Batsch, 2002; Dobbin and Zorn, 2005; Fligstein, 2001; Morin, 2006). To evaluate a pharmaceutical group, they analyse financial results, the pipeline and if the company has blockbusters. If the company has a lot of molecules in the last phase of their pipelines and many blockbusters protected from losing their patents, they give a 'buy' order to their respective investors (Figure 4.2).

The stock price of the company concerned will then increase, making it easier for the firm to acquire competitors or smaller firms such as biotechnology producers. But in cases where the opposite has occurred, for example when the pipeline is poor or if a group is dependant upon one blockbuster that will shortly face competition from generics, stock prices will decrease and the firm will become vulnerable to a hostile takeover. The Financial IR of the pharmaceutical industry has typically been 'financialized' for these reasons and because as corporations have sought to maximize shareholder profits they have become increasingly dependant upon the opinions of investors and analysts.

In short, in this industry, blockbusters, pipelines, mergers and acquisitions provide the links between its Financial and Commercial IRs and structure competition between the players from *Big Pharma*.

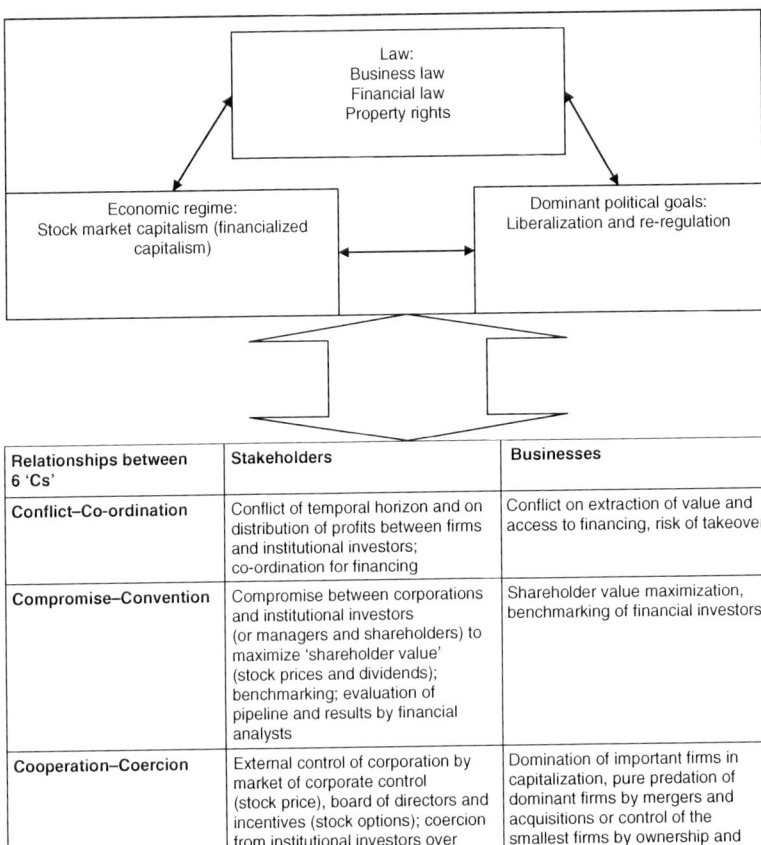

Figure 4.2 The Financial IR of the pharmaceutical industry

2.2. The articulation between the Financial, the Commercial and the other IRs

Having first shown that the US market is strategic for *Big Pharma* and blockbuster drugs, I will then analyse why increasing numbers of US and European firms have attempted to penetrate this market and undertaken political work to maintain 'pro-business' regulation in this country. The political work of the pharmaceutical industry is structured by two-pronged strategies of legitimization. On the one hand, many issues are problematized and then politicized around the argument that drugs contribute to better health. On the other, issues are frequently technicized around the idea that innovation is highly complex and costly because of 'the burden of regulation'. The best antidotes to this are seen as a strong patent system, unregulated prices and direct consumer advertising as a means of 'educating' patients.

2.2.1. The lobbying activity of Big Pharma and the institutionalization of the Commercial IR in the US

PhRMA is the principal US trade association but its membership is not restricted to American companies because it also includes many of their European and Japanese competitors (e.g. Sanofi-Aventis, GlaxoSmithKline, AstraZeneca and Takeda). Similarly, the main European pharmaceutical interest group (the European Federation of Pharmaceutical Industry and Associations, EFPIA) also contains American and Japanese members. In reality, all these groups have the same members and defend the same kind of regulations. PhRMA and pharmaceutical firms in the US finance numerous lobbyists in the House of Representatives and the Senate to protect the interests of pharmaceutical companies, especially the industry's patent, health care and unregulated price systems. Indeed, the pharmaceutical industry is the industrial sector which spends the most on lobbying in the US and has the most industry filings to the Senate – part of this financed by European groups such as Sanofi-Aventis or Novartis. Using data collected by the Center for Public Integrity, Tables 4.2–4.8 set out descriptive

Table 4.2 Pharmaceutical industry in the top 100 companies and organizations in lobbying

Rank	Names	Reported lobbying (in $ millions)
10	PhRMA	72.72
24	Pfizer inc	43.522
32	Merck and Co	40.71
36	Ali Lilly co	36.51
46	Glaxosmithkline plc	32.43
49	Bristol-Myers Squibb Co	31.76
61	Abbot lobaoratories	27.57
74	Wyeth	24.07
77	Biotechnology Industry Organization	23.61
80	Amgen	22.83
86	Johnson & Johnson	21.76
87	Schering-Plough Corp	21.1
99	Sanofi-Aventis	18.97
	Total industry	**417.562**

Source: Center Watch Database (Centre for Public Integrity).

Table 4.3 Money spent by pharmaceutical companies to directly influence US public policy

Category	Lobbying (in $ millions)
Federal lobbying	674
Federal campaign contributions*	87
State political contributions	46
527 donations**	10
Total	817

*Federal campaign contributions are from the 1998 cycle, which starts in 1997.
**527 donations from the top 20 pharmaceutical companies.

Table 4.4 Pharmaceutical lobbying in the US

Amount spent in lobbying since 1998	$675 millions
Number of lobbyists since 1998	3009
Former officials who registered to lobby since 1998	1014
Former members of Congress who lobbied	75
Bills lobbied	more than 1600

Source: Center for Public Integrity.

Table 4.5 Industries ranked by number of lobbying forms filed to the House between 1998 and 2004

Rank	Industry	Number of files
1	States, local governments and related organizations	13,776
2	**Pharmaceutical industry**	5433
3	Non-governmental organizations	5151

Note: If we are interested in industries, Pharmaceuticals comes first.

statistics about the lobbying activities of the pharmaceutical industry in the US (this database and its methodology are available online at www.publicintegrity.org). Unfortunately, this data covers only the 1998–2004 period. However, it provides a good idea of the influence of the pharmaceutical industry. More than 3009 lobbyists worked for the pharmaceutical industry between 1998 and 2004, an industry which spent more than $800 million to influence US policy over this period (Graph 4.2).

As many individual examples show, this lobbying activity has been very fruitful for the pharmaceutical industry. First, in 1980 the American

Table 4.6 Firms and organizations ranked by number of forms filed to the House between 1998 and 2004

Rank	Organization or firm	Number of files
8	PhRMA	303
11	Pfizer inc	262
25	Amgen inc	187
29	Bristol-Myers Squibb Co	165
30	Sanofi-Aventis	165
37	Glaxosmithkline plc	147
57	Schering-Plough Corp.	119
58	Wyeth	119
62	Merck & Co	116
67	Eli Lilly and Co	113
71	Novartis AG	111
73	Barr laboratories inc	109
75	Biotechnology Industry Organization	107
87	Genentech inc.	97

Table 4.7 Industries ranked by number of lobbying forms filed to the Senate between 1998 and 2004

Rank	Industry	Number of files
1	States, local governments and related organizations	13,571
2	**Pharmaceutical industry**	5397
3	Non-governmental organizations	5157

Note: If we are interested in industries, Pharmaceuticals comes first.

intellectual property regime was transformed by the Bayh–Dole Act, which permits industry–university partnerships to patent research products themselves, and this building upon the Chakrabarty decree of the US Supreme Court (1972), which permitted the patenting of biological entities (Coriat and Orsi, 2003a; Orsi, 2002). Further institutionalization took place in 1983 when, as a result of the political work undertaken by a coalition of pharmaceutical firms and patient representatives, an Orphan Drug Act was passed which, through tax credits, accelerated the development of drugs treating less than 200,000 people. Initially intended to be temporary, this legislation became permanent in 1997 through the FDA Modernization Act. Together, these three sets of rules were institutional preconditions for the development of biotechnology and the genomic paradigm which creates new technological and

Table 4.8 Firms and organizations ranked by number of forms filed to the Senate between 1998 and 2004

Rank	Organization or firm	Number of files
8	PhRMA	286
10	Pfizer inc	262
25	Amgen inc	185
28	Bristol-Myers Squibb Co	172
30	Sanofi-Aventis	166
37	Glaxosmithkline plc	147
57	Schering-Plough Corp	118
59	Merck & Co	117
62	Wyeth	116
63	Eli Lilly and Co	115
65	Biotechnology Industry Organization	113
79	Novartis AG	102
80	Genentech inc	100
82	Barr laboratories inc	99
86	Johnson & Johnson	97

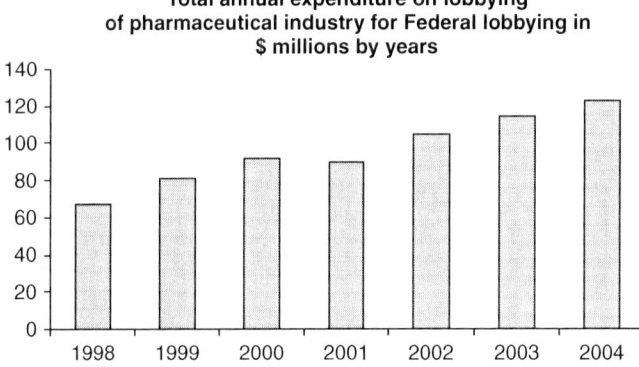

Graph 4.2 Growth of annual lobbying expenditures of the pharmaceutical industry in the US
Source: Center Watch Database (Center for Public Integrity).

growth opportunities for biotech and pharmaceutical companies (Coriat and Orsi, 2003a & b).

Second, in 1984, Senator Harry Waxman sought to encourage competition from generic drugs and to limit the price of ethical drugs. However, again the resulting legislation (the Hatch–Waxman Act of 1984, also called the Drug Price Competition and Patent Term Restoration Act) was a compromise between *Big Pharma*, Federal government and generic companies: '*The Hatch–Waxman Act established a regulatory framework that sought to balance incentives for continued innovation by research-based companies and opportunities for market entry by generic manufacturers*' (Federal Trade Commission, 2002). To enable earlier entry of generics into markets, amendments to the initial bill provided that certain conduct related to obtaining FDA approval, and which would otherwise constitute patent infringements, would be exempt from infringement liability under the patent laws. These amendments permitted the generic companies to file an Abbreviated New Drug Application (ANDA): if the generic companies could demonstrate that their products have the same active substances, means of administration, dosage form and strength and are bio-equivalent to branded drugs, they can obtain an ANDA without undertaking costly clinical trials. For *Big Pharma* the Hatch–Waxman Act established a five-year data exclusivity period and a total market exclusivity time of 14 years for new molecular entities. It also established that if a generic manufacturer claims a patent is invalid or uninfringed, the patent's owner has 45 days to file an infringement action which automatically ensured another 30 months of protection before an ANDA could be approved and generic competition could begin (paragraph IV on 'certifications'). In fact, as regards this law, in 75% of cases where *Big Pharma* have gone to court against generic manufacturers, they have obtained 30 extra months of protection (FTC, 2002): for example, GlaxoSmithKline successively obtained five 30-month stays of protection for Paxil.[3] Consequently, the protection of such companies is highly important, even if competition with generic manufacturers now exists as a legitimate part of the industry's Institutional Order (IO).

For a long time, the pharmaceutical companies have complained that the period for examining the files for marketing approval is too long. Since the introduction of the Prescription Drug Fees Act, however, companies have been able to pay fees for faster reviews. In 1997, after constant lobbying from *Big Pharma*, the Modernization Act reduced the time for FDA approval to 180 days, allowed manufacturers to disseminate journal articles describing the results of trials for unapproved uses of drugs and authorized six-month 'pediatric exclusivity' patent extensions. Indeed, because of the FDA Modernization Act, the mission of the FDA is changing, and especially now its role is '*to promote public health by promptly and efficiently reviewing clinical research and taking appropriate action on the marketing of regulated products in a timely manner (. . .) to participate with representatives of other countries*

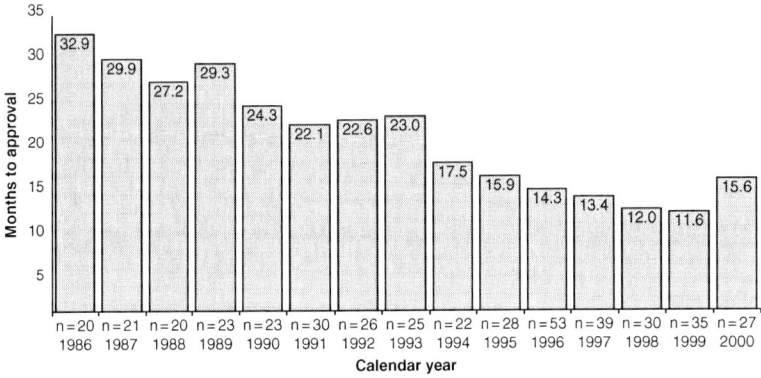

Graph 4.3 New drug approval time by year (median of total approval times in months)
Source: FDA.

to reduce the burden of regulation, coordinate regulatory requirements, and achieve appropriate equivalent arrangements' (FDA website: my emphasis). In addition, the FDA now eases restrictions on direct-to-consumer advertising of prescription drugs, allowing advertisements to refer consumers elsewhere to find risk information instead of including it in the ads themselves.[4] As we can see, these rules have led to a substantial decrease in approval times (Graph 4.3)

Pharmaceutical companies are also in favour of the reimbursement of drugs by states but are against price control. Indeed, the protection of unregulated price systems has always been a political objective of PhRMA. In 1994, after an important lobbying campaign, drug price control – part of President Clinton's health care project – was abandoned. In 2003, the Medicare Modernization Act offering prescription drugs benefits to Medicare recipients was institutionalized. However, this act also forbade Medicare from bargaining over drug prices with pharmaceutical firms. The pharmaceutical industry argues for (high) unregulated levels of pricing because of the cost of R&D, in particular using a study by Di Masi, Grabowski and Hansen (2003), which evaluates this cost at $800 million. However, this cost was estimated using the direct cost of development and an opportunity cost: the weighted average cost of capital, that is what a firm would have obtained if money had been invested in stock markets instead of in R&D. Consequently, this calculation was not based upon real expenditure. Nevertheless, the US administration accepted this line of argument and continues to cite the same study and its figure, thus legitimizing itself through the 'science' of neoclassical economists: a 'science' which is now used in all countries to explain why patents should be strong and prices high. Fundamentally, this is an indirect political validation of shareholder value by the State and a problematization of competitiveness and innovation in the pharmaceutical industry. A final effect of high prices and low levels of reimbursement is that more and more American people buy their drugs from Canada. In reaction, PhRMA and pharmaceutical companies have undertaken political work to forbid the import of drugs into the US by de-legitimizing them around the 'dangers of counterfeiting'.

2.2.2. The Commercial IR, the US market, the strategies of Big Pharma *and their articulation with the Financial IR*

This absence of control has made US drug prices the highest in the world (see Table 4.9).

For this reason, as well as those linked to the US intellectual property regime, this market is very 'business friendly' for pharmaceutical companies. First, the US market represented 49% of global sales in 2004 ($248 billion), the EU 28% and Japan 11%. More importantly, 72% of global sales of blockbusters in the world are made in the US alone. So, blockbuster drugs are in fact a construction of the US market's high prices and patent system. The strategy of *Big Pharma*, be it American or European, is to market blockbusters because they drive quick growth, increase profit rates and market share. Moreover, blockbusters generate enough profits for the self-financing of R&D. Therefore each *Big Pharma* company tries to capture a substantial share of the US market. To become a blockbuster, aggressive marketing is needed to target health care professionals (using drug representatives, training, advertising, etc.), insurers and patients (by direct-to-consumer advertising or 'consumer education'). European *Big Pharma* – for example Novartis, GlaxoSmithKline, AstraZeneca, Roche and Sanofi-Aventis – have also adopted a strategy based on

Table 4.9 Producer price index for drugs in several countries (100 = UK)

	1998	1999	2000	2001	2002
Spain	77	72	70	72	77
France	85	86	83	81	83
The Netherlands	na	na	83	84	92
Italy	88	82	82	85	86
Germany	109	103	94	90	94
United Kingdom	100	100	100	100	100
United States of America	188	213	241	205	194

Sources: PPRS, LEEM (2004).

blockbusters that entails increasing investments in the US market. For example, before its merger with Sanofi-Synthélabo, Aventis's US sales accounted for more than 49% of its total pharmaceutical sales in 2003. Sanofi-Synthélabo has also strongly increased its presence in the US: although in 1998 only 9.8% of its employees were in the US, by 2005 this figure had risen to 14.5%; sales in the US accounted for 35% of total pharmaceutical sales in 2004, up from only 12% in 1998. For Novartis, 46.6 % of its sales was in the US in 2005 (Source: annual reports; see also Montalban, 2007). More generally, evaluations carried out by financial analysts and dependency on blockbusters means that a permanent flow of new blockbusters and drugs in the pipeline is needed to avoid hostile takeovers.

Another important reason companies seek to penetrate the US market is the intellectual property regime which covers the *biotech* industry. Because of the specificities of US institutions in this field, it is dominated by US firms like Genentech, Amgen, Genzyme and Biogen-Idec. US *biotech* controls major parts of biotechnology's patents. Moreover, important financial markets and venture capital funds ease financing of start-ups. For *Big Pharma*, *Biotech* companies are more often suppliers of technologies, molecules or services, and sometimes they establish strong links with *Big Pharma* to develop their own drugs. Because of their small size and their financial needs, however, they are in fact highly dependant upon *Big Pharma*, who sometimes finance them or control an important share of their ownership. The latter can also easily acquire these companies. To use the language of this book, the Purchase IR in this industry is based upon cooperation and markets. The rules of this Purchase IR are again interdependent with drug and biological regulations and patent systems. Moreover, this Purchase relationship is also a Financial relationship for *biotech* because *Big Pharma* finance a lot of their research projects or create venture capital funds. Indeed, these Purchase relationships could be seen as a process of R&D outsourcing.

This relationship is partly rendered a public problem because Federal government financing for biotech is very important: first, through the Orphan Drug Tax Credit (which can amount to 50% of R&D costs); second, 85% of the National Institute of Health (NIH) budget ($28.6 billion in 2005) finances external projects and 88.9% are dedicated to life sciences (especially biotechnology). NIH has an agreement with *biotech* to undertake clinical trials or R&D. Some financing also comes from the National Science Foundation. In total, $132 billion was spent on the life sciences in 2005 by the US public sector. PhRMA and the Biotechnology Industry Organization (BIO, the interest group of small and medium-sized biotech firms) have consistently politicized the necessity to finance biotechnology using government funds and low taxes, arguing that biotechnology can increase innovation and permit better access to new medicine. In short, the same kind of legitimization through technicization has been adopted as for patent's protection of drugs. In addition, all these modes of financing are complementary with the new IPR regime, created by the Chakrabarty case and the Bayh–Dole Act, because they are incentives for attracting companies to the US. The relationship between *Big Pharma* and *biotech* is structured by these institutions and is very flexible and reversible, allowing firms to share and limit their risks and costs. *Big Pharma* are clearly dominant in this relationship, even if this is a typical 'market' relationship (Figures 4.3 and 4.4).

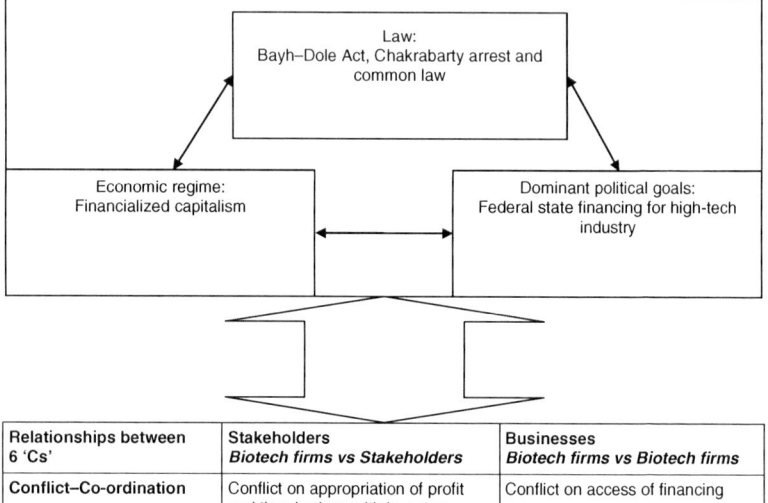

Figure 4.3 The Financial IR of the biotech industry and the Purchase IR of the pharmaceutical/biotech industry

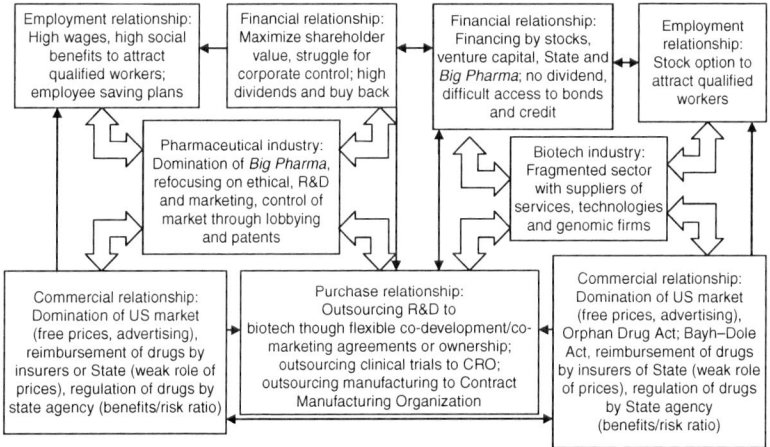

Figure 4.4 The pharmaceutical and biotech sectors

The institutional specificities of the US market and the domination of US firms also serve as benchmarks for the political work carried out by pharmaceutical companies in Europe. Moreover, the international institutionalization of patent systems is a critical issue for the pharmaceutical companies because of the important growth in generics and the lack of medicines in developing countries.

3. Political work in Europe and the WTO: The strengths and limits of 'exporting' US regulations

In several cases, the pharmaceutical industry has tried to influence national and European regulation and this especially in the areas of price control, clinical trials and patents. For the moment at least, however, European political compromises have been more 'health care orientated' and less 'business friendly'. In a context of globalization where shareholder value has become hegemonic because of change in the Financial IR, and where US markets and firms are increasingly in competition with European firms, since 1990 political work in Europe has been undertaken to enhance the 'competitiveness' of the European pharmaceutical industry by creating a more friendly business and institutional context which would be more attractive, both politically and commercially, to *Big Pharma*. In fact, because *Big Pharma* are multinational corporations, this political work has also been carried out by national and multinational companies. As a result, this work has been more orientated towards the maximization of shareholder value than to the promotion of health care. I analyse here the influence of political work of pharmaceutical companies on regulations in France, the UK and the EU. The main arguments for defending strong patents system, free prices, lower 'regulatory burdens' and the introduction of advertising (or 'consumer education') are presented by pharmaceutical companies as a means of delivering 'quality medicine'. But they are also increasingly framed as a means of halting the (supposed) decline of the competitiveness of Europe's pharmaceutical industry.

3.1. Pharmaceutical companies and their political work in France: Contrasting results

The French market is marked by not only the control of prices (by the *Comité Economique des Produits de Santé*, CEPS), no advertising on ethical drugs, a small OTC market, but also the reimbursement of all drugs by *l'assurance-maladie* (the health care system), which is part of the *Sécurité sociale*, the social protection system. From an historical point of view, the political compromise that structures the industry's Commercial IR is largely based on socialized medicine but predominately private health care professionals, a model which ensures growth of demand in volume, but with controls on prices. Moreover, advertising on ethical medicines is forbidden, and there is a specific tax on drugs which contributes to financing health care expenditure. Three conflicting features have recently structured political debates: first, the historical consensus on the necessity of a public health care system (be they on the political left or right, amongst patients, doctors and pharmaceutical companies, very few voices have been raised in favour of privatizing this system); second, the growth of drug and health care expenditure resulting in budget deficits for the *Sécurité Sociale* and pressures to limit prices, reimbursements, prescriptions from doctors and, recently, to facilitate generic drugs; and third, the competitiveness of the pharmaceutical industry in France (and therefore its 'attractiveness') is dependent upon higher reimbursements and higher prices, and greater numbers of prescriptions. The LEEM (*LEs Entreprises du Médicaments*, the main pharmaceutical interest group) has been arguing for several years for the higher reimbursement of drugs, increased (or unregulated) prices, less taxes (in France, there is a special tax for the pharmaceutical industry), more public research expenditure, the development of the OTC market and advertising on ethical drugs, strong patent protection and lower approval times. The LEEM remains favourable to a 'public' health care system,[5] but its main political work is devoted to 'attractiveness' and 'competitiveness', arguing that France loses market share in research, clinical trials and exports because of the lack of public R&D expenditure and its price system (which is partly true for clinical trials, but false for drug production) (Bélis-Bergouignan and Montalban, 2006; Moreau *et al.*, 2002). Since 2004, several reports have been published which underline the necessity to increase the competitiveness of French pharmaceutical and *biotech* companies (Marmot, 2004; Masson, 2004; Rexecode, 2004). The political work of these companies in France has had varying results. First, since 2004 the pharmaceutical and biotech industries have been considered as 'strategic' for France's competitiveness, and in so doing have obtained some new financing for biotech (increase of public expenses in R&D, the institutionalization of an *Agence Nationale de la Recherche*, the development of venture capital funds for biotech by the collaboration between Sanofi-Aventis and *Caisse des Dépôts et Consignations*); second, following an agreement between the LEEM and *Comité Economique des produits de Santé* covering the period 2003–2006, firms have obtained a little more freedom for determining their prices and some measures have been taken to accelerate administrative procedures for innovative drugs; third, the State has intervened to make the merger between Sanofi-Synthélabo and Aventis easier, and this following political work undertaken chiefly by Jean François Dehecq (ex-PDG of Sanofi-Synthélabo and PDG of Sanofi-Aventis) in a compromise between the financialization process (which has entailed mergers and acquisitions, and hostile takeovers to create shareholder value) and the Colbertist–Gaullian tradition of 'national champions' (Montalban, 2007). However, at the same time, because of increasing budget deficits, the Ministry of Health adopted a plan in 2004 to avoid public deficits by undertaking de-reimbursements and imposing lower prices on several drugs.

Because of these measures, politicizations have been attempted. For example, Dehecq wrote a newspaper article in *Le Monde* to call for much more public R&D and higher prices on ethical drugs. Meanwhile, Pfizer has threatened to delocalize its production plants if the French State does not develop a 'clearer and more stable' policy on prices and reimbursement.

3.2. The UK case: Promotion of the UK industry's competitiveness

The UK health care system is largely public through the National Health System (NHS). At the same time, the UK pharmaceutical and biotech companies are amongst the most competitive in the world (e.g. groups like GlaxoSmithKline plc, AstraZeneca plc and Shire pharmaceutical plc). The key trade association in the UK is the Association of the British Pharmaceutical Industry (ABPI). Political work engaged in by the ABPI and pharmaceutical companies has led to compromises that are much more business friendly than in France. First, the pricing system (Pharmaceutical Price Regulation Scheme) is based on the control of profits, not of prices. Instead, prices are decided by comparing those in other countries in order to achieve a sufficient rate of profits for pharmaceutical companies and their shareholders to invest in R&D. In practice, this system ensures a comfortable minimum of 30% of return on capital for ethical drugs. Second, since 2001 a Pharmaceutical Industry Competitiveness Task Force (PICTF) has been institutionalized by the UK government. Its objective is to promote the British pharmaceutical industry's competitiveness by creating a 'proper' institutional environment in the UK and Europe. This Task Force was created following a meeting between Prime Minister Tony Blair and the CEOs of SmithKline Beecham, Glaxo Wellcome and AstraZeneca in 1999. Moreover, since 2001, PICTF has been co-directed by Lord Hunt (health minister) and Tom McKillop, CEO of AstraZeneca, between 1999 and 2006. PICTF and the UK government have worked to protect patents and to favour business-friendly regulations in Europe. Finally, the UK government has institutionalized a Bioscience Innovation and Growth Team (BIGT), directed by Sir David Cooksey of Advent Venture Partners, to give recommendations on policy on research in biotechnologies. In summary, political work in the UK has obtained important results which favour the interests of the companies concerned, and this without restricting public health care interests.

3.3. EU political work

The competitiveness of the European pharmaceutical sector has become a key political question for the EU, as underlined by a report for the Enterprise Directorate-General (DG) of the European Commission written by a group of economists (Gambardella *et al.*, 2000).[6] Several political questions linked to competitiveness were raised due to the political work undertaken by The EFPIA and pharmaceutical companies at the EU level over the last few years: first, questions regarding the regulation of clinical trials and drugs (time for approval, protection of data exclusivity, advertising, etc.); second, orphan, biological and paediatric drug issues; third, questions of parallel trade and counterfeit. In all these areas, the EFPIA have tried to reduce 'the burden of regulation' in Europe, protect patent systems and limit administrative price control.

Indeed, around these three issue areas, *Big Pharma* has undertaken political work to adopt the same kind of regulations as in the US. First, the EU has adopted regulations on biological and orphan drugs. Second, two draft directives supported by the EFPIA and the European Commission's DG Enterprise[7] on clinical trials and marketing authorization were drawn up between 2002 and 2004. If adopted, these would lower the time of approval from 210 to 150 days, authorize direct-to-consumer advertising for some diseases, and create conditional marketing authorizations. After political work undertaken by associations of patients such as *Act Up* and independent medical reviews (e.g. *Prescrire*), the European Parliament rejected part of these directives. However, the directive on the protection of clinical data has been adopted, increasing this protection by two years (and by a further year if the company transforms its ethical drugs into OTCs) and thus the time when a generic firm can enter the market. This regulation created a new class of 'biogeneric drugs', which makes obtaining marketing authorization more difficult for generic firms on biological products whenever processes of manufacturing are different. In short, this represents a victory for *Big Pharma* over generic firms. Finally, the European Commission still seeks to make 'education for consumers' easier through the deregulation of advertising (Prescrire, 2006).

Second, as in the US, the EU has adopted regulations on orphan drugs and a stronger intellectual property regime for biological products. Behind this, again, lies political work undertaken by *Big Pharma*.

Third, the single market remains problematic for drugs because pricing procedures and levels of price are very different from one country to another. Consequently, the import of drugs by parallel trade is growing. At the same time, counterfeit drugs from China are more and more important. For this reason, *Big Pharma* are undertaking political work to forbid these practices in the EU, using very similar arguments to those used in the US to end imports of drugs from Canada.

3.4. Patents, WTO and TRIPS: Imposing on the poor the IPR regime of the rich

The relationship between the WTO and patents and the relationship between the pharmaceutical industry and the emerging countries have been played out around the issue of access to generic drugs for poor countries, especially for the treatment of AIDS. Through increasing the price of drugs and forbidding their production without a licence, patents limit access to treatment for the peoples of emerging and poor countries.

However, because of the prevalence of AIDS in these countries, the discovery of tri-therapy and the role of generic drugs, important political conflicts have emerged between *Big Pharma* (e.g. Abbott, Merck, Gilead and Novartis), who produce anti-AIDS drugs, on the one hand and public health care objectives on the other. This conflict of interests has necessitated the finding of political compromises through political work. The WTO is the organization and the political arena where bargaining and the construction of such compromises between *Big Pharma*, generic firms, and rich and poor countries have taken place.

In 1994, the TRIPS (Trade-Related aspects of Intellectual Property Rights) agreement was signed. It institutionalized an international IPR regime that was very favourable to *Big Pharma* because it imposed the same kind of patent protection as that which already existed in the richest countries, especially the US (Coriat and Orsi, 2003b; Sihanya, 2007). Of course, these rules have been defended by *Big Pharma* by deploying the same strategies of legitimization used in rich markets: 'patents are an incentive to innovate and to improve health'. Before the TRIPS agreement, patents on drugs were not institutionalized in several emerging countries such as Brazil, India, Kenya and Thailand. This absence encouraged the development of an important generic drugs industry in India and Brazil. In India, the Indian Patent Act forbade patents on drugs but authorized them on manufacturing processes, thus allowing the growth of a domestic generic industry. But TRIPS obliged India to change its national regulation of IPR and patents in 2005. Brazil was obliged to change its regulation in 1996 and Thailand in 1994 because they had a generic industry (Coriat and Orsi, 2003b). In the case of Kenya, the Kenya Industrial Property Act was passed in 2001.

These rules are highly favourable to multinational pharmaceutical corporations. All these rules offer *Big Pharma* legal resources with which to attack states or generic firms for not respecting the TRIPS rules. For example, Novartis brought a lawsuit against the Indian State over *Glivec* (an anti-cancer drug) because it accused India of distributing generic versions of Novartis's ethical drug (eventually, Novartis lost this lawsuit).

However, TRIPS was also partly a compromise because it also institutionalized a 'compulsory license' in cases of 'national emergency' which authorizes the import of generic versions of patented drugs by paying royalties to *Big Pharma*. The compulsory licence clause had not been used until 2005. However, since that year Brazil (2007), Kenya and Thailand have used this in what appears to be part of a process of de-institutionalization. Even if we can partly talk about a 'globalization' process linked to the constraints of the WTO and the TRIPS agreements, each country has nevertheless tried to manage the contradiction of interests as regards the local (national) political problem it has had to deal with.

4. De-institutionalization of the Commercial IR and the fight for control of *Big Pharma*: Causes and consequences of crisis

In 2004, a Merck & Co's drug, Vioxx, was withdrawn because it was claimed to have caused more than 27,000 deaths by cardiac problems in the US alone. This has been the most important sanitary crisis in rich countries since the Thalidomid affair. The company and the FDA were accused by David Graham, an expert from the FDA, to have masked the results of clinical trials and to have put pressure on him to give marketing approval for Vioxx. Since this case, the Commercial IR in the US has been de-institutionalized. This is partly because of the breakdown of the public health care/competitiveness compromise which previously had marked all this country's pharmaceutical companies. However, this has not been the only cause of this crisis.

4.1. The causes of the crisis

There are several causes of crisis and de-institutionalization of the Commercial IR. First, the pharmaceutical industry has been facing a decline in innovation and R&D productivity: R&D expenditures are growing, but the number of marketing approvals of New Molecular Entity by the FDA is declining. Since innovation is the basis for political compromises, without it a de-institutionalization of the Commercial IR becomes possible. Moreover, declining innovation has led to lower levels of profits (Graph 4.4).

Second, and because of the decline in R&D productivity, governments have increased pressures on prices and costs, some of them trying to favour generic competition. Most importantly, it is in the US that competition has been the highest: the FTC (2002) now forbids multiple 'automatic 180 days of protection' under paragraph IV of the Hatch–Waxman Act, and this because of the practices of *Big Pharma*. Consequently, since the end of 1990s, more and more blockbusters have suffered from claims of patent infringement from generic companies in India (Ranbaxy, Dr Reddy's), Canada (Apotex) and Israël (Teva). In addition, many blockbusters have lost or will lose their patents (Allegra, Zoloft, Zyrtec, Prilosec, etc.). Moreover, emerging countries and non-governmental organizations contest more and

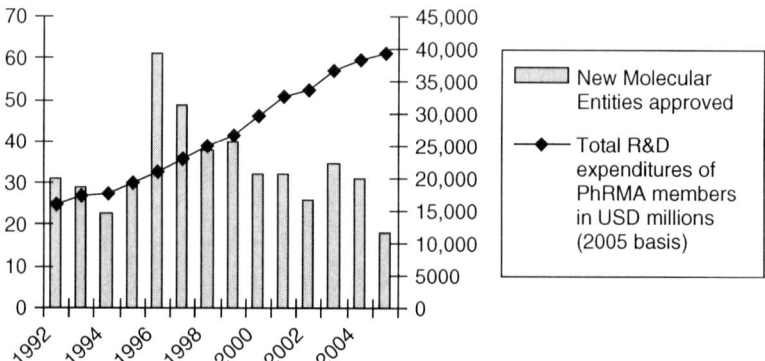

Graph 4.4 New molecular entities and total R&D expenditures of PhRMA members (in million US$).
Sources: FDA, PhRMA.

more frequently the role of patents in order to make access easier for the Third World. This political conflict is not regulated: decisions of the different courts are sometimes favourable to generic firms and local governments, and sometimes to *Big Pharma*. For example, Pfizer won its lawsuit against Ranbaxy over Lipitor (La Tribune 13/09/2007); Sanofi-Aventis won against Apotex over Plavix and Lovenox; Eli Lilly won against Ivax, Dr Reddy's and Teva over Zyprexa (Le Figaro 16/04/2005). However, Novartis lost its lawsuit against India over Glivec, and AstraZeneca lost against Eon Labs and KV Pharmaceuticals over Toprol (L'Expansion 18/01/2006). Overall, conditions are politically and economically decreasingly favourable to *Big Pharma*: several countries like Brazil, Kenya and Thailand have used compulsory licences since 2005.

Third comes the Vioxx case. Vioxx is a 'painkiller' (anti-inflammatory) made by Merck & Co which was expected to have no side effects. In 2004, Merck & Co voluntarily withdrew the drug because of the increase in cardiovascular problems linked to the drug. Indeed, as stated above, a scientist from the FDA, David Graham, has claimed this drug has been directly responsible for 27,000 deaths by heart attacks and that he suffered pressure from the FDA and Merck & Co not to reveal its dangers. Now, Merck & Co is facing numerous class action lawsuits and the FDA has been strongly de-legitimized. Consequently, the FDA is now more severe than before, which implies less marketing approvals. More generally, the pharmaceutical companies are now increasingly criticized and more class action lawsuits by patients have been taken against other pharmaceutical companies (which is a form of political work and public action).

4.2. Consequences of the crisis and political work by institutional investors

The main consequence of these different tendencies has been the decline of profitability of *Big Pharma* and the recent under-performance of the pharmaceutical industry (Graph 4.5).

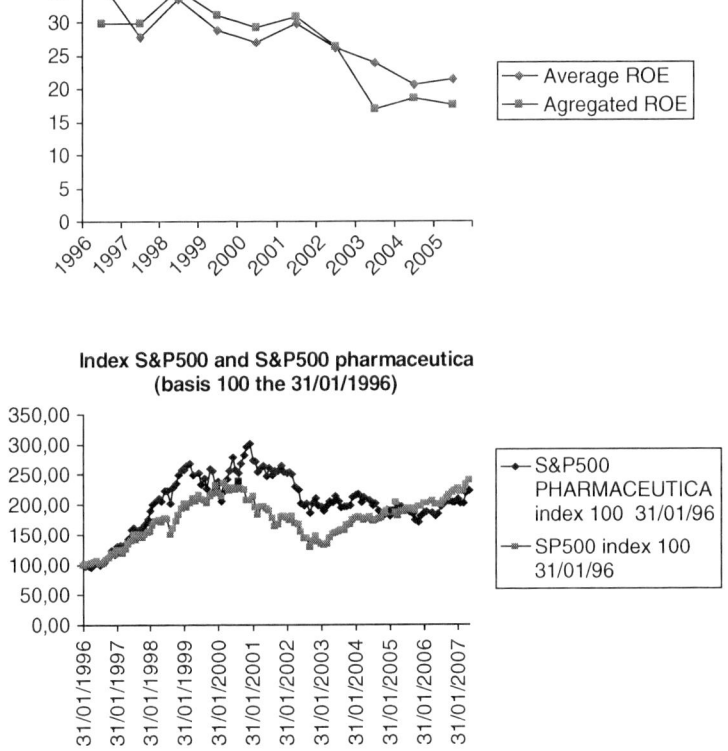

Graph 4.5 Decline of return on equity of the 15 biggest pharmaceutical companies by sales in 2004 (in %) and of S&P 500 pharma relatively to S&P500
Sources: Annual reports, Thomson financials.

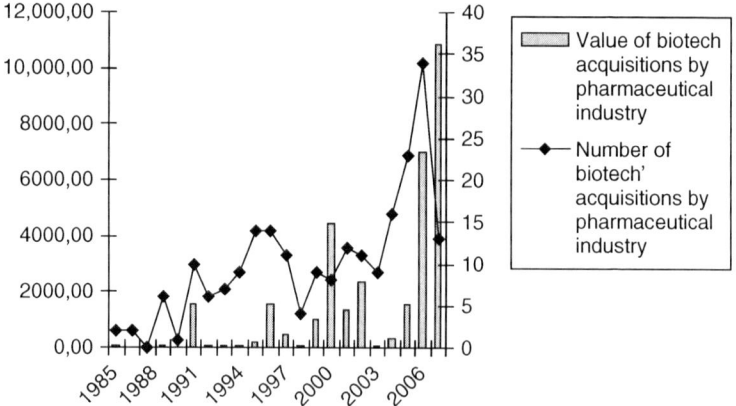

Graph 4.6 Acquisitions of biotechs by pharmaceutical companies
Note: Numbers of 2006 include period between January to May.
Source: Thomson financials.

This decline of profitability has had several consequences for *Big Pharma* strategies. First, a lot of *Big Pharma* companies have downsized their labour forces, been searching for a new business model and tried to outsource more and more of their manufacturing activities and clinical trials. To solve their problems, over the last three years Purchase and Financial IRs have been changing, leading in particular to increased acquisitions of *biotech* companies by *Big Pharma* (Graph 4.6).

Second, collective action has been undertaken by institutional investors to force *Big Pharma* to change: several CEOs have been fired[8], and some institutional investors have organized meetings with the pharmaceutical industry's managers and financial analysts to build new business models and, thus, change the respective expectations of CEOs and investors in shareholder value creation (Pharma Futures, 2004). They underline a contradiction between the short-term objective of maximization of shareholder value and the long-term objective of innovation. Other institutional investors recognize the contradiction between public health care (especially access to drugs for populations in developing countries) and the short-term objectives of creating value for shareholders. They are afraid of severe reactions by states that could 'destroy shareholder value'. Consequently, to protect shareholder value in the long term, these investors would like to force pharmaceutical companies to adopt 'good practices' as regards the poor, especially for HIV sufferers (Pharmaceutical Shareowner Group, 2004). However, the

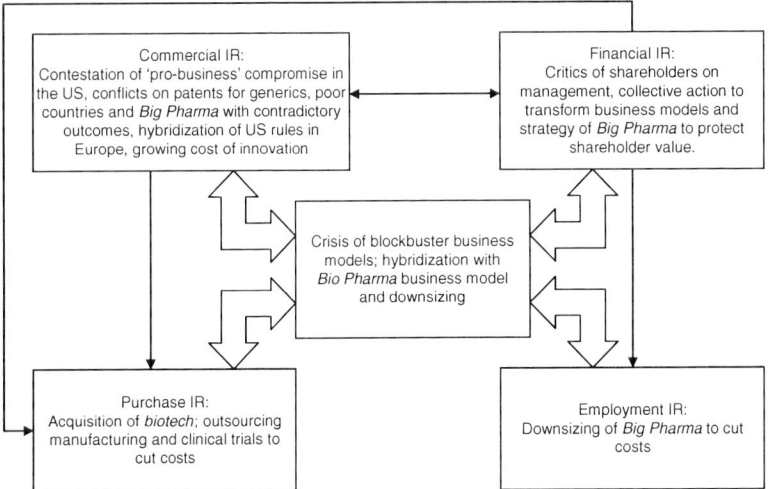

Figure 4.5 De-institutionalization, crisis of blockbuster business models and a new unstable Institutional Order

objective of shareholder value creation has not been abandoned. Without its politicization, and therefore without political intervention, there is little chance that things will change quickly (Figure 4.5).

Conclusion

Globalization in the pharmaceutical industry has been linked to financialization, the specificities of US markets and the power of multinational corporations. The pharmaceutical industry case shows that studying the social and political construction of markets is necessary to understanding strategies of corporations and, conversely, that analysis of these strategies is necessary to studying political processes. Even if clear trends have been defined as 'globalization', the *Politics of Industry* approach, in particular its multi-scale analysis, has shown that this process is not uniform. The various parts of the pharmaceutical industry are structured at different scales (national, supranational and international), which means that the outcome of bargaining can also be different. Differences in regulations between countries and between scales in a world where markets are more and more open have created economic pressure to transform regulations. But the outcome of the political work this has inspired remains largely unpredictable. Political work has meant that globalization has been partly undetermined and that national autonomy can exist, and this because rules change because of interdependence and bargaining between actors. For example, the *Politics of Industry* approach used in this chapter reveals that IPR and the regulation of drug and price systems are clearly political constructions which have important economic consequences. Competition in the pharmaceutical industry is largely determined by political work, as well as by the shape of collective, public or political action. Problematization and (de)politicization are continually used by the pharmaceutical industry to influence regulations. Different forms of politicization, for example through lobbying, problematization and lawsuits, are used by *Big Pharma* and corporations to control their market share and increase their profits by influencing the social construction of markets and political compromises. 'Capturing' American and European governments is necessary for *Big Pharma* to protect their profits and to obtain the financing of innovation.

Finally, the case of the pharmaceutical industry also reveals the conflict of interest between dominant and dominated groups (generics firms and others, etc.) and that political work by the former is a way of creating barriers to entry and maintaining the control of the market. Following Bourdieu (2000) or Fligstein (2001), we can say that financial capital, marketing and barriers to entry all participate in 'competition for the powerful to have power over the state' to 'define the frontiers of the field'. As such, they constitute the main sources of control over markets and shape the rules of competition. Following Fligstein, I conclude that the blockbuster-led strategies of *Big Pharma* and its domination structures are a 'conception of control', that is a shared representation of how industry functions and a form of symbolic violence between incumbent and dominated firms which guides actor strategies and political work. Overall, the institutionalized relationships which structure this industry are not only a means of co-ordinating firms in this sector with their respective stakeholders, but also structure competition between these firms, while favouring some types of strategies above others. At the same time, they institutionalize relationships of domination within the industry, both for its stakeholders and for its competitors.

5
The US Defence Industry Since 1945: Globalization Refused

Sylvain Moura

Introduction

Globalization is a crucial issue for the US defence industry because it entails considerations of national security and of military technological leadership over the world (US Congress, 1990). In this chapter I will show that these two issues have inhibited the globalization of this industry since 1945. More precisely, using the *Politics of Industry* approach, I will explain how its institutional architecture established during the Cold War has produced irreversible rules for the national mode of producing and selling military equipment.

Because of the specific role of the US State in financing the American defence industry (budget activity) and its simultaneous role as its own main customer (for war and defence activities), the two main Institutionalized Relationships (IRs) I will focus upon are the Financial and the Commercial IR. The core of our argumentation is to demonstrate that the industry's Institutional Order has not fundamentally changed since its institutionalization during the Cold War. This order still hinges on a specific hierarchy between these two IRs wherein the Commercial IR dominates its Financial counterpart. This is due to the political work undertaken over the years by specific stakeholders. As a consequence, and despite the end of the Cold War, the US defence industry still operates on a national basis. This in turn means that when compared to the rest of the US economy, or even defence in other countries, the globalization of this industry possesses distinct characteristics.

This chapter develops this thesis by unpacking the two IRs from an historical point of view. First, I present the characteristics of the US defence industry during the Cold War. I explain the way the Commercial IR became dominant, how the Finance IR had to fit with it and why this process occurred on a purely national basis. Second, I present the political work undertaken by representatives of the State during the 1990s in order to change this mode of regulation following the end of the Cold War. I emphasize in particular that this 'new deal' for defence policy attempted to introduce greater globalization. However, as the final part of the chapter demonstrates, political work by a variety of stakeholders has subsequently succeeded in preserving the traditional Institutional Order of the industry, thereby restricting the impact of globalization.

1. The Cold War era: A national defence industry

During the Cold War, US macroeconomics bore the stamp of *containment:* the main objective of US foreign policy. The ideology of containment aimed at stopping the extension of the Soviet Union and communist ideas, and this in order to promote instead capitalist values and American influence throughout the world. From the beginning of the 1950s, containment became a strong national political compromise supported by the considerable potential for national production of high-tech weapons it encouraged. Thus, the defence industry became one of the main tools for making containment possible as the US entered into an arms race with the Soviet Union. In this context, the defence industry quickly became oriented towards technological supremacy because of the Commercial IR's structuring effects upon its Institutional Order. Moreover, this order became sustainable because its Finance IR was able to fit financial resources with the technological ambitions of its Commercial opposite number.

1.1. The Commercial IR and the arms race

During the Cold War, 'the arms race' described competition between the Soviet Union and the US for military supremacy (Hartley and Sandler, 1995). Within the Commercial IR, two main rules were established in order to favour this end. The first dealt with the technological escalation of military equipment while the second sought to compensate for the lack of competition in defence markets (Figure 5.1).

1.1.1. The technological race
Since the 1950s, American sociologists have demonstrated that the objective of large-scale production of high-technology weapons was the

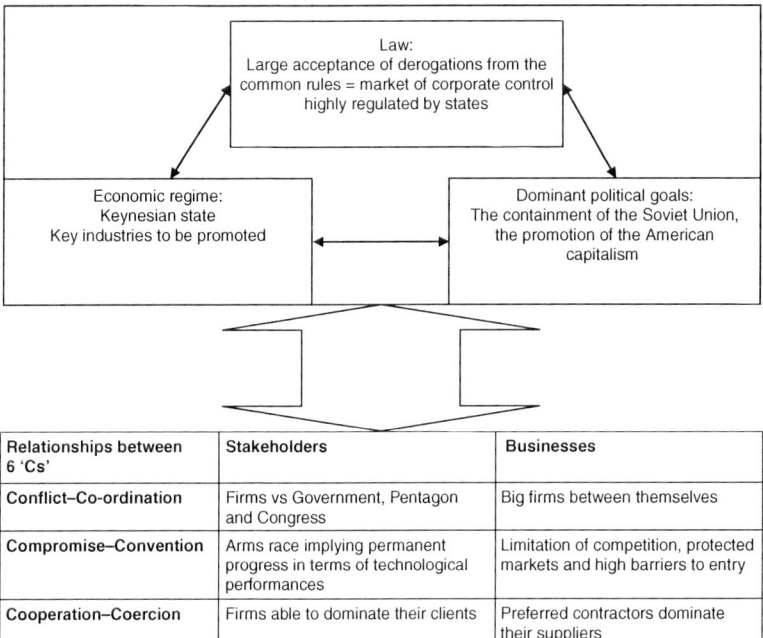

Figure 5.1 The Commerical IR in the US defence industry during the Cold War

common interest of stakeholders in the defence industry, a set of actors who interacted within what they called 'the military industrial complex'. At the same time, this common interest provided the defence industry with internal legitimation (Buzan and Herring, 1998; Gleditsch and Njolstad, 1990). Many of the major military contractors were clustered in only a relatively few congressional districts. Consequently, their representatives in Congress sought to influence military procurement policies in order to be re-elected. Companies obviously supported this policy because it encouraged growth of the defence market. Moreover, a strong defence industrial base was framed as the necessary 'partner' of a powerful military force. Indeed, it was argued that military leaders could engage forces with fewer risks of defeat if their technology was efficient. For these reasons, congressmen and women came to possess considerable global influence through their efforts to preserve American interests in international negotiations. In sum, the goal of high military technology created a common way of thinking and acting for most, if not all, defence industry stakeholders.

At the same time, this goal was used to legitimate the 'militarization of high technology' throughout the entire nation (Tirman, 1984). The majority of American people were convinced that the development of the nuclear arsenal was the best solution for facing up to 'the Communist threat' (Davis, 1971). As a consequence, this quest for high-tech military equipment gave the defence industry the opportunity to mobilize extra-industry networks in order to further legitimate the industry's internal modes of operating.

Significantly, according to this 'two-sided' strategy of legitimation, military technology had to be defined and produced nationally: the Pentagon's suppliers were all American and provided equipment to all the segments of the defence industry (nuclear, sea, land, space, sky, electronics and communications). Moreover, arms programmes involving international cooperation were avoided because the risk of sharing technologies and of foreign procurement were not seen to be compatible with the national autonomy of the defence industry (OTA, 1991; Reppy, 1983). In short, the US defence industry grew on national foundations, and globalization was not a pertinent issue. Indeed, this question 'made no sense' during the Cold War.

1.1.2. Markets without competition

The technological race also had a major impact upon the organization of defence markets. Indeed, the goal of competition failed in these markets because the technological objective created 'preferred contractors' for the Pentagon, and this for two reasons. First, the US defence market possessed legal international barriers to entry because of the autonomy of US technology. More than 95% of the Pentagon's purchases were produced within the US. National companies were protected not only by the Pentagon's decisions, but by export regulation (the Buy American Act, International Traffic in Arms Regulations and other specific regulations about defence exports). As a result, foreign companies were almost invariably excluded from bidding for US defence contracts, a characteristic of this industry which was obviously a serious obstacle to globalization.

Second, in practice, national contractors were nearly always preferred to foreigners because of their reputation in general and, more particularly, the history of their Research and Development (R&D) performance. Successful performance by an R&D contractor depends upon the development of technical skills. For this reason, a company that receives one contract in a given R&D field tends to be in a better position to win the next one than a newcomer with little or no previous experience (Kucera, 1974). The result was that, in 1968, 90% of the Pentagon's and 98% of NASA's contract awards were negotiated without competitive bidding (Davis, 1971).

1.2. The Finance IR and the sustainability of the arms race

Because of the technological race, US defence production was characterized by high sunk costs (huge investments in R&D, low returns due to its relatively small scale of production, etc.). In order to make the arms race sustainable, the Federal government had to take on the cost of investment through massive public spending and a system of contractual incentives for individual companies. Within the industry's Institutional Order, this trait emphasized the domination of the Financial IR by the Commercial one. In terms of macroeconomics, this order was made sustainable through the application of Keynesian economic policy and its legitimation of an interventionist state.

1.2.1. High public military spending

The development of technological capacity within the US defence industry was largely maintained by the Federal defence budget. Obviously, this characteristic reinforced the lack of international competition because the government preferred to pay for a national capability rather than buy in foreign technology. Between 1960 and 1987, public defence spending as part of GDP was between 5% and 9%, the highest rate for the main NATO countries (SIPRI, various years). Moreover, an average of 57% of total Federal expenditures on R&D went to the defence sector and its allies, a rate that reached 80% in the early years of the Cold War (*National Science Foundation's* website). Finally, private companies did not have to fund for themselves the financial investment required for innovation in defence R&D.

1.2.2. Technological contractual incentives

To complete this set of incentives for innovation, the standard US weapon acquisition process pushed firms to focus upon technological performance more than on the cost of the programme concerned. The contractual incentive was technological, not financial, and this in accordance with the main objective determined within the Commercial relationship. According to the Office of Technological Assessment (OTA, 1992), the majority of defence contracts were of a cost-plus-reimbursement type, which meant that the government not only paid the contractor its costs of R&D or production, but also picked up the bill for any cost overruns. In other words, quality, not price, was the priority. In short, the government was prepared to foot the bill if costs rose (Ball and Leintenberg, 1983).

1.2.3. Keynesian public policy

This public financing of private investments occurred within the trans-industry context of Keynesian management of US economic policy. According to this vision of economic development, the Federal government was authorized to intervene directly in industries such as defence because the dominant thinking was that purely market-driven policies would fail to sustain the health of the economy. Moreover, this framing considered that the stimulation of growth within certain industries would, in accordance with the paradigm of 'spillover', result in growth for the economy as a whole.[1] Spillovers refer to a situation in which a defence R&D programme produces results which give a significant boost to civilian industries (in terms of product and production processes). Thus, in 1970 in this industry there were an average of 7.4 scientists, engineers and technicians in the R&D field for every 100 workers in production. In contrast, the rate was 1 to a 100 in the rest of manufacturing (Melman, 1975).

Overall, for the US defence industry the political compromise over containment generated a specific Institutional Order. It eliminated the question of globalization because it was based on a purely nationally defined Commercial IR. The fall of the Berlin Wall in 1989 marked the 'official' end of the Cold War, even if from a military point of view the US had largely won this war a few years earlier due to President Reagan's remilitarization plan (the Strategic Defence Initiative launched in 1983). The year 1989 nevertheless heralded important change in US defence policy and considerable upheaval of the defence industry's Institutional Order. Indeed, at that time, a door seemed to open for a more globalized US defence industry (Moran, 1990).

2. The post–Cold War era: Impetus for a more globalized defence industry

Indeed, as of 1989 the Federal government announced its aim to reform its defence policy and thus to modify the Institutional Order of this industry. The principal argument of government representatives was that the disappearance of the Soviet threat ended the justification for such high public defence budgets in general, and programme cost overruns in particular. More fundamentally, this problematization also contested the spillover paradigm. The reason for this was that during the 1980s innovation dynamics had reversed the pattern of spin-off from military research towards civilian sectors: now the dynamics were more of a 'spin-on' type (from civilian to military). Finally, the changing ideology for general economic policy had an important role in a movement for changing the defence industry's Institutional Order built during the Cold War. Duménil and Lévy (2004) and Fligstein (1990) show that in terms of macroeconomics, neoliberalism had by then become hegemonic by replacing the post-war Keynesian compromise. In particular, under the Reagan Administration, the reduction of the interventionist state's role in the economy and the enhancement of competition through the deregulation of markets became part of an ideology for a 'thinner' state which was no longer supposed to support the private costs of industrial production.

These changes had consequences within the defence industry. Indeed, in this case the Federal government dominated all the arguments for problematizing a contestation of the Cold War Institutional Order and for implementing new rules in its Commercial and Financial IRs. A first step was to denounce this traditional order so as to make change of its rules possible. A second step was to devise new rules in their stead. This process of deinstitutionalization of the two IRs entailed political work inspired by the goal of breaking the Commercial IR's dominance and setting up instead a system based on financial considerations of profitability. In sum, a struggle began to impose cost considerations for military production which, in analytical terms, would fit with the industry's new Institutional Order. Consequently, globalization suddenly appeared possible for the US defence industry for two reasons. First, more international collaborations to share production costs (Finance IR) were to be sought. Second, more international competition during procurement was to be striven for in order to decrease prices (Commercial IR).

2.1. The Finance IR and the peace dividend

Since the end of the Cold War, the Federal government's struggle against programme cost overruns and the desire to reduce the defence budget were the issues around which the Cold War regulation of the Financial IR came to be contested. In this new context, more international cooperation on military programmes seemed unavoidable, thus introducing reflection about globalization as a means of reinstitutionalizing key rules and procedures.

2.1.1. The decline of defence budgets

Between 1988 and 1999, US public defence spending fell by about a third and came to represent only 3% of GDP in 1999, whereas it had been 5.7% in 1988. This trend seriously affected the Federal defence R&D budget: it decreased by 27% between 1989 and 1996. Due to this drop in public financial commitments to the defence industry, national industrial production fell by 47% between 1989 and 1996. The direct consequence was that the national production of military products (evaluated in terms of sales) also fell by 47% in constant dollars (SIPRI, various years). One way for the military companies to recover from this situation was to boost exports by opening new markets. In other words, such sales could have been the first step towards a more globalized American defence industry.

2.1.2. The struggle against programme cost overruns

For defence contractors, challenges raised by the peace dividend were aggravated by a new 'contractual' defence policy introduced by the Federal government. Faced with cost overruns exacerbated by the practice of cost-plus-reimbursement contracts, the Congress had already passed the Tax Reform Act in 1986. This placed new constraints upon the Pentagon to increase usage of fixed-price contracts – a type of arrangement which corresponds most closely to the contractual relationships that prevail in market environments: a contractor promises to supply specified goods and services at a cost which is financed by the government and which is not subject to adjustments. Consequently, development and production cost overruns were to become the sole responsibility of the contractor. Moreover, Defence Secretary W. Perry introduced several measures in 1994 in order to generalize fixed-price contracts and verify their implementation. Overall, the change inspired by the end of the Cold War was transformed into arguments used by the State to justify the deinstitutionalization of rules which governed the Financial IR. Advocates of change then proposed that a coherent means of reinstitutionalizing this IR would be to enable increased globalization through greater international collaboration.

2.1.3. The 'need' for international collaboration

The reduction of public expenditure on defence and the desire of the many actors within the Federal government to make savings fuelled new initiatives for the US administration to share investment in weapons production with foreign partners. Thus, as early as 1986, the Nunn–Roth–Warner amendment created the possibility for the US government to share the financing of defence R&D with NATO member states, and this throughout the stages of each weapons programme. This principle was applied, for example, to the F35 fighter programme, the most expensive military programme in history (in 2007, the estimated cost was $308 billion, including 40 billion for the first stages of R&D). In a context of cost control, the Department of Defence (DoD) opened the programme up to international cooperation, in particular to share investments in R&D. Thus far, Canada, Australia and some European countries have committed approximately $4 billion to this activity.

2.2. The Commercial IR and competition

Expressed in the terms employed throughout this book, henceforth various actors encouraged the US defence industry's Commercial IR to adapt to changes in the Institutional Order as a whole and, in particular, to institutionalize change in the rules of the Financial IR. As a consequence, and using globalization as an argument for reform, the Federal government attempted to inject into its procurement practices the concept of 'duality' and the principle of competitive bidding.

2.2.1. Duality

In the Commercial IR, defence policy-makers have tried to impose a new conception of technology upon weapons producers. Considering that the spillover paradigm did not produce concrete results in many cases, and had more generally been challenged due to new knowledge being produced about weapons production processes (Cowan and Foray, 1995), the Federal government engaged in political work which invented, then promoted, a principle of 'duality' in order to modify the public procurement of defence goods.

Duality – or 'dual-use technology' – consists of integrating civilian components into military equipment to reduce their cost through benefiting from the lower prices generated by competitive markets. More precisely, duality comes from Bill Clinton's campaign promises to reduce the public defence R&D budget, which were partly inspired by proposals formulated in 1990 by the Carnegie Commission. In order to enact these promises, the Pentagon implemented a number of plans to establish duality, in particular the Technology Reinvestment Project (1993) and the Technology Dual-Uses programme (1997). In addition, Defence Secretary W. Perry took legal measures to increase the use of civilian components in the field of microelectronics, leading to, in spite of the defence contractors' protests, Texas Instruments becoming the prime contractor of the latest Federal programme in this field. Moreover, the Pentagon changed the name of its principal agency of fundamental research from DARPA into ARPA, thereby reflecting its new orientation towards duality by dropping the word 'defence'.

Introducing duality thus provided an opportunity to develop globalization within the US defence industry in two ways. First, it meant there should no longer be any reason to forbid a foreign company supplying civilian components to US defence markets, especially if the components are technologically commonplace. Second, the government sought more industrial collaborations with foreign companies (e.g. Japanese) when they are considered to be 'ahead' in some civilian sectors such as microelectronics. As a consequence, it was hoped that collaborations would be profitable to the technical competitiveness of American defence products (Lorell, 1995).

2.2.2. Competitive bidding

The other change in the Commercial IR corresponds to the new national defence policy's objective of introducing compulsory competitive bidding. The aim was to make the defence market more competitive in order to decrease programme costs, and this through obliging defence agencies to choose the cheapest proposals. In this way, the 'symbiotic link' between these agencies and contractors (Kucera, 1974) was to be made more slack, and this because the goal was no longer to push back the frontiers of military science but rather to build acceptable technology at a lower cost.

Since the end of the 1990s, this argument allowed BAE Systems (UK) to reinforce its position as an important contractor for the DoD since the 'American nationality' of firms was no longer a criterion. In 1999, the company was not in the top 100 of DoD's contractors, but had risen to number 8 by 2006 (DoD's website). This change therefore looks like a clear sign of globalization within the American defence industry.

Overall, the intermediate conclusion is that throughout the 1990s, the end of the Cold War sparked or accelerated important changes in the US national defence policy due to initiatives taken by the Federal government. This process of deinstitutionalization of the industry's traditional Institutional Order and the setting up of a renewed one was based upon the policy concepts, and concomitant problematizations, of 'the peace dividend' and 'competition'. Consequently, and for the first time since 1945, this trend appeared to globalize the US defence industry in three ways: globalization of sales through competition for exports, more international collaborations and globalization of the Pentagon's suppliers. Nevertheless, since the late 1990s, the reinstitutionalization of rules within the commercial and the Financial IR have not produced all the anticipated results and, therefore, globalization of this industry still remains largely incomplete.

3. The post–Cold War era: Incomplete globalization

Because of political work undertaken by various stakeholders, the historic mode of regulation developed during the Cold War has been used to resist reforms and, ultimately, transform plans to globalize this industry into a failure. More precisely, political negotiations and compromises have encouraged the pursuit of practices in this industry which have meant that the Commercial IR still structures its Institutional Order. This is mainly due to continued commitments to technological performance. Consequently, the order's Finance IR has had to go on adapting to its Commercial counterpart, which has meant that, at least thus far, it has continued to reserve most public financing for American companies. From the point of view of globalization, this has resulted in a failure to achieve the aims of enlarging the list of suppliers to the Pentagon and boosting international collaborations.

3.1. Political work by stakeholders

The defence companies, the Federal government's executive branch, the financial community and Congress are the four main sets of stakeholders in this industry. Each has engaged in political work in order to retain the supremacy of US technological military in the world, and this because favouring traditional modes of regulation has been framed as part of their 'common interest'.

3.1.1. Defence manufacturers

Managers of companies in this industry have actively defended the Cold War Institutional Order by problematizing calls for change, both through discourse and alliance-making, around arguments of technology. Discursively, they have argued that the decline of public procurement and the Federal government's desire to impose duality are harmful to the development of knowledge and skills in the US defence industry. They have underlined that innovation requires maintaining and improving such knowledge and skills by launching new programmes or by retrofitting existing equipment, two practices whose scale has been drastically reduced since the collapse of the Soviet Union. Not surprisingly, these firms have ardently supported the different wars entered into by the US since 1990 and actively participated in convincing decision-makers about the necessity of high-tech defence equipment research in order to win 'the battle against terrorism' throughout the world. In particular, they have sought to transform 'the domination of space' concept into a new technological objective, arguing that it would lead to military supremacy and security for the civil American economy (now heavily dependant on electronic transactions and communications). Moreover, company managers have denounced the principle of duality, emphasizing their incapacity to adapt to it and the risk it poses for their position in markets.[2] Indeed, some have even threatened to exit some segments of the defence industry and thus cause a loss of skills for the national defence industrial base.

Whenever this basic type of political work has not proved sufficient to maintain the traditional Institutional Order, managers have not hesitated to interact with the Federal government in a confrontational and politicized fashion. The case of the C17 aircraft is a prime example. Because Congress has chosen not to pay Boeing for a new version of this aircraft, since 2006 the company has been closing lines of production and firing workers. For Boeing, much of its political work has entailed threatening the government with redundancies of 5500 employees and arguing that the opportunity cost of stopping production should dissuade Congress from freezing its budget. According to representatives of Boeing, if Congress stops financing the C17 programme, the nation will lose all its capability to build military cargo planes. This would mean that if the US needed this type of plane in the future, it would have to restart production of the C17 and therefore take on the cost of rebuilding production lines and training new workers. In short, future costs would be so high that it is worth continuing to finance production of the C17. The company's political work against the Congress won the support of the Air Force Secretary M. Wynne in October 2007. Since then, he has been arguing that more C17s are needed because many cargo aircraft in the nation's fleet are too old and unreliable to use. He has also added that restarting a shut-down C17 line would take up to four years and cost 'tens, not single-digit billions of dollars' (*Chicago Business*, 24 October 2007).

Moreover, political work undertaken to fight 'duality' has centred upon the public budget for R&D investment in defence. Specifically, managers have argued that if they have to self-sponsor R&D costs, the Federal government should be held responsible for the problem of the opportunity costs of losing national capability. Between 1994 and 1999, calculated as R&D expenditure/net sales, the average 'R&D effort' of the Big Five US defence companies (Boeing, General Dynamics, Lockheed

Martin, Northrop Grumman and Raytheon) fell from 3.4% to 2.3% each year (companies' annual financial reports).

3.1.2. The executive branch

Faced with the proposed reforms, the Federal government's position has been ambiguous and even sometimes in flagrant contradiction with the problematization constructed some years earlier to modify this industry's Institutional Order. This becomes apparent when one examines the attitudes of successive US Presidents on the one hand and of the DoD on the other.

In spite of the end of the Cold War, Presidents Clinton and Bush II have not given up a permanent state-of-war stance. Constitutionally, the president has a key role in national security policy. But, their ability to build support in Congress, to control and direct the national security establishment and to gain public acceptance of policies is a direct consequence of their leadership style (Sarkesian *et al.*, 2005). In accordance with the interventionist tradition of most American presidents, Presidents Clinton and Bush I and II have been in favour of US hegemony, that is preserving the dominant US global position in the world, including, and thanks to, military power: the Gulf war in 1991, repeated bombings of Iraq between 1993 and 2000, military interventions in Somalia in 1993 and in the Balkans in 1995 and 1999, and wars in Afghanistan in 2001 and in Iraq since 2003. This doctrine follows on from the strategy of containment by continuing its heritage of supremacy and implying for military staff the ownership of the best weapon systems in the world (Posen, 2005).

Lastly, because of the fear of skill-loss, since as long ago as 1993, the DoD has decided to support national companies by encouraging its five prime contactors to start a mergers and acquisitions process (M&A). Their argument has been that in order to protect company profitability in a shrinking market, a means must be found for them to remain in defence activity. However, the risk of this strategy is that the concentration of national supply increases the market power of big defence contractors and thus clashes with the competition principles promoted since the end of the Cold War by actors such as W. Perry (Defense Secretary, 1993–1997).

3.1.3. The financial community

The financial community (institutional investors, banks and financial analysts) has also played a key role in the reinstitutionalization of the historic relationship between the Commercial and the Finance IR within this industry's Institutional Order. This has centred upon the judgements of financial analysts regarding the financial health of defence companies. The reduction of the defence budget and the wave of M&A have put defence contractors in bad financial shape because they now have to borrow liquidity and contract long-term debt assets in order to pick up the cost of inter- and intra-company reorganization. Indeed, defined as Long Term Debt vs Total Equity, the average 'Big Five's' long-term debt ratio has risen from 18% in 1992 to 80% in 1997 (companies' annual reports). Consequently, financial analysts have become cautious about defence companies because they forecast a decrease in the shareholder value creation in the near future. Reimbursement of debt prevents these companies from giving cash to stakeholders through dividends and stock repurchases. The effect of this negative evaluation was to stop the Big Five's stock prices increasing in 1997 and then cause their decline thereafter (Graph 5.1).

However, and paradoxically, this situation has also turned out to have positive effects for these defence companies. In fact, their bad financial position has prevented them from taking on the full cost of investment in defence production. To get out of this deadlock, in 1999 the then Deputy Secretary of Defence J. Hamre recommended an increase in the Pentagon's budget. In addition, P. Aldridge (Undersecretary of Defence for Acquisition) visited Wall Street in June 2001 with the aim of restoring the confidence of analysts in defence stocks and underlining that the Administration would be supporting the defence industry once again. Aldridge's political work was initially centred on communication. He announced to the analysts that the unfavourable reforms for defence contractors were to be suspended. Moreover, he promised

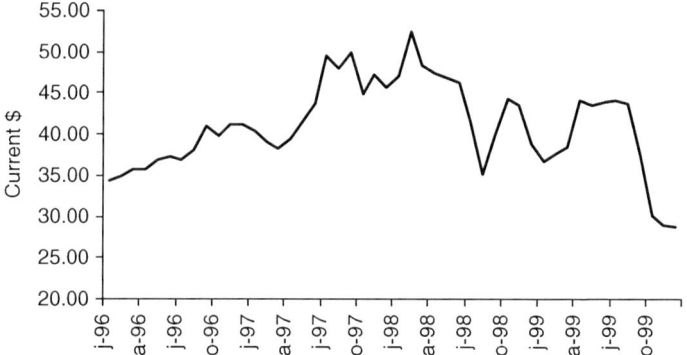

Graph 5.1 'The Big Five's' average stock price
Source: Thomson Financials Database.

to set up measures to improve company profits: more funding and increases in contractual premiums. Therefore, and before the attacks of September 11, 2001, the Federal government was already committed to a mindset and concrete policies of rearmament. Indeed, according to Sarkesian *et al*. (2005), by 2000, the government and Congress had agreed to increase defence spending, although they disagreed over its amount.

3.1.4. Congress

Congress's role is vitally important to the structure of the US defence industry. The president may be the commander-in-chief of the armies, but the Congress has the power of the purse. This was obvious in 1993 and 1994, when it obtained an increased reduction of the defence budget. Nevertheless, since the end of 1990, the number of congressmen and women in favour of an increase in the military expenditure has been growing for two reasons. First, some have been convinced by defence companies that high and constant military expenditure guarantees employment in their electoral districts. For example, after the Second World War, industrial consolidation in states such as California and Virginia was broadly linked to the defence sector. In 2005, these two States still received respectively 12% and 11% of the Pentagon's total direct expenditure (DoD website). Moreover, the defence industry has deliberately bolstered this argument by choosing subcontractors from throughout the US. For example, the controversial F22 programme is entailing industrial activity in 45 states. Second, since the attacks of September 11, a high level of Federal capital expenditure for homeland security has been used as an argument during electoral campaigns.

All this political work has had determinant effects upon the reinstitutionalization of rules in the Commercial and the Financial IR. This in turn has played a major part in resisting change to the industry's traditional Institutional Order and, therefore, its globalization.

3.2. The Commercial IR and the consecration of 'National Defence Technology'

Within the Commercial IR, the idea that high technology in the defence industry should be invented and implemented on a national basis has largely been reconfirmed and even reconsecrated. This is largely due to political work undertaken by a number of actors which has resulted in the retention of barriers to entry into the national market, and this in order to preserve national R&D and production capabilities. Consequently, the export market has remained the only real avenue for globalization of the Commercial IR (Figure 5.2).

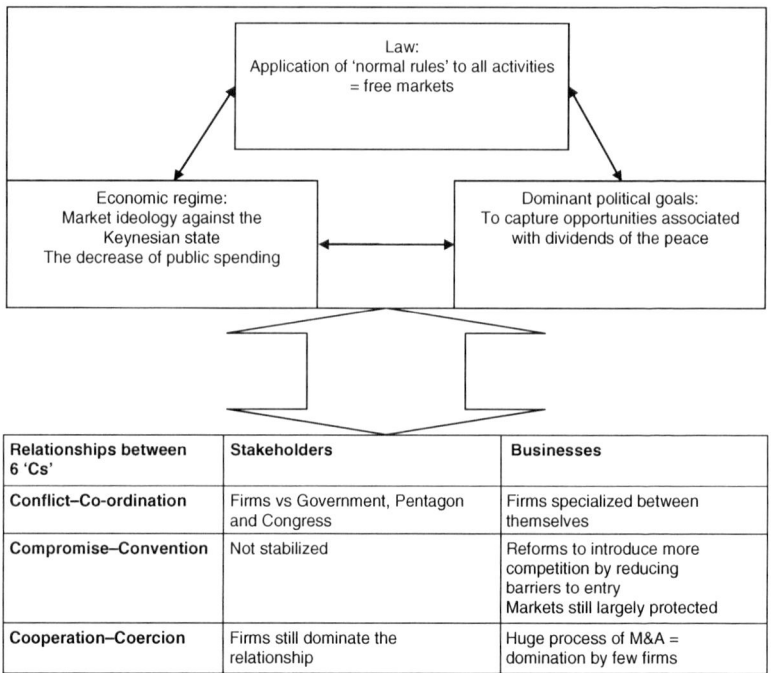

Figure 5.2 The Commercial IR in the US defence industry after the Cold War

3.2.1. A national defence market with barriers to entry

The US defence market has become increasingly protected from foreign companies. Indeed, since the 2004 presidential campaign, Congress has dramatically applied its Buy American Act to the defence industry. Nowadays, the consequence is that most of the Pentagon's purchases are 'American proven':[3] the DoD's prime contract awards outside the US still amounts to only about 5% of its total contract awards. This has meant, for instance, that, in 2006, 82% of the Big Five's defence sales were to the DoD (companies' annual reports). Moreover, in 2005, a group of congressmen and women (made up of both Republicans and Democrats) succeeded in getting a proposal accepted that China should be recognized as a threat to the national American interest. As a consequence, the purchase of electronic components from this country for military purposes, or military cooperation, has become much more difficult.

The overall result of this renewal of protectionism is that in 2006 no non-American company managed any of the 45 most costly defence programmes for the Pentagon (the only exception being BAE Systems as co-contractor with Boeing for the T45 Goshawk training aircraft programme). The only way to become a prime contractor for a foreign company is to be associated as subcontractors with American companies (e.g. EADS and its association with Northrop Grumman to build aerial refuelling planes for the US air force).

BAE Systems has also chosen to acquire American companies in order to obtain American 'nationality' and therefore the right to bid in the US defence market. If, superficially, this strategy seems to have been a success, in reality it provides further evidence for an incomplete process of globalization: in 2006, BAE Systems received only 1.56% of the Pentagon's total R&D funding for its list of top 100 companies, compared with 70.4% for the Big Five. As mentioned above, BAE Systems has become the eighth biggest supplier to the Pentagon, but it is not involved in strategic R&D activity. Moreover, the workforce of the American facilities and plants that BAE acquired since 1999 has no contact with its British counterpart and the latter is forbidden to work in the American plants of the group for reasons of 'defence secrecy'. As a consequence, BAE's presence in the US has not provided the UK with access to American military technologies.

3.2.2. *The boost for exports*

Finally, the only real globalization of the US defence industry that has occurred concerns American sales around the world. Because of the crisis in demand that hit US defence markets during the 1990s, exports became vital to the continued selling of military products.

In order to boost exports, the Defence Security Cooperation Agency (DSCA) has used direct grants to customer states *via* Foreign Military Financing. This fund can purchase products directly from American companies and then attempt to sell them on to foreign customers. This practice clearly favours company profitability. According to Nielsen (2005), exports bought by the FMN from defence firms are four times more than the exports they sell directly to foreign governments. Moreover, the US government makes loans and financially encourages foreign governments to buy American products. For instance, the sale of 48 F16 aircraft by American Lockheed Martin to Poland in 2003 was accompanied by a $3.8 billion loan from the American Federal government to its Polish counterpart. Lastly, the recent wars have 'combat proven' the efficiency of American weapons, thus providing an important commercial argument in their favour.

Overall, between 2000 and 2004 the US was, alongside Russia, the biggest exporter of arms in the world for conventional weapons (31% and 32% of market share: SIPRI, 2005). During the same period, the DoD's purchase of defence equipment and services from foreign companies decreased from 2.4% to 1.7% of its total purchases (GAO, 2006). In short, the re-affirmation of the technological goal within the industry's Commercial IR has not been compatible with the reforms engaged during the first few years after the end of the Cold War. Here, as in the Financial IR, the globalization of the US defence industry has therefore been decidedly limited.

3.3. The Financial IR and the war dividend

The increase of public defence spending and the retention of cost-plus contracts put a brake upon any growing need for international collaboration in order to share the costs of defence production. Again, then, the anticipated effects of globalization have not transpired. In fact, this situation reveals once more the persistence of the industry's traditional Institutional Order wherein its Financial IR encourages the production of high-tech weapons on a purely national basis.

3.3.1. The increase of public defence spending

Since 1999, public defence spending has stopped falling. On the contrary, it has increased from $310 billion in 1999 to $478 billion in 2006 (in constant 2003 US$: SIPRI, 2006). In 2004, public military spending as a part of GDP reached 4%, thus matching Cold War levels. Indeed, between 2001 and 2006, total Pentagon's funding for the industry rose by 103% from $145 to $295 billion (DoD's website). A major result has been an increase in the Federal R&D support received by firms: this budget is set to rise by 85% between 2001 and 2009 in constant dollars (Filder, 2005).

Moreover, the institutionalization of the collective norm for technological supremacy has been accompanied by the extensive use of cost-plus contracts, and this despite the Administration's desire to switch to fixed-price contracts during the 1990s. A study by Makinson (2004) shows that only 66% of the contracts signed by the Pentagon between 1998 and 2003 were of the fixed-price type. Moreover, the proportion is lower for the Big Five with an average rate of only 57%. Indeed, this figure falls to 50% and 47% for Northrop Grumman and Lockheed Martin respectively, because these companies are involved in programmes which entail a major part of strategic R&D for the military capabilities of the country.

As regards international collaborations, their use has not been as important as expected. First, amongst the Pentagon's 35 most expensive programmes, only that of the F35 is collaborative. Second, even this programme has not been based on the principle of an equal footing between partners, thus illustrating another facet of the rejection of globalization. Instead, Congress has even adopted legal measures to limit British access to the source codes of technologies in order to retain technological supremacy within the US and to use public financing for improving national capabilities. For these reasons, British actors have been struggling against American protectionism not only to obtain better access to American technology, but even to be able to define their own F35 specifications.

Conclusion

Since the Second World War, the history of globalization within the US defence industry has proven to be a highly incomplete process. During the Cold War, the doctrine of national defence promoted a form of technological isolationism in order to win the arms race against the Soviet Union. In spite of the end of the Cold War, political work undertaken by the industry's stakeholders has succeeded in maintaining the principle of military supremacy. This is still firmly rooted in the cognitive frames and in the practices of the actors and has thereby driven the development of the industry. As a consequence, the defence industry's globalization is still untypical of that of the rest of the American economy: low imports, a national industrial base and very limited cases of international cooperation due to the protection of 'national technological progress'.

I have reached this conclusion by applying the *Politics of Industry* model to the study of the two main IRs which structure the US defence industry: the Commercial and the Financial. In so doing, I have been led to emphasize that this industry's Institutional Order is based upon an institutionalized hierarchy wherein the Commercial IR overwhelmingly dominates its Financial counterpart. Although reforms initiated by the Federal government during the 1990s were intended to globalize the industry, this did not occur because governmental actors failed to rebuild an institutionalized hierarchy where the rules of the Commercial relationship would no longer have been dominant. In a word, the globalization of the US defence industry in 2007 looks nothing like the one anticipated 10 or 20 years earlier.

Overall, the rules institutionalized within this industry's Commercial and Financial IRs reveal a specific diffraction of macro-level globalization which can be explained only in terms of the political work undertaken at the meso level. These political processes have entailed collective action which has frequently been conflictual. Nevertheless, their cumulative result has been a sectorization of globalization, that is a distinct form which differentiates this phenomenon from its classical expression at the macro level or in other industries.

6
Globalization, Scottish Fisheries and 'Political Work': Global–EU–Local Dialectics

Caitríona A. Carter

Introduction

Like other fishing communities around the world, the Scottish industry faces global pressures of limited and diminishing resources. Collapses of North Sea herring (1970s) and Grand Banks cod (1990s) stocks have had severe impacts on the pelagic and whitefish sectors (Couper and Smith, 1997: 118). More recently, collapses of North Sea cod stocks resulted in further de-commissioning of the whitefish fleet, reducing it by 50% between 2000 and 2003 (Seafish, 2003). As well as the effects that diminishing resources are having on fishing activity in Scotland, international policy shifts on food prices and deregulation of international trade have also had repercussions for local fishing practice (Friis, 1996). This is because, over time, ownership of processing plants and sales contracts between fishers, merchants and processors have become increasingly globalized through the extension of the supply and demand food chain beyond local configurations. For a long time, reaction to these processes of 'global re-structuring of fisheries' (Symes, 1998: 254) has been analogous to others around the world, with commentators reporting fishers self-representing as 'victims' of global forces (Symes, 1998: 254–255).

Yet, unlike other international fisheries, but in common with other European Union (EU) fishing regions, these global challenges faced in Scotland have been experienced through the prism of the EU's Common Fisheries Policy (CFP). Under CFP rules, the EU holds exclusive authority to conserve marine and biological resources in its common seas. For the Scottish industry, therefore, the EU regulatory context is significant in any assessment of global–local dynamics because global impacts upon production, inter-firm relations and commercial relationships are all refracted by CFP rules. Consequently, reactions to 'the global' are bounded by reactions to 'the EU'. Indeed, like other fishing regions in Europe, there have been long and persistent periods of conflict and failure through the breakdown of catcher–EU manager relationships, during which time fishers were labelled 'immoral' and blamed for diminishing resources through over-fishing and breaking of laws. Similarly, lack of compliance with fishing quotas has been a regulatory feature acknowledged by catchers themselves as past industrial behaviour.

However, recent changes made by actors within the Scottish fishing industry challenge this view of fishers as 'victims' and demonstrate that relationships between the global and the local are far more complex than the standard narrative has assumed. More precisely, since 2001, there has been a noticeable change in Scotland in the framing of the 'problem' for fisheries management and how to achieve a 'sustainable' fisheries in the light of global challenges. Moving away from what is referred to as a 'command and control' approach, actors have begun instead to institutionalize different sets of practices which collectively build activities towards 'sustainable fisheries production' (Crean and Wisher, 2000: 471–473).

To evaluate these changes in the Scottish fisheries industry, and the transformative role of 'global–local dialectics' (Fløysand and Lindkvist, 2001: 113) therein, I apply the *Politics of Industry* approach set out in Chapter 1 of this volume. A first aim of this approach is to respond to a central scientific methodological concern to clarify the object of research, namely how to define an 'industry' in this context. Here, we start from the supposition that industries such as fisheries are highly structured entities, or 'Institutional Orders' (IOs) (Carter and Smith, 2008), and can be studied as four sets of Institutionalized Relationships (IRs). IRs shape actor strategy within their own institutional 'logics' of norms, rules, expectations and compromises, and systematize actor negotiation within four 'spaces of mediation' – Purchase, Commercial, Employment and Finance.

To explain change through examining processes of institutionalization (and re-institutionalization) unfolding within each IR, a second aim of the approach is to study these relationships as sites within which 'political work' is invested in by actors – either to bring about change or to preserve stasis in the IR's configurations and competitions as outlined below. In the case of Scottish fisheries, two types of competition to be examined can be distinguished: a competition between stakeholders around questions of reglementation over access to resources on the

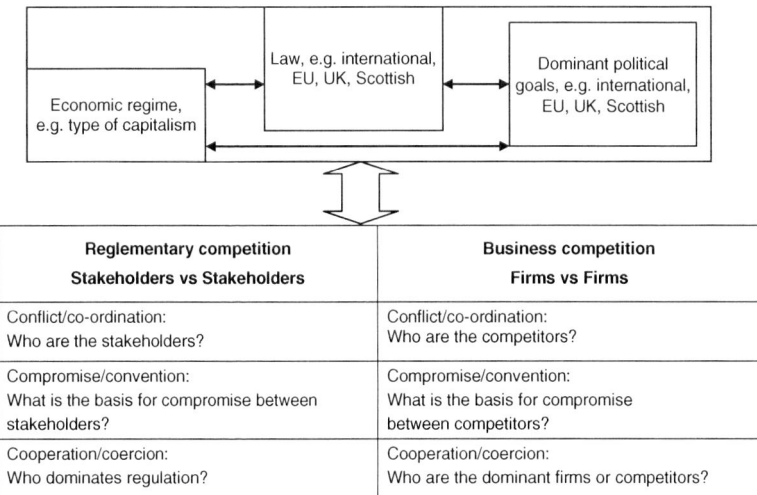

Figure 6.1 Studying an IR (fisheries)

one hand; and, occurring simultaneously, a business competition entailing commercial operators who compete for profit and/or resources on the other (see bottom part of Figure 6.1). Indeed, one of the characteristics which marks this industry as distinct from others presented in this volume is that extensive reglementary competition has constantly occurred between public and collective actors who battle to set policy instruments (e.g. quotas). Lastly, it is acknowledged that both types of regulatory competition are situated within a broader institutional context, including trans-industry rules, horizontal measures and meta-conventions which either apply to the sector, or from which actors have negotiated derogations (top part of Figure 6.1).

When applying this approach in the case of the Scottish fisheries industry, a first step in assessing the cause of change (or its absence) has thus been to apply the concept of 'political work'. Here, political work has been studied as three simultaneous processes – the marshalling of arguments; the construction of alliances; and the activation of both through 'problematization' and 'politicization' to bring about change in reglementary and business competitions. More specifically, in the case of Scottish fisheries, this has entailed the following:

- identifying conservationist, economic, scientific, social and marketing arguments and their prominence within the industry;

- questioning whether Scottish actors have worked either to form alliances and/or new types of industrial communities and organizations, or to bring about change in membership in existing ones;
- questioning the extent to which shifts in, and activation of, discourse towards sustainable fisheries production have resulted in durable institutional change which is favourable to actors across the IO.

In so doing, and in keeping with this approach to studying an IR, I have assessed whether there is evidence of a shift in underlying relations and behaviour within the industry away from conflict towards co-ordination, or from convention to compromise, or from coercion to cooperation. What evidence is there of 'successes' of new inter-organizational relations and interdependencies?

Overall, three features of change within this industry are apparent and will structure the organization of material in this chapter. First, due to the extensive institutionalization of Scottish fisheries within EU arenas resulting from transfers of regulatory authority to EU institutions, any study of how global–local dialectics have been mediated through the political work of Scottish actors would be incomplete without initially examining regulatory bargains underpinning the CFP and which refract those dialectics. Consequently, in Section 1, I will set out the key global challenges facing the fishing industry, the ways in which these have been refracted through the prism of the rules of CFP and opportunities thereby created for political work by local actors. Second, since the initial operation of the CFP in the 1980s, the focus of Scottish activity, both in terms of mobilizations of arguments and in the building of alliances, has been within the Purchase IR. In fisheries, the Purchase IR is centred upon rules which regulate the obtention of the product. These include, inter alia, rules which determine access to natural resources; quantitative rules which set the amount of fishing effort permitted; rules which categorize the type of production, for example, type and size of fish/type and size of net; rules which control inter-firm competition for resources. That actors have invested in political work within these relationships is perhaps not surprising given the scarcity of natural resources. What is striking, however, are the number of significant changes brought about more recently within the Commercial IR over rules of marketing and selling of product (i.e. fish). In Section 2, I thus critically assess this political work which has taken place in Scotland. I show that where change has occurred within the Scottish fishing industry this is particularly unexpected given the commonly held view that the CFP acts to constrain political choice at local levels. In this section, and using the approach outlined above, I will demonstrate that EU constraints are not all-encompassing, but pertain more to the Purchase, rather than the Commercial, IR.[1] Third, starting from the investigative position that local 'knowledge' is critical in explaining the impact of globalization on local capitalism (Fløysand and Lindkvist, 2001: 120), I argue throughout that not only is local knowledge generated by political work, but, more precisely, that it can be transformative when accompanied by actor deployments of sector–territory arguments. Actor references to 'territory' can be powerful tools both in the mobilization of resources and in the construction of legitimate arguments to bring about re-negotiations of compromises and re-setting of regulatory instruments (Carter and Smith, 2008).

1. Refracting the global: The EU's CFP

Before examining the political work of actors within the Scottish fisheries industry, it is important to first evaluate the different institutionalizations of the Purchase and Commercial IRs as they have occurred within EU arena through the creation and implementation of the CFP. In this section, I thus apply the approach as set out above to demonstrate the way in which EU negotiations have institutionalized both IRs and in so doing have established norms, rules and expectations which refract global problems as they have been experienced in Scotland.

1.1. EU institutionalization of the Purchase IR: Stakeholders vs Stakeholders

The central issues over which reglementary competition has been conducted in the Purchase IR of the EU fisheries industry are the determining of rights of access to common fishing grounds and agreeing the quantity of production in a global context of diminishing supply. In particular, reglementary challenges have centred on how to prevent an overexploitation of fish resources and instead achieve a sustainability of stocks (Hanna, 1998). To these ends, EU actors have invested in an extensive institutionalization and re-institutionalization of reglementary competition of the Purchase IR on an EU scale. Here, I set out key elements of their political work as they pertain to conflict vesus co-ordination of stakeholder competitions (for details see Carter, 2007).

1.1.1. Initial institutionalizations of reglementary competition

Competition between European countries over custody of natural resources clearly pre-dates the EU, with disputes over the exercise of a state 'sovereignty' of the seas and territorial clashes over 'ownership' of fishing grounds being part and parcel of Europe's maritime history (Wise, 1984: 68). Attempts to regulate competing territorial claims on an international scale also pre-date the EU, commencing in the late 19th century and accelerating after the Second World War with the international sanctioning of ownership of 'parts' of the seas by coastal states (Farnell and Elles, 1984: 5). Indeed, it was only when international thinking on control over resources recognized a new type of sea territory – an 'Exclusive Economic Zone' (EEZ) – that a 'common' EU resource was acknowledged through the claiming of an EU-EEZ in 1977 (Farnell and Elles, 1984). The declaring of these seas as 'common EU goods' thus marked the start of the institutionalization of the EU Purchase IR, with the extension of a Community regulatory authority over a sea area up to 200 miles from the coasts of coastal states (Couper and Smith, 1997: 115: Leigh, 1983: 63).

From this point onwards, problematizations over method of regulation and hierarchy of authority within the Purchase IR have both been subject to political compromise and conflict within EU policy-making arenas and, at times, adjudicated upon by the European Court of Justice (ECJ) (Wise, 1984). With regard to the method, levels of fishing effort and Member State (MS) quantities of production are decided upon through regulatory instruments of Total Allowable Catches (TACs) and national quotas negotiated by MSs on a yearly basis (Leigh, 1983: 88–89). This process is also accompanied by a programme to reduce catching capacity through re-structuring fleets (Coull, 1999: 351). Significantly, the particular institutionalization of the TACs and quota quantitative method in an EU context determined the hierarchy of reglementary authority within this IR. First, TACs assigned an exclusive authority over EU resources to the European Commission, which was 'alone in a position to come forward with quota proposals for the entire Community' (Farnell and Elles, 1984: 107). Second, the particular institutionalization of the instrument further required that MSs determine their own proposals on 'TACs and quotas' (TQs) by species and fishing areas, including a trade-off position (i.e. ranking of TQs by species). This organization of the instrument thus created new types of numerical-based competition between MSs within the Purchase IR over rights to acquire 'common EU goods'. This in turn necessitated national governments to take political decisions over frequently conflicting coastal community interests within their jurisdiction (Symes and Crean, 1995).

Third, quantitative regulatory methods additionally accorded a specific role for science – and the scientific community. In its institutionalization of marine biological advice, EU practice differed from that of other international regimes. This is because the provision of scientific advice, at the heart of the quantitative approach, has taken different forms in different management systems. For example, in Canadian fisheries the authority to do so has fluctuated, whereby epistemic scientific communities (Haas, 1992) have sought to influence public authorities and become increasingly interconnected with them:

> such epistemic communities have little influence unless they can convince others of the superiority of their particular policy advice.
> (Wiber, 2005: 136)

By contrast, this type of competition between scientific communities was not initially a feature of EU regulation. As Commission officials writing at the time stated, with its limited resources and expertise, the Commission required the authority of a regular independent advice on which to base its proposals (Farnell and Elles, 1984: 114–115, 167). The provider of this advice came to be the International Council for the Exploration of the Seas (ICES) and contracts were signed between the EU and the ICES to regularize this relationship in the Purchase IR. The legitimacy of this advice – and its provider – was premised on a conviction of its superiority derived from an uncontested vision of quantitative science as 'objective' and constructions of scientists as 'distant' from politics (Wilson and Hegland, 2005: 21). Through the regularization of provision of scientific advice constructed as 'independent', actors thus sought to de-politicize the question of its legitimacy within the decisional process and, in so doing, granted ICES a key role in regulation.

Significantly, whereas scientists were viewed as legitimate 'holders of knowledge' about 'common EU goods', at least in the first institutionalization of the Purchase IR, fishers were not. Indeed, the institutionalization of EU regulatory arenas was premised upon an unstated but implicit construction of fishers' role in the industry derived from neoclassical economics as one of 'exploiters' of the common resource.

According to this perception, fishers' 'natural' behaviour – to fish without care for the future state of resources – had to be controlled through regulation. Accordingly, the catching sector was not initially given a formal reglementary role within this IR. Instead, fishers were assigned a consultative role to be conducted within the arena of Commission committees. As a result, actors at the heart of industry – namely fishers – were placed 'outside' decisional arenas institutionalized within the Purchase IR. From the point of view of our approach, therefore, it is possible to view initial EU institutionalizations of 'how' and by 'whom' the common property of EU fisheries would be distributed as putting in motion two core types of reglementary competition between stakeholders:

1. Fishers vs The EU
2. Fishers vs Scientists

1.1.2. Refracting the global: Political work and re-institutionalization

Since its institutionalization in 1983, and in common with other international fisheries management regimes, the Purchase IR of the EU industry has been faced with a number of global challenges. Predominant amongst these have been collapsing fish stocks. Up until the reform of the CFP in 2002, EU rules within the Purchase IR shaped management interpretations of these global pressures and this through the aforementioned institutionalized regulatory paradigm with its emphasis on 'top-down' instruments based on quantitative definitions of the health of stocks (Degnbol, 2003: 47; Nielsen *et al.*, 2004: 153). This created a situation where management of 'global shocks' was refracted through the reglementary competitions this approach institutionalized. In a situation of crisis, conflict underpinning these relationships was not contained as actors sought instead to politicize these competitions. Conflictual competition thus came to dominate industry negotiations resulting in overall policy failure and ever-decreasing fish resources.

For example, throughout the 1990s, hostilities between fishers and the EU resulted in collective catcher mobilizations to contest the quantities of production agreed by 'centralist' decision-making processes. Challenges were mounted against the social and political constructions of science and knowledge which had underpinned CFP processes for assessing the biomass of common resources. Until the end of the 1990s, in addition to fishers taking direct action, these mobilizations were also 'passive' in the sense that they also consisted of non-compliance with quota levels, regarded by catchers as invalid (Deas, 2006). This in turn bolstered managers' and scientists' perceptions of catchers as 'exploiters'. Problems such as these were not unique to the EU. For example, scholars document distrust between biologists, managers and fishermen in New England (Hanna, 1998: 29) and a lack of representation of fishermen in Canada (Wiber, 2005: 137). In the EU, global problems played out within EU rules and structures fostering a regulatory climate which responded initially to these challenges through conflict, convention and coercion. This occurred because the construction of science as 'objective' had institutionalized a separation of the 'scientific community' from the 'catching sector', a separation reflected in discussions within European Commission committees which were described on interview by catchers, scientists and Commission officials alike as 'confrontational'. The exclusion of fishermen from decision-making was, it was argued, a primary cause of the lack of compliance with rules, perceived by catchers as unsuited to their fisheries (Nielsen *et al.*, 2004: 153; interviews). In turn, lack of compliance further fuelled conflict with managers who accused catchers of being primarily responsible for failing fish stocks.

Whereas both the general way in which EU fisheries was managed and the problems which the 'modern' system created were also ones experienced by other international fisheries systems (Nielsen *et al.*, 2004), it is through reform that both the importance of the EU refraction of the global and the specificities of its institutionalization become most apparent. First, in 2002, the EU was mandated by its own rules of access to undergo a reform. Second, in the run-up to reform the Commission was expected, in keeping with the norms and codes of EU trans-industry projects of 'Better Regulation' and 'good governance', to conduct a wide consultation of stakeholders on questions of substance. During these processes, actors invested in important political work which resulted in re-problematizations within the Purchase IR (Carter, 2007). The first stage of this political work was the re-problematization of the territory of the EU common estate into distinct fishing regions – for example, the North Sea – understood to be fished by collective groups of catchers who shared a sense of guardianship of resources. The second stage was the re-problematization of the 'knowledge' of the production of these regions and, in particular, a re-assessment of the 'type' of knowledge required to accurately assess the biomass of stocks within a region's fishery (interviews). As I will set out in Section 3, this political work included within it shifts in management and scientific discourses which re-framed fishers as holders of important types of 'qualitative' small-scale biological and commercial knowledge (e.g. water temperature, stock migrations, discards, landings – Deas, 2006). Co-ordinated usage of this knowledge would enable more accurate interpretations of biological large-scale data to be undertaken by scientists (Degnbol, 2003).

Although they did not cause the regulatory instrument of TQs to be abandoned, these re-problematizations within the Purchase IR did result in a re-institutionalization of the rules for the provision of advice for setting levels of fishing effort and therefore quantities of production. In addition to the role ascribed to ICES, new EU arenas of Regional Advisory Councils (RACs) of stakeholders were set up to co-ordinate reglementary competitions in the provision of advice on the setting of instruments. This provision of co-ordinated advice would be achieved through both the re-institutionalization of 'old' relationships between fishers and scientists and the enabling of new types of relationships within RACs – for example, between RAC members: fishers, community networks and environmental NGOs – for the regulation of the fishery concerned, for example, the North Western Waters RAC. In addition to the reglementary competitions detailed above, a third competition was thereby institutionalized:

Fishers, NGOs, community networks, scientists vs Each other

From a worldwide perspective, the fact that the European Commission and EU Council not only recognized but institutionalized fishers as legitimate holders of a 'qualitative' or 'soft' knowledge of natural resources and production constituted significant change. Further, certain features of RACs distinguish the EU from other international fisheries systems, for example Canada, where these types of approaches have been dismissed by the epistemic community as 'soft science' (Wiber, 2005: 138). Additionally, the role accorded to environmental NGOs as members of RACs also contrasts with other regimes, such as the US, where the structure of management has been slower to accommodate a broader set of interests (Hanna, 1998: 29). Re-institutionalization through RACs has thus been an important process within the Purchase IR. RACs are new and additional arenas for the mediations of reglementary competitions amongst a broader set of actors. For example, debates on managing collapsing fish stocks – such as North Sea cod stocks – are now also refracted through RACs and hence through co-ordinated stakeholder competitions.

In the case of Scotland, therefore, a first set of questions emerges from our overview of change in the Purchase IR. EU reglementary competitions are no longer solely ones of conflict. In this evolving context, we must question whether local discourses resonate with these changes or whether we find evidence of political work to resist them. How have these processes of re-institutionalization been experienced in Scotland in terms of Scottish actor engagement both in their shaping and in their current operation?

1.2. EU institutionalization of the Purchase IR: Firms vs Firms

As we have seen, CFP rules play an important role in refracting global challenges through the prism of the reglementary competitions they institutionalize. With regard to business competitions between commercial operators over profit and/or resources, here too the EU intervenes to manage inter-firm relations by providing for collective structures in the form of Producer Organisations (POs). POs were initially created to enhance the common market organization of fishery products and EU financial aid was provided to producer groups if they decided to organize themselves in this way (Phillipson, 1999: 79). EU Council regulations 'frame the parameters within which POs must operate' (Phillipson, 1999: 81) and cover their anticipated market role which is to adjust supply to demand through, inter alia, improving product quality, ordering marketing regimes to ensure continuity of supply and implementing market intervention mechanisms such as the withdrawing of products (Phillipson, 1999: 81). In short, rules on POs structure business competitions between firms as follows:

Fishers vs fishers

Because POs in different MSs display distinct characteristics and have adapted their functions to the local IO of which they are a part (Phillipson, 1999: 80), compromises underpinning inter-firm competitions will differ from MS to MS and from PO to PO. This is particularly the case when one takes into consideration the role played by UK POs in sectoral quota management. For although since 1992 all EU POs can be assigned the authority to manage quotas (Phillipson, 1999: 81), the UK is unique in being the only MS whose POs have engaged in this practice since the start (Phillipson, 1999: 82). In the case of Scottish POs, therefore, CFP rules play an important role refracting what are commonly voiced as global solutions in quota management to address regulatory problems caused by lack of compliance with quotas. This is because in regulating 'shortfalls in command and control approaches...one of the most common solutions is to advocate the establishment of private property rights' (Gibbs, 2008: 115). Rights regimes apply instruments of Individual Transferable Quotas (ITQs) whereby catchers can buy and sell quotas on an open market:

> the underlying assumption of rights-based regimes is that rights holders will now have positive incentives to ensure the biological sustainability of the stock.
>
> (Gibbs, 2008: 115)

Examples of acclaimed strong regimes applying ITQs are New Zealand (Hughey *et al*., 2000), Iceland and Australia (Couper and Smith, 1997: 117).

Yet, because ITQs are a form of privatization of the 'common estate' or 'the public ownership' of resources, they have sparked political debate (Hatcher *et al*., 2002). For example, commentators have questioned the extent to which quotas become the individual property of catchers or whether their content is being held 'on behalf of' public authority and can be reclaimed by government. Additionally, critical concerns have been voiced over the effects of ITQ systems on the re-structuring of fleets when their implementation has resulted in a contraction of the industry and a concentration of capital to favour large companies, putting small vessel owners out of business. Applying ITQ systems in certain types of small-scale fisheries, it has been argued, has the potential to de-stabilize coastal communities through causing high levels of local unemployment. Finally, with regard to questions of sustainability, others have pointed to the lack of evidence demonstrating a clear link between ITQs and greater sustainability of stocks and a lack of a correlation between ITQ systems and habitat quality issues (Hatcher *et al*., 2002).

Within the current application of the CFP, how this global debate is resolved in an EU context, and how any resolution subsequently affects business competitions between firms, is, for the moment at least, a matter for MSs and, in the case of Scotland, also for POs. This is not to say that EU rules have been silent on these matters. For although the type of 'regulatory orthodoxy' (Wiber, 2005: 136) adopted by the EU was similar in its generalities to that adopted by other fisheries regimes (such as Australia, New Zealand and the US), nevertheless its application has been linked to other dominant political goals:

> in the European case [it was more complex], a first priority ... [was] not only the distribution of stocks, but the social and economic nature of the fisheries.
>
> (Couper and Smith, 1997: 117)

To evaluate the EU's commitment to protecting traditional fishing rights and the socio-economic stability of coastal regions, it has become commonplace to refer to negotiated principles of 'qualified access' to stocks and 'relative stability' in annual allocations of resources as illustrations thereof (Farnell and Elles, 1984). This has recently been demonstrated in EU debates on rights-based management whereby Scottish MEPs have linked discussions on relative stability to discussions on ITQs (Fishing News, 18 April 2008). Here, I wish to address only this specific global–EU–local dialectic through studying the competitions institutionalized around local choices on types of quota management. Given that Scottish POs have the opportunity within the frame of EU rules to take local decisions on whether or not to privatize quotas, I hypothesize that studying their choices will be critical in any assessment of local applications of EU regulatory capitalism.

1.3. EU institutionalization of the Commercial IR

As I have shown above, CFP rules intensively institutionalize the Purchase IR of Scottish fisheries. Additionally, regulatory choices made by MSs acting collectively in the EU's Council of Ministers have also institutionalized relationships governing commercial practice which in turn have set in motion different types of competition in this IR within which Scottish operators have been able to intervene.

Initially, EU regulation in this IR affected both reglementary and business competitions between two sets of actors: Catchers (producers) vs Processors. Over time, we have seen both retailers and large supermarkets enter into these competitions as shown below:

Producers vs Processors
producers and processors amongst themselves and both vs large supermarkets

Additionally, the balance of power between stakeholders and firms in both types of competition has changed and this partly because of reform of EU regulations. To begin with, along with TQs, a central pillar of early institutionalizations of the CFP in the 1980s were rules on common market organization, including rules on pricing and controls on EU imports. On the whole, these rules tended to be protectionist to producers over processors (Farell and Elles, 1984: 130–133). This weighing of business competitions in favour of producers has changed, however, and in particular throughout the 1990s. According to Friis (1996), EU action affected change in two main ways. First, through its engagement in the international de-regulation of trade, the EU gradually increased its imports resulting in reduced prices until the mid-1990s, and this despite a falling volume of catch. Second, reform of the CAP also contributed to lower prices (Friis, 1996: 178). Given that consumer choices are based on 'weighing quality and price', fish prices must 'keep pace with those of alternate food products which compete directly with fish', for example, chicken (Friis, 1996: 179). Both types of de-regulation have thus had effects, all be they indirect, on the balance of power between producers and processors, and between both of these groups of actors and retailers in determining price formation. Whereas formerly this process was dominated by producers, now multinational retailers dominate as 'the internationalization of the retail trade [has added] to the retail sector's negotiating power' (Friis, 1996: 181, 184).

In this trans-industry de-regulatory environment, supermarkets have mobilized to legitimate their dominance through claiming ownership of knowledge of consumer preferences: 'to obtain advantage over the food producers in terms of a much more detailed and comprehensive knowledge of consumers' quality demands' (Friis, 1996: 182). Actors have thus exploited opportunities presented through the de-institutionalization of the Commercial IR to alter patterns of power in both reglementary and business competitions.

Given these significant global changes in the 1990s, the final object of my research concerning the Scottish industry has been to question the extent to which these latter patterns of domination have been re-institutionalized. To what extent is this IR dominated by supermarkets and/or multinational processors? Is there scope for local political work in the Commercial IR, for example in price formation? In particular, these questions are raised in a context where this IR has also experienced some global institutionalization through the setting up of worldwide instruments which create market incentives for local industry which are independent of EU rules – for example, the international joint initiative by the multinational corporation Unilever PLC ('one of the world's largest buyers of fish' – Long, 1999: 147–148) and the NGO WWF to set up an eco-labelling system accredited by a Marine Stewardship Council (Long, 1999; Symes, 1998: 255) (Figure 6.2).

In summary, the Purchase and Commerical IRs of the Scottish fisheries industry have been significantly institutionalized within EU arenas. Global impacts in Scotland are consequently refracted, first through negotiated interpretations and solutions to those challenges within these arenas. This institutionalization has not been static, however.

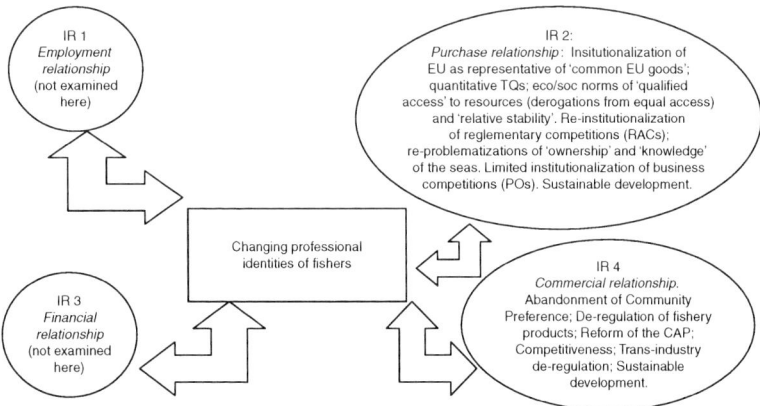

Figure 6.2 The EU IO of fisheries

In both IRs examined, the norms and compromises underpinning intra-industry competitions have been subject to political work bringing about a process of re-institutionalization, which in turn has resulted in a changed refraction of global influences.

2. Interpreting EU refractions of global fisheries: The 'political work' of the Scottish fishing industry

In this section, and following from above, I examine political work conducted by actors within the Scottish fisheries industry. In so doing, it should be noted that Scottish fisheries is not a homogeneous industry, but consists of a number of distinct fishing constituencies, for example, Northeast Scotland, Northwest Scotland, and Shetland. Additionally, production has been centred on different types of fisheries: whitefisheries, for example, haddock, monkfish, cod; shellfisheries, for example, nephrops (prawns/langoustine), scallops; pelagic fisheries, for example, mackerel, herring. Collectively, Scottish vessels land the highest volume (c.68%) and have the highest value of landings in whole of the UK, although, since the 1980s, there have been shifts in both the quantities of landings between fisheries and their respective commercial values. Furthermore, for some species, for example nephrops, an excess of Scottish landings over imports exists (the Scottish catch represents 60% of the world's catch), whereas for others, for example, cod, landings are topped up by imports. For all these reasons, interpretations of the 'global' differ across the industry.

Despite these differences, however, common Scottish political work can be detected. More precisely, we can identify changed political work whereby the building and transferring of local knowledge is increasingly being framed within a sustainable fisheries production model. This model claims to set three goals to attain sustainable fisheries production:

1. establishing congruence of eco-system and governance boundaries;
2. re-shaping relations between human beings and the environment through new systems of governance – which includes establishing enabling institutional structures, processes of negotiation and participation of users;
3. A re-programming of markets (Crean and Wisher, 2000: 471–473).

Recent reforms in Scotland – which are documented in this section – can be understood as attempts to move the Scottish approach to fisheries management towards the SFP model. This is not to say that this has been achieved, nor that all three goals outlined above are ones which are shared by all actors across the industry. Rather, problematizing fisheries 'in this way', as opposed to any other way, tends to dominate actors' assessment of recent choices made in the face of global challenges. Moreover, this shift in thinking has driven actors to vocalize new arguments and form new collective organizations in both the Purchase and Commercial IRs.

The overall aim of this section is twofold: to explore this political work and to demonstrate that it has not been static, but has responded to shifts in international and EU thinking; to show that this work has been underpinned by a constant tension between the conservation of natural resources and the survival of local communities.

2.1. Problematization and politicization of the Purchase IR: Stakeholders vs Stakeholders

As I set out in Section 1, CFP institutions put in motion three significant reglementary competitions in the Purchase IR

1. Fishers vs The EU as representative of natural resources, common goods and the interests of future generations;
2. Fishers vs Scientists as holders of knowledge about natural resources and common goods;
3. Fishers, NGOs, community networks and scientists vs Each other.

Since 1999, political work invested in by Scottish actors has brought about change in all three competitions. This has occurred through strategies of problematization, that is change in ideas, and politicization, that is the forging of alliances. At the heart of this political work has been the re-problematization of professional identities of Scottish fishers. As I argued above, the 'command and control' approach to fisheries management contained within it an implicit construction of fishers as 'exploiters' of natural resources who had to be controlled through both quantitative and coercive institutions. Enforcement was a matter for MSs: in Scotland, the Scottish Fisheries Protection Agency (FPA) was established in 1991 to carry out this task in the seas off the coast of Scotland and in its ports (Coull, 1999: 347).

This construction of fishers as exploiters of a common resource, who ruthlessly fish for economic gain and without care for future generations, merits further consideration. For lack of compliance with quotas has in the past been a major obstacle to the effective management of Scottish fisheries (Coull, 1999: 347). Indeed, for a long time it was suspected (Nuttall, 2000: 112), and more recently openly acknowledged by fishers, that fishing rules were being extensively broken through 'black landings' of fish. Yet, compliance is a complex phenomenon for it goes to the heart of the professional identity of fishers and the conceptualization of their industry. This is because compliance with regulatory institutions is strongly intertwined with conceptions of their legitimacy – in the way they are both designed and talked about. Those who broke the rules argued that they had conflicts of interest over dumping quality fish and regarded landing 'black fish' as 'necessary and legitimate': 'nobody knows what they should do, whether to land fish illegally or throw it overboard' (Nuttall, 2000: 113). However, not all catchers broke the rules. Indeed, many regarded this practice as 'immoral' given that a large number of skippers, for example, in the northeast, were also senior figures in the Church (Nuttall, 2000: 112). Breaking the rules thus not only caused conflict across the industry, but also brought about splits within fishing communities (Couper and Smith, 1997: 118). Indeed, because of the constructed links between fishing and representations of territory (Carter and Smith, 2008), when fishers were defined as 'dishonest' this had broader effects in local communities who felt tarnished by the same brush:

> In north-east Scotland... to be seen as unskilful, to be labelled as dishonest and to be accused of poor seamanship in official reports, has

an effect not only on the skipper and crew, but also on the wider community and social and economic contexts that derive their essential and respective identities from fishing.

(Nuttall, 2000: 114)

Against this background, since 1999, actors have mobilized to make significant changes to this regulatory practice. This political work was led in early 2000 by the Scottish Fishermen's Federation (SFF). SFF argued that an underlying cause of policy failure in Scotland was this representation of catchers as 'rogues', rather than 'joint custodians' of the sea (interviews). Re-claiming professional identities as ones of 'guardians of resources', SFF embarked upon strategies of politicization of this new identity in order to de-politicize old reglementary competitions. One of these strategies was geared towards the re-building of alliances with scientists. This involved a number of different enterprises – for example, for the first time, SFF began to pay scientists to provide fishers' associations with scientific advice; SFF also engaged a scientist to enable them to examine science in a 'more refined' way (interviews). This shift in approach was one which went from 'condemning to refuting the science' (interviews). Significantly, new alliances were subsequently institutionalized with the setting up of the North Sea Commission, under whose umbrella scientists and fishers were brought together in the form of a partnership to explore new ways of managing North Sea fisheries.

These politicizations of new identities were successful in finding a common cause with scientists because the shift in catchers' discourse found resonance in the already changing discourse of the regulatory science community (Hanna, 1998: 29). Since the mid-1990s, scientists had recognized a problem with their non-biological data and, in particular, had acknowledged an absence of data generally on the ways in which fishermen were adapting to quotas (Schwach et al., 2007). This included a lack of accurate information on the numbers of fish discarded and catch recordings, which rendered bias in the calculations, for example in the North Sea cod assessments at the end of the 1990s (Schwach et al., 2007; interviews). Aside from biological explanations, part of the reasons accounting for bias was that stock assessment predictions had been based on rationalistic assumptions of human behaviour (e.g. by adding 'capital' to the model in the absence of commercial data – interviews). Calls were made within the scientific community for the need to 'model the human element' (interviews). Moreover, greater engagement of catchers was viewed by scientists as necessary in order to aid in the interpretation of data.

A good example of this common cause was the political work carried out by fishers and scientists over Scottish langoustine quotas. Scottish nephrops had consistently been set a very low quota and, partly as a consequence, black landings of prawns were commonplace. In 2005, it was decided that catchers would work with the Fisheries Research Service in Aberdeen to develop improved data on nephrops' reproduction and recruitment using a TV survey technique. The results of this targeted biological marine survey were presented in the form of scientifically grounded arguments to present a case to the European Commission for an increase in quota. The results were that, in 2006, the nephrops quota for the West Coast of Scotland was raised by 36% (32% for the North Sea) – levels of fishing effort which reflected what was being caught already. The increased quota was legitimated by a biological survey using peer-approved techniques and was of a scale not possible for ICES. The success of this political work stemmed from the joint perception of the nature of the 'problem' shared by catchers and scientists alike grasping the complexity of compliance. In short, reglementary competition which had been one of conflict was now turned into one of co-ordination.

This work through the generation of new marine biological knowledge, specific to the fishery concerned, has more recently been accompanied by a number of other instruments. First, Scottish POs have internal codes of conduct of members not to over-fish a quota and have disciplinary powers, for example fines (NC, 2006). At times, internal organizational tensions have been such that the desire to protect membership (and quota) through safeguarding a cooperative and consensual mode of functioning and the desire to deliver a strict management regime to members to guarantee compliance have not always been easy to reconcile (Phillipson, 1999: 87). Yet, a commonly held view is that 'this system by involving fishermen directly in dividing up the quotas effectively incorporates a measure of self-policing' (Coull, 1999: 354). Second, and in response to arguments made by collective organizations such as Sea Fish Authority, stricter regulatory instruments have been enacted (Seafish, 2005). There has been a proliferation of new regulatory instruments to ensure compliance: computerized log books onboard vessels; computerized landing declarations; records of first sales of fish; 'Buyers and Sellers' register; transport documents. Instruments such as these are the outcomes of political work in Scotland (and in the UK as a whole) which, rather than relying on coercion and the role of the FPA to police the seas, are aimed at institutionalizing compliance through regulated cooperation.

Politicizations of new professional identities have also driven strategies of action to re-institutionalize both EU and Scottish regulatory arenas. With regard to the former, finding common cause with the English/Welsh/Northern Irish Fishermen's Federation (the NFFO), SFF played a strategic role in the reform of the CFP in 2002 and in the setting up of the RACs. During this period, Scottish actors heavily invested in collective political work with others both from the UK and other MSs (e.g. Spain) to bring about change in EU arenas. Once again, at the heart of their argument for transformation was the re-construction of the fishing industry as an organization of production. Moreover, territorial arguments were deployed not only to justify the boundaries of new policy arenas created by RACs, but also to lend support to the desire for change – for example, the SFF argued that it was not only fishers who wanted transformation, but the 'broad church of thinking in Scotland' (interviews). Finally, and since their establishment in 2004, Scottish actors have also mobilized to be active engagers in RACs. Indeed, the UK is the only MS to have two 'national' industry representations as members. Scottish representatives hold key positions and have been pivotal in driving new types of deliberation conducted within them (Carter, 2007).

Within Scottish regulatory arenas, here too actors have conducted political work to institutionalize new partnerships. For, even though scholars continue to describe the UK's stakeholder engagement practice as 'ad hoc lobbying [rather than] formal representation' (Mikalsen and Jentoft, 2008: 170), in Scotland this is changing. A central outcome of a collective marshalling of arguments towards creating a sustainable fisheries production approach has been the institutionalization of a new advisory partnership – the SeaFAR strategy and advisory group – bringing together managers, catchers, processors, environmental NGOs, retailers and consumers. To legitimize the institutionalization of this arena and resources put to policy delivery, powerful evocations of the territorial significance of the fisheries industry to Scotland have been repeatedly made: 'Scotland's fishing industry has a long and proud past and sea fishing has always been a part of Scottish life' (Ross Finnie MP: part of speech given at the inauguration of the North Sea RAC). Moreover, catchers' eligibility to be members has been legitimized by shifts in the dramatization of their identities and regulatory practice away from non-compliance towards 'appropriate' strategies of engagement (interview material). This specific institutionalization has been accompanied by other initiatives since Scottish political devolution in 1999. Resources have been deployed by the former Scottish Executive, now

Scottish government, to re-shape industry relations through establishing enabling regulatory structures and increased participation of users. This is recently evidenced by the negotiation of the Scottish Conservation Credits Scheme by the Scottish government at the December EU Council meeting (2007) whereby it was agreed that Scottish fishers could be awarded 'days at sea' for complying with conservation measures.

In summary, strategies to problematize and politicize professional identities away from 'exploiters' of a resource to 'custodians' of that resource have enabled fishers to re-define their relations with the scientific community, public authorities and the rest of the industry. With regard to their re-defining of relations with other actors across the industry, for example processors, political work in the Purchase IR has begun to have repercussions for the Commercial IR (see Section 2.2). Overall, this work has been geared towards ensuring a multi-positionality and omnipresence of Scottish actors from across the industry in arenas setting rules regulating the obtention of the product. In particular, parallel engagement within RACs and the SeaFAR partnership has made a tremendous difference to the management of the industry. Whereas in the past industrial behaviour operated on the basis of conflict, today work is geared towards co-ordination of activities in a plethora of arena. This shift in the reglementary competition has had staggering results: Seafood Scotland now claim a '99%' compliance rate in Scottish fisheries practice.

2.2. Containing conflict through co-ordination in the Purchase IR: Firms vs Firms

Although reglementary negotiations over resources have been important drivers of regulation and actor coalitions, political work has also occurred around business competitions within the Purchase IR. As I stated above, EU rules on POs institutionalized inter-firm relations as follows:

Fishers vs Fishers

The local application of these rules in Scotland has resulted in POs which tend to be 'favourably disposed in terms of the strength of their managerial, administrative and financial capacities and on the basis of close regular contact maintained with their members' (Phillipson, 1999: 87). There are currently eight Scottish POs, the most prominent of which is the Scottish Fishermen's Organisation (SFO). Membership consists of fishing vessel owners registered in the economic area assigned to the PO and finance comes from membership fees, landing fees and company earnings (Phillipson, 1999: 89). For these reasons, there are differences between the respective bargaining power of POs and also between their members. Indeed, POs are commonly constructed as 'exclusive enclaves for larger capital and quota holders' (Phillipson, 1999: 84), whereby large POs are seen to dominate inter-firm competition. These patterns notwithstanding, conflict between them is co-ordinated through collective organizations, such as the Scottish Association of Fish Producers' Organisations (SAFPO) and Seafood Scotland (see below).

The central work carried out by POs is sectoral quota management. PO quota management started in the UK as early as 1984, the initiative taken by the Shetland PO (Phillipson, 1999: 82). In Scotland, as in the UK, quota management is shared between public authorities and the POs. The government is responsible for the management of the quota for the non-sector and vessels under 10 m within their territory: POs are responsible for quota management of their members. Since 1999, UK quotas are allocated according to the system of Fixed Allocation of Quotas (FAQ). These were fixed in 1999 based on historical catch records between 1996 and 1999.

Given that POs across Scotland are responsible for quota management for their members, a key concern has been to determine how best to administer them. In this context, quota trading has become part and parcel of quota management, but takes different forms. In Scotland, quota trading of a type practised by English vessel owners – whereby substantial quantities of quota were sold to Dutch, Galician/Basque and Icelandic companies (who currently own the majority of the fishing industry in England, with the exception of the South West) – has not been prevalent. Rather quota trading has tended to occur within POs. This has taken the form of 'ring fencing' track records (e.g. Shetland FPO; see Phillipson, 1999: 83), that is when fishers leave the industry the opportunity arises for POs to retain their vessel's track record and hold it permanently by the PO either in a pool or for individual distribution (Phillipson, 1999: 83). POs also implement policies to enable their members to swap or lease quotas (see Nautilus Consultants, 2006, for details). Some POs, for example, adopt a 'pool' system, some an Individual Quota system and others a 'pool plus' system, combining elements of pooling and individual quota management (Nautilus Consultants, 2006). The system adopted can also be linked to the type of fisheries – for example pelagic fishers have deployed individual quota management tools, nephrops fishers the pool system and the white fish sector a mix of both (Nautilus Consultants, 2006).

In 1999, concerns were raised that 'fixing the track records [could] signify another step towards...ITQs' (Phillipson, 1999: 89). This end point has not materialized, however. Rather what we find is a variety of practices. Officially, there is no 'quota trading' in that actor perceptions are that there is no legal entitlement to what is bought and sold – quotas remain 'public property' of the government (interviews). This is a 'grey area' in the UK: discussions over property rights have dominated debates on whether to move to a fully ITQ scheme. More recent debates on tradeable quota rights within West Coast shellfisheries reveal the seriousness with which actors discuss the implications of ITQs for local communities (and resonate with local struggles elsewhere, for example Nova Scotia: Wiber, 2005). For example, in a survey conducted on the West Coast nephrops industry, arguments were made weighing pros and cons of ITQs:

> if fishing rights...are freely tradeable they are more likely to end up in the hands of the most efficient businesses...but not necessarily benefiting west coast economies.
>
> If part of the available fishing rights are protected for local businesses (e.g. via the non-sector quota system)...there may be less profit generated by the nephrops fishery, but more of it may remain in west coast communities.
>
> (Seafish, 2006: 2)

In Scotland, the debate for ITQs is constantly couched in these terms of their potential impact on local fishing communities. This being said, it is also the case that current practice is premised more on convention than compromise over potentially conflicting approaches. Indeed, the question raised by the survey revealed that political work had not been conducted towards negotiating a compromise between local benefits and total profits (Seafish, 2006: 2). The recent launching by the European Commission of an EU-wide debate on rights-based management might provide new impetus for actor investment in political work of this kind to clarify local choices for mixed practices in fisheries management systems.

Political work has been embarked upon by POs to seek to optimize fishing opportunities for their members (NC, 2006), that is to increase the supply side of fishing. When this occurs, inter-firm competitions are shifted into the reglementary dimension of the Purchase IR. This political work has resulted in POs becoming active in policy shaping and, in particular, in discussions over levels of fishing effort and stock assessments in quota setting. The establishment of the RACs has provided a new opportunity for POs to perform this function and one which has been seized. When exercising this role, POs shift from being managing/marketing organizations to representative/'political' organizations and act as the interface between the two types of competition within the Purchase IR.

Overall, we can summarize two key features of Scottish inter-firm competitions within the Purchase IR. First, these competitions have been institutionalized both through the rules of quota allocations, including the continued role for public authority in managing quota for the under 10 m sector, as well as through the internal rules governing POs. This institutionalization has put in motion two expressions of business competition – the first between non-organized small-vessel owners and large-vessel owners organized in POs; the second between members of POs, whereby PO codes and practices dominate how competitive struggles are resolved. Second, the privatization of the local in response to global pressures of sustainability has not occurred in Scotland to the extent it has in other jurisdictions, for example, the Netherlands. Once again the examination of the political work of Scottish POs, as well as that of local fishermen, provides the key to explaining resistance to full privatization (Figure 6.3).

2.3. Political work and the institutionalization of the Commercial IR

As I stated in Section 1, although the Commercial IR has been refracted to some extent by EU policies, this has not occurred to the same degree as that of the Purchase IR. Nonetheless, EU regulation has structured two types of competition within it:

1. Producers vs Processors;
2. Producers and processors amongst themselves and Both vs Large supermarkets.

For many years, the Commercial IR of the Scottish fishing industry consisted of price mechanisms and individual contracts for the selling of fish. Recently new and important political work has been invested in by actors which has led to the first institutionalization of this IR in

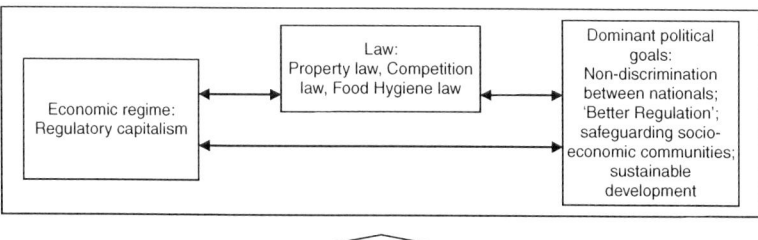

Relationships between 6 'Cs'	Stakeholders	Businesses
Conflict–Co-ordination	Still fishers vs The European Commission as a representative of natural resources, common goods, interests of future generations Increasingly fishers alongside Scottish government, scientists, NGOs (WWF), community networks as co-holders of knowledge of the common resource	Still firms vs Firms (between MSs); Firms vs Firms (within Scotland and the UK) Increasing conflict between over 10 m sector vs under 10 m sector
Compromise–Convention	Enduring convention of TQs Increasingly challenged convention of EU quota distribution principles affecting Scotland, e.g. relative stability New compromises on (re)-constructions of professional identities, knowledge and territorialized ownership of resources (RACs, SeaFAR)	Increasingly challenged conventions of EU and UK quota distribution principles, e.g. relative stability, FAQs inter-firm struggles mediated by compromises over rules and norms of POs Unresolved debates on ITQs
Cooperation–Coercion	EU sets regulatory instruments based on advice supplied by ICES and now, but to a much lesser extent, RACs Compliance increasingly framed as cooperation, not coercion	Large POs and large fishing companies dominate

Figure 6.3 The *Purchase IR* in today's Scottish fisheries industry

Scotland. This finding about political work in the Commercial IR is particularly significant given the competition over limited resources within the fisheries industry and inter-professional struggles triggered by EU rules – and marks the Scottish fisheries case out in contrast to others in this volume, for example, that of the French foie gras industry. Overall, this political work has been conducted within an active strategy to re-programme markets to sell sustainable fish and has centred on three issues: quality, price and sustainability of product.

Until 1999, processors and producers mainly pursued parallel strategies within the Commercial IR. With regard to processors, their engagement in this IR has traditionally been a unilateral one – for example, individual firms seeking to obtain fish on contract arrangements rather than through auction (Coull, 1999: 355). However, as the Scottish processing industry has contracted over the years, so too has its organization become less disparate and fragmented (interviews). As part of this process, Scottish processing has collectively organized through the Scottish Seafood Processors' Federation (SSPF), which has a representative role and shapes policy through its membership of the SeaFAR partnership. Similarly, although producers have tended to engage unilaterally in the Commerical IR, changing strategies are apparent here also. For, whereas in England POs have done little to actively intervene in the market or conduct 'added-value' activities in addition to their quota management role (Phillipson, 1999: 86), in Scotland the two largest POs have adopted active as well as passive marketing strategies. For example, the largest PO, the SFO has established a separate subsidiary processing company, Braehead Ltd; Shetland FPO is 'a major shareholder in Shetland Catch (the largest pelagic processor in the UK and a major trader in this product area)' (NC, 2006: 10).

Although separate approaches have thus been the dominant way of managing issues within the Commercial IR, recently they have been brought together through political work, whereby actors politicized a 'common cause' in commercial activities. Its origins can be traced to actor problematizations of sectoral dilemmas in the whitefish fishery in the mid-1990s, when a marketing crisis for haddock occurred because excess tonnes of haddock were withdrawn from the market to be processed as fishmeal. At that time, it became clear that there was no collective industry body which could have addressed this crisis in a different way. The existing Sea Fish Industry Authority was a UK-wide body and did not recognize this sectoral issue as a public UK problem but rather as a local sectoral problem. No problematization of a 'Scottish' interest was recognized. Since then, to render these sectoral issues public problems, actors have mobilized around re-definitions of the 'public' in whose interest action required to be taken. Actors argued that what was needed was a separate organization which would recognize and address 'Scottish' interests in fisheries marketing. The organization which was subsequently established to carry out this work is Seafood Scotland (SFS), a Trade Association, which started functioning in 2000.

Producers – led by the SFO – thus began to politicize the need for a Scottish inter-professional organization to co-ordinate strategies in response to endogenous global impacts within the Commercial IR. The institutionalization of the SFS has further continued through political work which is rooted in an ongoing construction of its necessity to enable co-ordination of conflict arising from refracted global shocks in the Purchase IR. Initial issues over which actor struggles were mediated within SFS were quality and price of fish. Both of these sets of political work have been conducted in reaction to EU quota cuts in whitefish and de-commissioning of the fleet in 2000 and 2003. During this period, the whitefish fleet was cut by 50% (Seafish, 2003). In its examination of fishers' practice following both sets of de-commissioning, SFS made a number of observations which would subsequently guide its work. First, that there was evidence of fishers behaving as 'exploiters' and not thinking about the market or quality of product, but just 'racing to sea to fish as much as they could'. This behaviour was reflected also in their presentation of fish – for example, over-filling six stone boxes with eight stone of fish was common practice. Second, the behaviour of fishers failing to comply with the quotas had resulted in 'black landings' and the operation of two markets (official and 'black'). Yet, fleet re-structuring was unfolding at a time when, as I documented above, re-problematizations of professional identities were already taking place and which were to drive change in the Commercial IR too. On the one hand, the fleet was much slimmer. On the other, actors describe those operators remaining as fishers whose 'mindset was altered' and in keeping with broader changes taking place: 'the people left were the better guys' (interviews).

Within this changing IO, actors within SFS began to problematize and politicize the Commercial IR within a sustainable fisheries production model and the need to re-progamme markets. Actors refer to this political work as a 'quality drive'. In 1999, scholars writing on the UK industries reported that 'quality and value issues have tended to give way to those of quantity and volume' (Phillipson, 1999: 84). Indeed, discussions on quality had already begun within the European Commission, UK fisheries Departments and the Sea Fish Industry Authority in the mid-1990s (Phillipson, 1999: 84–86), but had not produced any durable change:

> icing of fish at sea was uneven...temperature control at most port auctions was poor; and in summer especially there were serious losses in quality along the distribution chain.
>
> (Coull, 1999: 355)

In the context of a changing discourse within the Commercial IR, SFS began to establish quality schemes for those who had not been forced to exit the industry. A vessel could become 'accredited', whereby it was benchmarked by SFS and awarded a (confidential) grade by comparison with its competitors with regard to the quality of its practice in, for example, icing, washing of fish, gutting. Within this process, individual fishermen acted as 'pioneers', for example, one fisherman began to weigh and grade his fish at sea and others began to do the same.

Beyond such changes in individual practice, in order to politicize strategies of action premised on quality, stakeholders were keen to repeat arguments linking quality to price:

> The link between financial reward and quality must be strong in order to move towards an overall higher standard of quality and maximise earnings from the fishery
>
> The question of paying a pack-out rate, or some other mechanism to give skippers a clear financial incentive for better quality product, should now be addressed by a suitable industry group.
>
> (Seafish, 2006: 5)

Arguments were made that one could catch less but attain a higher price, and these encouraged fishers to invest in quality practices, including weighing and packing at sea, onboard ice-making, smaller box weights:

> Despite the economic difficulties there has been some investment, with 50% of those surveyed investing in quality on board practices in the last 12 months.
>
> (Seafish, 2003)

Quality schemes started for whitefish sector were subsequently extended to pelagic and nephrops (prawns). As mentioned above, prawns had had a high number of black landings with fishermen catching above the quota and being pursued by the Fish Protection Agency. This began to change. Rather than continue with a strategy of non-compliance, the successfully obtained increase in quota documented above meant that these levels of illegal landings no longer occurred. Moreover, the quality drive was supported by changes in technology (installation of satellite tracking systems) and new policy instruments, such as the 'Buyers and Sellers' register. As one interviewee put it, there was now 'nowhere to hide'. Additionally, this change in practice has been sustained through an increasing number of direct contracts between catchers and processors/retailers away from auction.

According to commissioned reports, political work invested in this IR has been successful in its re-orientation of fishers' practices to catch for the market, that is to encourage fishers not to come in all at once or all on a Friday: 'there has been a shift of influence towards the market throughout the value chain' (Seafish, 2005). What has been recognized is that whilst it is true that the prices of fish products are determined by many different factors 'operating at all scales and throughout the fish chain' (Phillipson, 1999: 87), there are choices which could be taken locally to effect price. For, although scholars document falling prices in fisheries up until 1998, recently in Scotland the price of fish has risen dramatically in some fisheries, for example in haddock, where recently falling prices across the industry have not been seen, and langoustine, where there is a high demand.

The second element of political work conducted by actors through the SFS has been to generate knowledge on consumer preferences and facilitate dialogue between different parts of the industry on the environmental sustainability of operations (Seafish, 2005). From this perspective, in the last two years, the quality of product has been linked to a sustainability drive and one which is supported by processors, environmental NGOs and supermarkets (retail sector). As part of this political work, the concept of a 'quality' product in fisheries no longer refers solely to quality in harvesting but has been linked to proving that fishing practice is 'sustainable'. This was reported on interview as a response to a 'global' demand: 'in the global market, one has to be green': data to prove 'greenness' has to be robust. Indeed, two central challenges have been posed for retailers in matters of sustainability – first, whether to keep buying from Scotland; and second, how to brand fish on fish counters to indicate responsible sourcing of product. With regard to the former, processors looking to sell in global markets have requested evidence of provenance. Currently, most Scottish processors will buy Scottish products first and foremost, and in the whitefish sector they top up, for example, from the Faroe Islands and Iceland. In the nephrops sector, the bulk of landings are native. With regard to the latter, provision of accurate data indicating provenance to enhance traceability of responsible fishing is essential (Seafish, 2005). Pilot projects have been run, for example Scottish processors Young's Bluecrest on tailed nephrops (Combes and Myers, 2004).

Importantly, large retailers such as Sainsbury's, Tesco, Morrison's and Marks and Spencer have become leaders of political work to politicize sustainability. However, supermarkets do not act independently from global discourses. Pressure has been placed on them by NGOs, such as Greenpeace, for example through its 'league table' of supermarkets. The game of sustainability or 'being seen to be green' is also now something to which both French and Spanish retail sectors are beginning to react, albeit slowly compared to that of the UK sector. This is encouraging fishers to provide evidence of their sustainable practice. The key is to 'establish information channels into the end user market to improve perception of UK caught fish' (Seafish, 2005).

In all of this, the overlap of political work in this Commercial IR and that conducted in the Purchase IR has brought about significant change. The creation of the SeaFAR partnership to co-ordinate reglementary competitions in the Purchase IR has also had significant effects on the political work conducted within the Commercial IR. Its contribution results in part from its broad membership and its uniqueness as 'a partnership with a market face' 'unlike any other in EU' (comments made by a range of EU actors at a conference on the Scottish Seafood Industry held in Brussels in February 2007). Further, the types of deliberations conducted within SeaFAR have helped the tone of discussions conducted within SFS Board meetings: 'in 2003 there used to be big punch ups between processors and fishers... that has all changed now' (interviews):

> When asked what issues are facing the west coast nephrops sector, most processors identified the low quantity of nephrops available. Only one in five companies interviewed cited lack of communication, knowledge and trust between fishermen and their customers (the processors and/or exporters).
>
> (Seafish, 2006: 4)

The SFS can and has carried on the work started by SeaFAR – for example on nephrops – and in ways to contain business competitions between firms identified above. Indeed, SFS not only represents the big trawlers, but extends the membership of its working groups to small creelers thereby engaging them in local choices over markets and accreditation. In this manner, a greater proportion of fishers can be involved in the making of local choices, whose effects impact on broader industry considerations of management of common resources and preservation of local communities.

In summary, political work in the Commercial IR has recognized the limits of that conducted within the Purchase IR, given that debates over common resources always remain unresolved due to uncertainties over the supply of fish. The overall aim of this work has been to expand the 'seafood consumption market through product innovation and marketing' (Seafish, 2005), whilst at the same time placing an emphasis on sustainability. In undertaking this political work, stakeholders and firms alike have been supported by public authorities in Scotland, and in particular the Scottish government. Indeed, changes in the Commercial IR in fisheries resonate with that experienced in other sectors in Scotland and have recently been brought together within the new national policy on 'Scotland Food and Drink', which is part of an overall Scottish government national strategy for promoting Scotland in global markets. Consequently, in this IR too, our approach identifies successful strategies

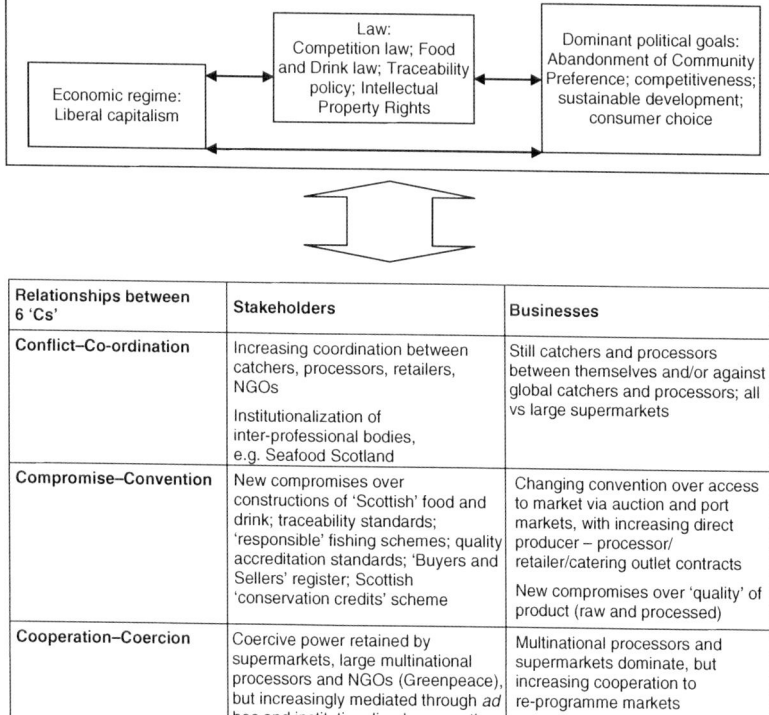

Figure 6.4 The *Commercial IR* in today's Scottish fisheries industry

of both problematization and politicization to bring about behavioural and attitudinal changes in sustainability. This is not to suggest that patterns of domination have altered; nor that they are always co-ordinated. Rather, political work undertaken by coalitions of actors has aimed both to generate knowledge about consumer preferences to be held by producers and processors vs large supermarkets and to contain the inherent conflict underpinning inter-professional competitions (Figure 6.4).

Conclusions

In this chapter, we have examined changes made within the Scottish fishing industry to move fisheries management away from a 'command and control' approach towards sustainable fisheries production. To do this, we have applied the *Politics of Industry* approach as set out in Chapter 1 of this volume to analyse transforming 'global–local dialectics' (Fløysand and Lindkvist, 2001: 113). The specific application of this approach as adopted in this chapter has been to give prominence to sub-state territories as venues for global and EU regulation, as well as coalitions of actors who seek to influence regulation on wider stages. In doing this, first two analytical conclusions are drawn: that in the case of Scottish fisheries, global–local dialectics must be studied as refracted through the prism of the EU's CFP; that only by applying clear analytical concepts such as 'political work' can research accurately capture the causalities of the linkages between globalization and European integration across different industrial scales.

Secondly, the application of this approach demonstrates that in bringing about change in their industry, Scottish fishers have invested in political work to re-define their relations with scientists, public authorities and other actors across the industry. At the heart of this political work has been a core strategy to re-problematize and politicize professional identities of catchers. I have shown how fishers re-problematized and politicized their professional identities as 'custodians', not 'exploiters', of the seas and in so doing institutionalized a changed perception of the organization of fisheries production. Whereas initially such political work centred on re-shaping struggles within the Purchase IR over access to and management of resources, it was not contained there. Rather, changed professional identities and relations across the industry also enabled actors to institutionalize new sustainable strategies within the Commercial IR in the marketing and selling of Scottish fish. Finally, political work was not only carried out in local arenas: Scottish fishers have devised and implemented political strategies to find common cause with fishers from other parts of the UK, other MSs and other stakeholders (e.g. scientists) to bring about change in reglementary competitions in EU arenas as well. In so doing, they have radically shifted their response to global challenges and can no longer be identified as 'victims' of globalization.

Finally, this study reveals that there is an important relationship between 'community' vs 'market-driven' approaches to fisheries management, on the one hand, and the institutional links between EU policy making and local community commercial activities, on the other. These are not separate processes but rather are shaped by a global/EU/local layering of institutions. Indeed, the significance of sustainable fisheries production is that it fundamentally recognizes that local choices can affect applications of regulatory capitalism. I have also shown that the extent to which the 'global' results in de-regulatory capitalism depends on the type of political work conducted by actors within the Purchase and Commercial IRs. In Scotland at least, it was not found as in other systems that 'the internationalisation of seafood markets...has distanced fishermen from local connections' (Hanna, 1998: 29). From my research, I thus hypothesize that when political work intersects sector–territory dialectics with global–local dialectics it can bring about significant institutional change. Exploring these links in more detail would be a fruitful area for future research.

7
The Transformation of the French Foie Gras Industry: Globalization, Intellectual Property Rights and Industrial Domination

Bernard Jullien and Andy Smith

Although this has undoubtedly escaped the notice of most consumers, over the last 15 years foie gras has become more abundant and less expensive. Behind these trends lies an industry within which the daily industrial and commercial practices of duck producers, manufacturers and retailers have been deeply transformed. At the root of this modified 'productive system', however, lies the emergence and institutionalization of a new normative and cognitive framework for this industry. This process began in the late 1980s when concerns began to be systematically raised in the South-West of France about the effects of unregulated international trade upon the quality of the foie gras on the market, the veracity of its geographical labelling and, indirectly, the lowering of its price. More precisely, producers and manufacturers from areas such as the Périgord began to contest and politicize a practice, common at the time, which consisted of importing liver from Eastern-bloc countries such as Hungary, processing it in the South-West of France, and then labelling it as a product of this region. In so doing, these actors allied themselves with representatives of other foodstuffs (e.g. Jambon de Bayonne, Jambon de Parme, Pruneaux d'Agen) who were similarly outraged at the fraudulent 'passing off' of their products. After lengthy intra- and trans-national negotiations, in 1992, this alliance then convinced a sufficient number of national governments in Europe to pass a European Union (EU) regulation (2081/92) creating a system of Protected Geographical Indications (PGIs) for food products. Indeed, through establishing geographical names as intellectual property rights and creating a European register of PGIs, this legislation provided protection to makers of labelled foodstuffs in two ways:

1. against usurpation of a PGI by firms from outside their territory;
2. against products made in the territory in question but which fail to meet the specifications laid down during the registration of the PGI.

For a book that seeks to tease out the precise relationship between 'globalization' and the regulation of industries, PGIs provide an illuminating object of study for two main reasons. First, the growth of intra- and extra-Community trade in the 1980s – a trend often associated with 'globalization' – gave rise to calls for the development of new legal and political regulatory frameworks. In the case of the EU, the completion of its single market through the removal of tariff barriers, competition policy and the mutual recognition of product norms constituted a hegemonic political project which both liberalized numerous industries and re-regulated them at the scale of the EU (Jabko, 2006; Majone, 1996). However, a number of industries also sought to subtract themselves from the general rules of the single market by obtaining derogations, of which PGIs constitute a clear example. Similarly, in 1995 the Uruguay Round of the General Agreement of Tariffs and Trade (GATT) also liberalized wide swathes of global trade whilst creating the World Trade Organization (WTO). Again, however, a certain number of derogations to the neo-liberal agenda were established, in particular through the agreement on Trade Related Aspects of Intellectual Property and Services (TRIPS), an accord which includes provision for the EU's system of PGIs. In short, be it intra-Community or 'global', trade across national borders has consistently been used to justify and legitimize the institutionalization of PGIs as a set of laws and norms which take their ideological inspiration not from 'free market economics', but from traditions of regulated capitalism and industrial policy.

Having analysed directly elsewhere the controversies which have surrounded the introduction of PGIs in the EU (Smith, 2007) and the WTO (Smith, 2008), this chapter now seeks to tackle them from the angle of how these norms shape the regulation of precise industries – in this case foie gras. In so doing we shall concentrate upon the second reason why examination of PGIs can shed new light upon the relationship between globalization and the regulation of industries: because it encourages research to focus upon how trans-industry legislation, norms and procedures set in supranational arenas are translated within industries which themselves are cleaved in a number of ways (firms, professions, territories, etc.). As has been shown in preceding chapters on car retailing and wine in particular, studying the political work this process of translation entails enables research to generate new, detailed and meaningful knowledge about the 'thickness' of the relationship between globalization and the manner contemporary industries have come to be regulated.

Based on research into the institutionalization of the French foie gras industry as a whole (Cuntigh and Smith, 2005; Cuntigh *et al.*, 2005; Jullien and Smith, 2004), this focus upon political work leads us to develop an explanation of the domination of this industry's Institutional Order (IO) in two stages. Sparked by changes in the Purchase Institutionalized Relationship (IR), and heavily influenced by the EU's regulation on PGIs, the first saw the IO displaced in a matter of years from one based on relatively autonomous artisans to a Taylorized order of intensified production (Section 1). However, five to ten years later, this order has been subject to deinstitutionalization and reinstitutionalization, this time caused by change that occurred first in the industry's Commercial IR and, more recently, by the emergence of a 'reinternationalization' of the industry's largest processing firms (Section 2). On the basis of this longitudinal analysis, the chapter concludes by reflecting upon the causes of change in the IOs observed, the evolution of policy instruments such as PGIs and their usage over time, and how this feeds back into general trans-industry debates about the regulation of European and global trade.

More generally, this chapter argues that the case of foie gras highlights how, within specific industries, 'globalization' can become the heart of a political enterprise with its own set of objectives, arguments and alliances. Moreover, given that such an enterprise is frequently seen as unacceptable by many productive and commercial operators, globalization almost inevitably engenders competing political enterprises of resistance. In this way globalization has given rise in this industry, as in many others, to a dialectic not dissimilar to that identified by Karl Polanyi in his classic book *The Great Transformation* (1944). Indeed, the foie gras industry will be shown to be an emblematic example of the dialectic with which 'globalization' is almost invariably associated:

i) By generating resistance 'globalization' constantly gives rise to the production of new institutions.
ii) Because the creation of new institutions takes place in different negotiating arenas and encompasses different geographical scales, it

causes actors to modify their respective strategies depending upon where they conduct their political work. This in turn strongly tends to renew and exacerbate regulatory difference throughout the world.

1. From artisanal to intensive Taylorized production (1990–2002)

Until the late 1980s, virtually all French foie gras was produced by small, family-centred farms which reared and finished ducks, processed their liver, then packaged and sold it through specialized shops. In short, agricultural production was relatively extensive and manufacturing was not highly specialized (Figure 7.1). Significantly, the Purchase IR was symbiotic: producers and processors of ducks were one and the same actors. Consequently, competition was mainly between numerous small producers supplying highly similar products. Because the latter were expensive and demand was not very price sensitive, this example of 'perfect' competition did not engender strong pressure on prices until the arrival of newcomers from Eastern Europe.

In the space of less than ten years, however, this industry came instead to be structured around a Taylorized productive system that entailed, on the one hand, the intensive rearing of ducks and, on the other, the emergence of large specialized processors. Although technological

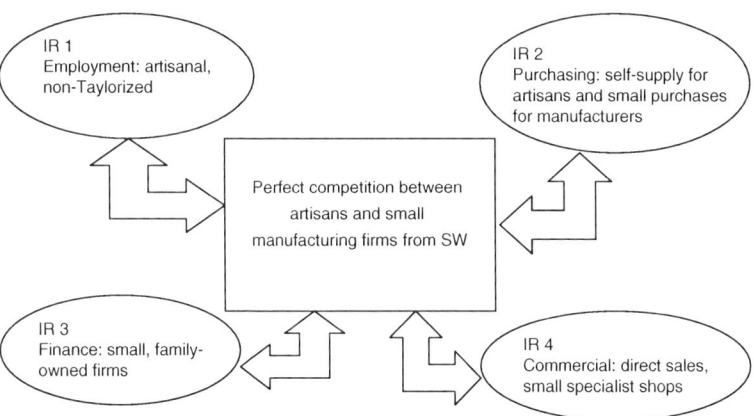

Figure 7.1 The foie gras industry in 1990: The productive system at its initial stage

innovation played an important role in this change, our research identified no automatic functional causality. Rather, it is the examination of the political work involved in reshaping problems of collective and public action in this industry (Section 1.1) and those pertaining to its Purchase IR in particular (Section 1.2) which enables the precise causes of this industry's transformation to be ascertained. The change in the firms of the French foie gras industry has been outlined in Table 7.1.

Table 7.1 Change in the firms of the French foie gras industry

	1995		2001	
	Firms	production (%)	Firms	production (%)
Firms producing ducklings				
>1,800,000 ducklings	3	36	6	63.7
1,000,000 to 1,800,000 ducklings	3	21	5	16.7
500,000 to 1,000,000 ducklings	6	24	6	14.5
1,000,000 to 500,000 ducklings	10	15	5	5.0
<100,000 ducklings	+/− 15	4	<5	0.1
Total	+/− 40	100	<30	100
Abattoirs				
>800,000 ducks	5	36	14	82.5
400,000 to 800,000	7	22	3	6.0
200,000 to 400,000	8	14	7	6.5
<200,000	Approx. 100	28	Approx. 40	5.0
Total	14,500,000	100	26,700,000	100
Foie Gras manufacturing firms				
>400 tonnes	5	48	8	76
200 to 400 tonnes	4	21	4	11
100 to 200 tonnes	5	11	3	5
<100 tonnes	41	19	53	8

Source: *Rapport économique, marché du foie gras*, CIFOG.

Throughout these processes, the translation of the EU's regulation on geographical indications into a PGI for foie gras has been a central issue. Nevertheless, it is important to underline from the outset that we have studied the whole of the French foie gras industry, and not just foie gras produced under PGI rules and conditions. This is because, contrary to the assertions of many economists interested in PGIs as part of 'localized productive systems' (Torre, 2000a & b), we argue, PGI production is in direct competition with non-PGI production. Consequently, it cannot be analysed as an autonomous 'niche' industry. Instead, it is important to understand why and how some producers, manufacturers and distributors have chosen to follow PGI rules and support their institutionalization, whereas others patently have not. Indeed, most of the firms involved in PGIs do not sell all their products using these labels and thus constantly strive to manage the coexistence of different types of products in their productive and commercial portfolios. Moreover, the choice to use PGIs or not is reversible and stems from comparisons between the two options in order to cope with market and productive problems.

1.1. The emergence of foie gras as a collective and public problem

Not included in the Common Agricultural Policy, nor the subject of specific French laws or policy measures, the French foie gras industry's sole normative constraints until the early 1990s were a range of EU-inspired hygiene and environmental standards introduced over the course of the preceding decade. By its end, however, this relatively lightly institutionalized productive system had become confronted with two new dilemmas.

The first concerned usurpation of geographical-origin names that gave notoriety, and therefore commercial advantages, to foie gras produced in the South-West of France, and micro-regions such as the Périgord in particular. As mentioned above, because no specific legislation banning such practices existed at the time, names like 'Périgord' were consistently being used with impunity either directly by Eastern European manufacturers or more indirectly by manufacturers from the South-West of France who bought in duck liver from countries such as Hungary. Initially, these practices were framed as meriting collective protests to be channelled through associations (e.g. the *Association foie gras du Périgord*: AFGP), farming unions and local chambers of agriculture. However, from being an issue for collective protest, in the early 1990s the question of usurpation rapidly became one of public action. This public problem then became highly politicized around three themes fraught with symbolism:

1. deceiving the consumer;
2. danger to public health (the 1985 Chernobyl incident was used by French producers to stigmatize Eastern European competition as 'unsafe');
3. the threat to traditional and authentic agricultural and culinary practices.

Rather than develop each of these themes individually as we have elsewhere, here it is more important to grasp how the impetus for their cumulative problematization stemmed from the political work undertaken to make them overlap as part of one single set of norms, instruments and logics of action.

The second dilemma facing representatives of the French foie gras industry concerned collective and public reaction to three technological innovations that began to heavily influence methods of duck production from 1990 onwards. First, the invention and widespread adoption of artificial insemination encouraged specialization and therefore separation between duck rearers and finishers. Second, the invention of pneumatic feeding machines led to the introduction of ground maize in the form of paste as the dominant form of duck fodder. Cheaper than whole grain feed and faster to administer, this paste encouraged the emergence of duck producers who no longer processed their own raw materials but sent them instead to specialized manufacturers. Finally, whereas hitherto it had been thought that transporting ducks large distances before slaughter was detrimental to the quality of their liver, new methods of transport enabled distances from farm to abattoir to be extended, thereby further encouraging separation between production and processing. Overall, these innovations added up to an intensification of rearing and finishing techniques on the one hand, while encouraging the development of specialized manufacturers on the other (Table 7.2).

Faced with this radical change in productive system, collective action organizations such as the AFGP, which had begun their existence as vehicles for reacting to usurpation and 'excessive' EU hygiene and environmental standards, suddenly became mobilized in order to restructure a sector marked by expanding production, new manufacturers and

Table 7.2 Change in foie gras production between 1995 and 2006 (in tonnes and growth in %)

	Production	Growth (%)	Production	Growth (%)
1995	9,768	nd	10,386	na
1996	10,289	5.3	10,800	4.0
1997	11,163	8.5	11,685	8.2
1998	12,969	16.2	13,463	15.2
1999	14,490	11.7	15,017	11.5
2000	15,185	4.8	15,766	5.0
2001	15,848	4.4	16,431	4.2
2002	16,981	7.1	17,570	6.9
2003	16,457	−3.1	17,018	−3.1
2004	17,390	5.7	17,945	5.4
2005	17,551	0.9	18,086	0.8
2006 (e)	18,578	5.9	19,105	5.6

Source: OFIVAL, who in turn depend upon the SCEES.

resegmenting markets. However, it is at this stage that a new regional-level interprofessional body – the PALSO (*Palmipèdes du Sud-Ouest*) – was created and became a vehicle for responding simultaneously to all the dilemmas outlined above. As will be shown below, the actors who dominated the PALSO ensured that its principal political work in the early 1990s was devoted to supporting the introduction of EU legislation on PGIs, obtaining a PGI for foie gras for the whole of the South-West and ensuring that the product specification for the latter fitted with the expansionary objectives of the organization's largest members.

1.2. The Purchase IR as the locus of institutionalization and domination

This book's analytical grid allows one to understand the principal cause of both the PALSO's 'victory' and of the reinstitutionalization of the French foie gras industry this caused. Although the Employment IR changed considerably during this time because new divisions of labour were created, and supermarkets became much more heavily involved in the industry's Commercial IR, the real driving force for change was a modification in the internal balance of the Purchase IR. Within the latter, a set of farmers new to duck production and using new rearing methods created an alliance with large-scale manufacturers, each of them linked to farmers by contracts and classical elements of agricultural vertical integration (notably involving animal foodstuffs, veterinary advice, etc.). It is thus via the Purchase IR that a change in the capitalization of

190 The Transformation of the French Foie Gras Industry

the foie gras industry, its Finance IR and, more generally, the financing of agriculture in South-West France began to have considerable effects upon collective action and public policy. This central importance of the Purchase IR can in turn be understood only by grasping how and why it became the locus of intra- and extra-regional negotiations over the specifications for a 'Sud-Ouest' PGI (Figures 7.2 and 7.3).

During both these sets of negotiations, the alliance of new intensive producers and large manufacturers argued successfully in favour of a relatively lenient set of product standards as regards issues such as length of rearing and finishing periods, type of feeding and so on. It was anticipated that such leniency would be accepted by the French authorities and the European Commission. But it was also anticipated that by imposing few extra costs on operators from the South-West this leniency would allow them to successfully compete with other new entrants to the foie gras market (notably from the Pays de la Loire) whilst forbidding

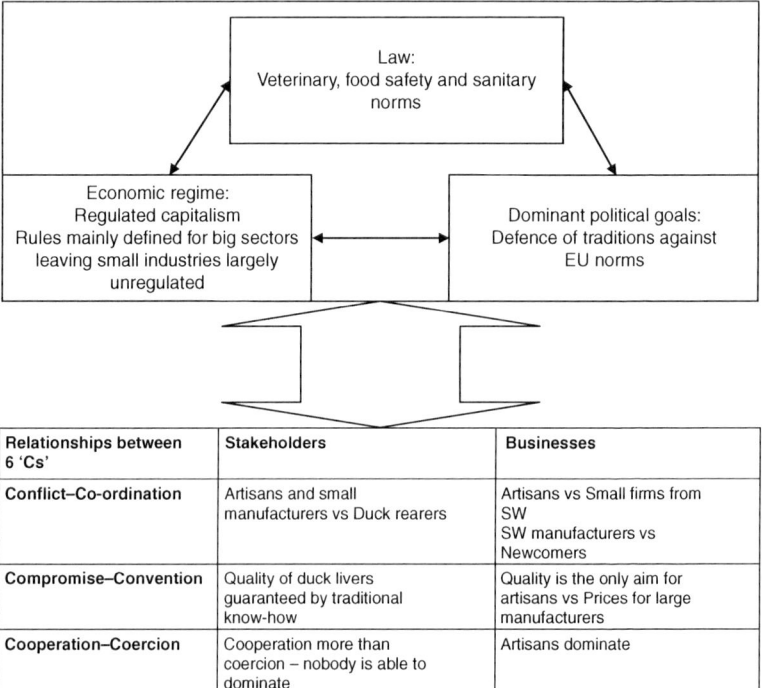

Figure 7.2 The traditional purchase IR in the foie gras industry

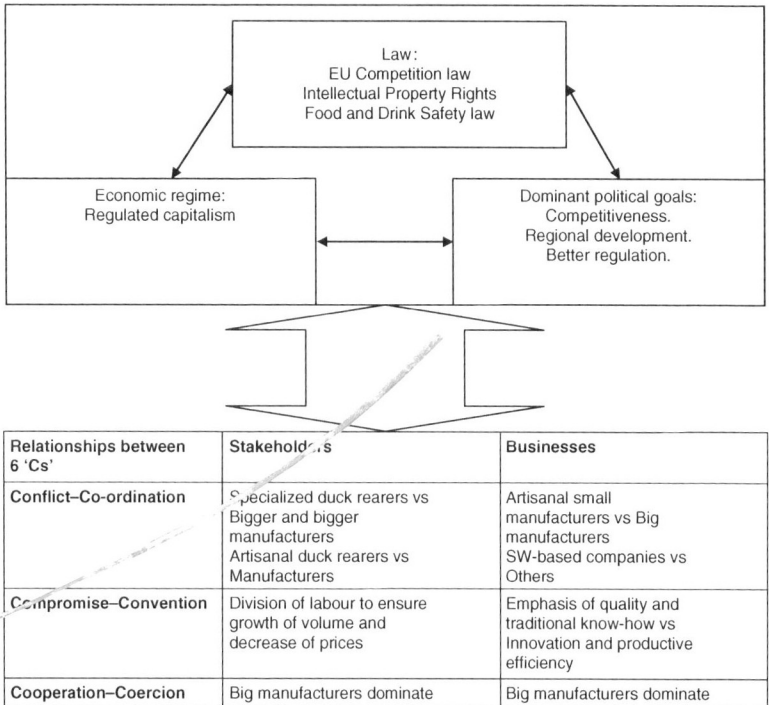

Figure 7.3 The purchase IR generated by PGI's adoption and changes during 1990s

such newcomers from using the South-West name or references to this region when marketing their product. As Table 7.3 highlights, whereas in 1990 producers from Pays de la Loire and Brittany accounted for only 3.2% of French foie gras production, by 2002 this figure had risen dramatically to 22.5%. Conscious that producers from the South-West were having great difficulty competing with these challengers because of their higher costs of production, representatives of this region framed the PGI as a means of ensuring they could at least use an institutionalized image of their product to increase its price.

With these aims in mind, political work was successfully carried out within the French ministry of agriculture and the European Commission in order to gain official backing for the desired specification. In order to achieve this aim, arguments were developed which connected a PGI for foie gras to the protection of 'tradition' and public support for rural development in areas hit hard by the reform of

Table 7.3 French foie gras production by region

	1990		2002	
	Tonnes	production (%)	Tonnes	production (%)
South West	5,031.8	95.8	11,665.0	71.0
Aquitaine	3,718.4	70.8	7,761.0	47.2
Midi Pyrénées	1,313.0	25.0	3,904.0	23.8
West	168.1	3.2	3,697.0	22.5
Pays de la Loire	120.8	2.3	3,016.0	18.4
Britanny	47.3	0.9	692.0	4.2
Total	5,252	100	16,429	100

Source: Scees, CIFOG.

the Common Agricultural Policy. These arguments were channelled through long-standing extra-industry networks which previously had frequently been mobilized in order to defend the interests of French farmers in general and those of the South-West in particular.

The product specification institutionalized in the PGI gave protection to all producers and processors from the South-West. However, in order to establish the detail of this specification, first a single set of standards had to be adopted within the region itself. This was far from easy to achieve. Indeed, the political work carried out to institutionalize the PGI within this region can be explained only in terms of the domination of artisanal producers by the alliance of new intensive duck producers and the large processing firms. First, leniency over product standards, quality and the ability to compete directly with new entrants from the Pays de la Loire were not objectives shared by artisanal producers. Indeed, nearly all the latter were dismayed that the PGI's specification would decrease the quality of foie gras from the South-West because it demanded so little of producers and processors. Secondly, many artisans were scandalized by the fact that their image of extensive, small-scale production and its association with the traditions of South-West France was now to be used to sell intensively produced foie gras which, they allege, could be made anywhere (Figure 7.4). Small wonder then that artisans came to see the PGI as an act of 'treason' which had subverted the very goals of the EU regulation: 'the Offical Journal states quite clearly that the value added of a PGI must come from the quality not the quantity of production. However, the types of production and organization authorized by the PGI's specification has had quite the opposite effect!' (interview with an artisan, 2003).

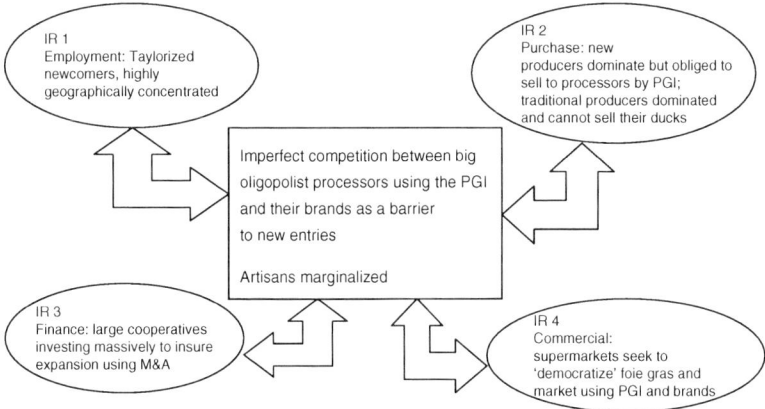

Figure 7.4 The foie gras industry after intensification and introduction of PGI (1995–2002)

This is not the place for a full account of the forms of domination which have caused the manner through which the French foie gras industry has come to be institutionalized. Rather it is important at this stage to underline that the victory of the intensive and expansionist political enterprise can best be explained by examining how the framing of the PGI as a collective and public problem took place on the one hand, whilst a series of intra- and extra-regional alliances were being built, activated or reactivated on the other. More generally, in this section we have seen how a whole series of 'technical' or 'commercial' issues came to be problematized and in some cases politicized. This political work was inextricably linked to changes in the institutions which structured the production and the manufacturing of foie gras and, in so doing, the transformation of an artisanal set of activities into a Taylorized and institutionalized industry.

2. A Commercial IR–inspired shift to retailer domination

At the end of the 1990s and the beginning of the new century, the progressive introduction of a PGI for 'foie gras du Sud-Ouest' coincided with a period of high prices and vastly increased sales for this product. These trends intially strongly consolidated the political and industrial resources of the hegemonic alliance of new producers and large manufacturers. However, when, in 2003, the market for foie gras reached a

Table 7.4 The average price of unprocessed foie gras (1998–2006)

	1998	1999	2000	2001	2002	2003	2004	2005	2006
Price (Euro/kg)	21.04	20.57	21.94	21.99	19.32	18.74	20.13	21.08	21.65
Change (%)	−3.7	−2.2	6.7	0.2	−12.1	−3.0	7.4	4.7	2.7

Source: Service des Nouvelles du Marché (Toulouse).

point of saturation, this alliance was severely shaken and, in part, began to unravel. This time the driving force for change was the Commercial IR (Section 2.1), which subsequently contaminated the other IRs (Section 2.2). Since 2003, the alliance dominating the industry's IO has thus undergone significant conflict and witnessed a shift in the locus of much decision-making from the Purchase to the Commercial IR. Nevertheless, the durability of its main protagonists suggest that the order as a whole remains institutionalized largely along the lines established from the mid- to late 1990s (Table 7.4).

2.1. From change within the Commercial IR...

The traditional Commercial IR for the foie gras industry is shown in Figure 7.5. This industry's Commercial IR between 2002 and 2008 needs to be unpacked in two ways, both involving the increased role of supermarkets in the distribution and sale of foie gras.

First, one needs to understand that French supermarkets have been experiencing a new and intense round of competition amongst themselves and with new entrants (hard discounters).

Whereas at the end of the 1990s supermarket chains such as Carrefour were seeking to raise their prices for food by emphasizing their 'quality', since then falling turnover and pressure from shareholders have frequently led to the abandonment of this strategy in favour of price cuts and less sophisticated marketing. Within this change in the cognitive framing of commercial conditions for each firm, goods that had previously been heavily promoted by supermarkets as 'quality' products, such as foie gras from the South-West, suddenly were made to compete on price (i.e. with foie gras from the Pays de la Loire). Consequently, the positive welcome that had initially been given by supermarkets to labels that guaranteed product 'quality' and 'origin' (PGIs but also Label Rouge, 'bio' or 'green' products) transformed itself into scepticism about

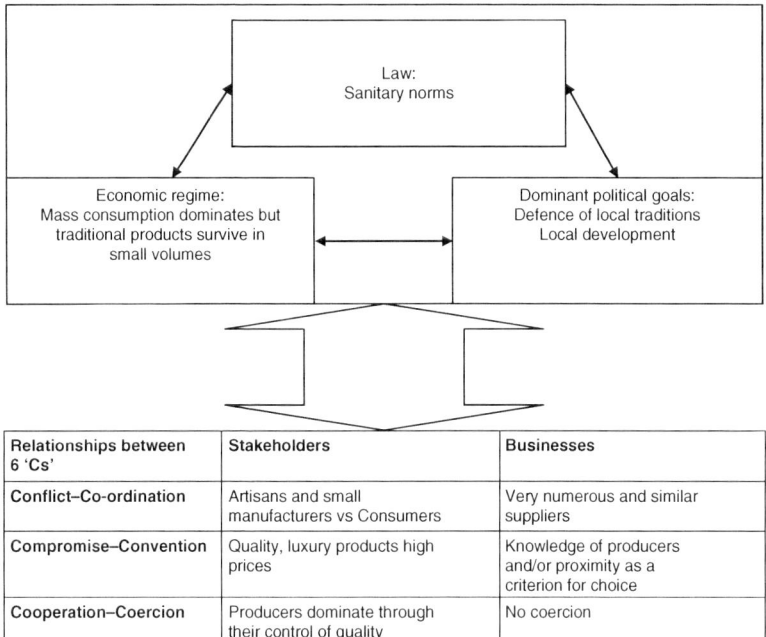

Figure 7.5 The traditional commercial IR for the foie gras industry

their commercial value. In their place, internal policies in favour of the supermarket's own brands received new impetus and a preference was now often expressed for a set of minimum standards on quality, lower even than that established by the PGI.

However, this change in the supermarkets' approach to labels in general, and to PGIs in particular, cannot solely be attributed to intra-supermarket reflection and decision-making. Rather this change took place at a moment of an industry-wide food debate over the banalization of food labels which also involved representatives of collective action organizations and public authorities. According to representatives of supermarkets, whereas previously the consumer had received relatively little information about the food they were purchasing, he or she was now faced with a plethora of labels and had little means with which to establish a hierarchy amongst them. At least for the *Foie gras du Sud-Ouest* PGI, this unpeaceful coexistence between different types of label contributed to a sharp fall in the price differential that had previously been attributed to it. Consequently, supermarket buyers found

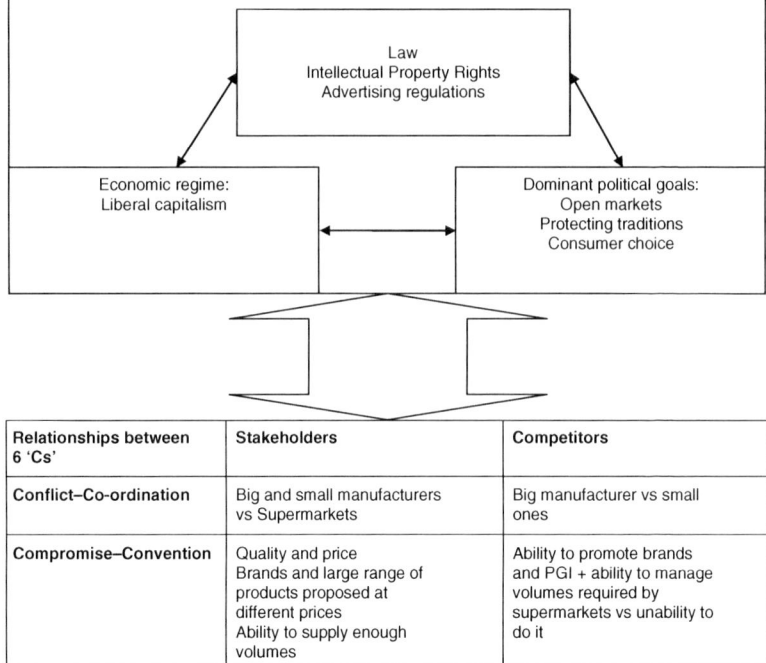

Figure 7.6 The Commercial IR associated with PGI and changes of the Foie Gras Industry

themselves a new and powerful argument for cutting prices paid to manufacturers. In short, the major supermarket chains in France not only criticized the PGI as a means of increasing their influence over the Commercial IR of the foie gras industry, but in so doing also delegitimized the previous practice of regulating the PGI solely within the Purchase IR (Figure 7.6).

2.2. ...to contamination of the other three IRs

Indeed, this change in the Commerical IR quickly contaminated the other three IRs. As indicated above, the first to feel its impact was the Purchase relationship. Made to compete intensely for market share, the four main manufacturers of foie gras in the South-West distanced themselves not only from one another but also from representatives of producers. This crack in the hegemonic alliance that had previously dominated the interprofessional body (PALSO) even led one large manufacturer, Delpeyrat, owned by one of the two largest SW cooperatives (Maïsadour), to publicly defect from the PGI for a significant part of its product range. So, despite initial pressures from large agricultural cooperatives to maintain the rules and market structures provided by the PGI, this major manufacturer decided to adopt a strategy that seemed likely to weaken the alliance. The initial principal result of this change was a drop in prices paid to producers and the introduction of uncertainty in the Purchase IR. Whereas producers had previously benefited from strongly guaranteed prices and volumes if they adhered to PGI rules, as of 2003 both were made conditional on 'market conditions'. Even for producers that did not follow Delpeyrat's (partial) exit strategy, such a move was seen as an opportunity to weaken the constraints associated with the PGI as it showed that opportunities to stay in business without the PGI existed. In so doing, an important change was introduced in the Purchase IR: it had not been a market relationship, but it suddenly became one. Competition between duck producers then became de facto whilst cutting prices at this level was not a sacrifice demanded of processors even if they used the PGI (Figure 7.7).

Again, rather than a direct and unmediated relationship between producers, manufacturers and supermarkets, our research highlights the role of institutions, as well as the collective and public actors who refract

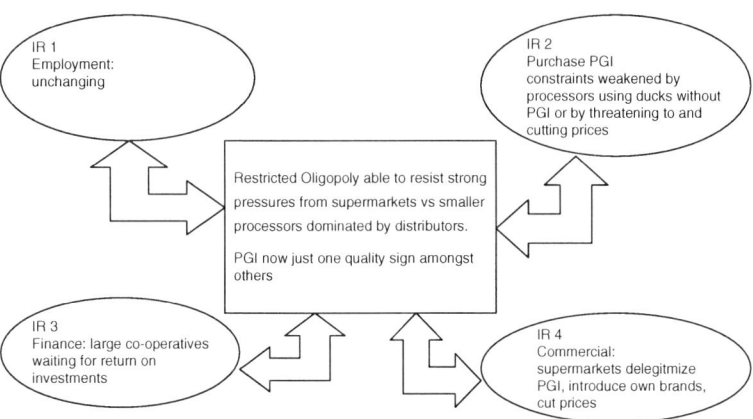

Figure 7.7 The foie gras industry after 'banalization' of the PGI

their influence, in the structuring of change within the foie gras industry. This can be observed first from the point of view of collective action by producers and manufacturers. Within the national and regional 'interprofessional' bodies which co-regulate this industry, supermarkets have no direct presence or role. However, given their importance for the industry as a whole, they are nevertheless omnipresent in the reflections and discourse of the interprofession's dominant representatives. What is striking is that the latter appear to have given up any chance of including supermarkets in the organized deliberations which participate in the co-regulation of their industry. Indeed, not only have producers and manufacturer representatives failed to engage with their interlocutors from the distribution milieu, they have not equipped themselves or their organization with the analytical means (e.g. detailed studies of markets and supermarket practices) to even begin an in-depth exchange with such actors. This way of framing the industry's problems reflects problematizations inherited from the past which see the selling of a

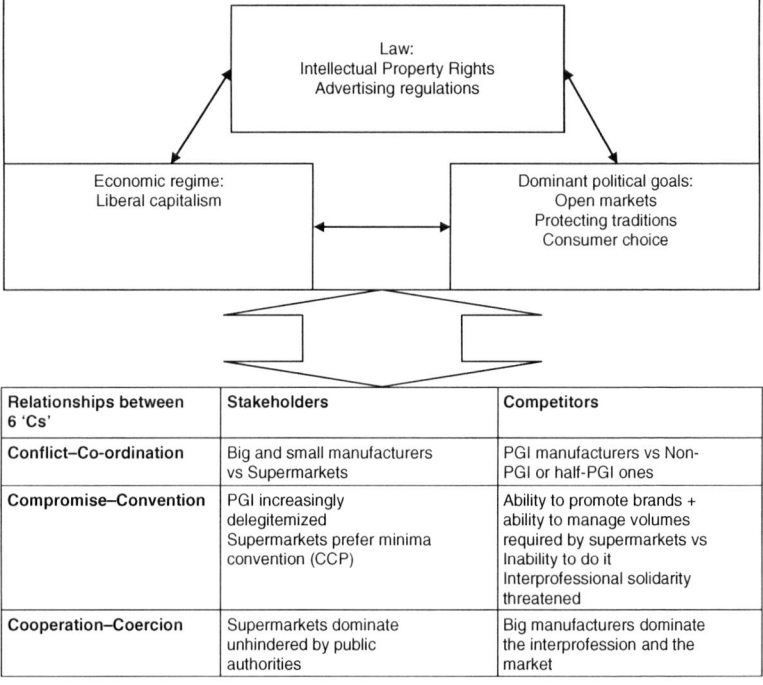

Figure 7.8 New Commercial relationship in foie gras industry

product as the sole preserve of retailers. Such a framing also reflects a political choice made as much by public as collective actors to consider that the industry must simply submit to the preferences of the supermarkets rather than engage with them in a risky, but potentially mutually beneficial, sustained dialogue.

The second angle through which the IO of this industry has facilitated the rising power of supermarkets in this industry concerns the role played by representatives of public authorities. These bodies (in particular the *Institut National des Appellations d'Origine*: INAO) seem unable to develop a stabilized doctrine on PGIs that would assist them in administering PGIs in a coherent and consistent manner. More fundamentally, this absence of doctrine prevents representatives of public authority (in particular the French State) from imposing norms and interpretations of norms on supermarkets in the name of the public interest. The new Commercial IR in the foie gras industry is shown in Figure 7.8.

In summary, the current IO that structures the foie gras industry is still marked by a 'producer-based culture' within which little room is left for commercial reflexivity. Indeed, even the main manufacturers in this field continue to think about their industry essentially from the angle of norms that govern the production of liver, and in particular those inscribed in the *Sud-Ouest* PGI's specifications.

Conclusion

This chapter has endeavoured to show how and why the French foie gras industry, and indirectly that of the rest of the world, has been radically transformed over the last 20 years. Although technological innovation and the generalized opening up of markets play their part in this story, the fundamental cause of change has been the political work carried out to institutionalize the industry around a set of norms and rules designed to encourage intensive and expanded production. As we have underlined, ironically this expansion has been facilitated and then legally protected by the introduction of an EU regulation on PGIs which most of the actors involved in its negotiation considered was originally intended to support the extensive production of quality products in the face of the trading and commercial challenges raised by 'globalization'. In this case, globalization has ultimately served as a register of legitimization for actors who have sought to introduce an instrument of public policy for a plurality of reasons which extend way beyond questions of international trade. Indeed, the PGI examined here has not fundamentally changed trading patterns, nor has it facilitated exports.

Rather it has provided a rationale, as well as legally backed norms and procedures, for changing the power relations within the industry's IO. In short, and as we have seen elsewhere in this book, the recent history of foie gras demonstrates again how collective and public attempts to resist the supposedly negative effects of globalization can lead to consequences that only careful industry–by-industry, and IR–by-IR, analysis can reveal.

At least in the case of foie gras, however, it would be wrong to consider that the consequences of resisting globalization through the PGI regulation were entirely 'unintended'. If many public actors were indeed surprised by what the foie gras industry has since become, a closely knit alliance of producer and manufacturer representatives clearly have always seen a PGI for the *Foie gras du Sud-Ouest* as a policy instrument through which to redesign this industry along expansionist and protectionist lines. As in other chapters, we have also seen how the power of this alliance of actors has not simply flowed from their structural advantages and resources. Rather through simultaneously, and generally astutely, marshalling their arguments and interdependencies, the members of this alliance have steadily built, shored up, then renewed their position of hegemony in this industry. Indeed, although political work in this industry has recently undergone a shift of emphasis from the Purchase to the Commercial IR, this alliance has in general adapted to this change and ensured that its domination has not been threatened by any serious challenge.

The final conclusion we wish to make on the basis of this case study concerns how intra-industry usages of public norms, such as PGIs, also shed light on the ambivalence and sometimes outright confusion which can surround their political defence within the EU and at the WTO. When the EU regulation was first negotiated, its advocates were at pains to underline that geographical indications were not protectionist policy instruments but instead were legitimate and necessary intellectual property rights. Nearly 20 years later, this assertion appears less easy to make and the case of foie gras certainly seems to play into the hand of PGI-sceptics within the EU, such as the Danish government (Smith, 2007). Not surprisingly, this scepticism is even stronger amongst representatives of states outside the EU, in particular the US and Australia, who see PGIs as not only protectionist but 'neo-colonial' (Smith, 2008). Indeed, the stalemate in WTO negotiations on this point since the 1995 TRIPS agreement serves as yet another reminder that 'globalization' can be, and constantly is, used to justify highly contrasting visions of contemporary capitalism and how it ought to be regulated.

8
Conclusion: The Politics of Industry and Globalization

Bernard Jullien and Andy Smith

This book has sought to renew and revitalize research on phenomena frequently synthesized with the term 'globalization'. It has done so by treating the latter as both a process and a powerful vector for legitimizing regulatory change within specific industries.

Studied as a process, we have certainly seen that globalization encompasses a number of trans-industry trends, in particular the WTO-inspired reduction of tariffs and other barriers to trade, the liberalization of markets through competition policy and the financialization of capital – what Saskia Sassen calls 'the self-evidently global scale' (2007: 82). Above all, however, our empirical analysis has also shown that globalization is a process which actually takes effect through its translation within specific industries. Notwithstanding the potential power of trans-industry norms and political projects, industries remain highly structured by their respective Institutional Order (IO). Moreover, given that these orders are made up of interdependent sets of Institutionalized Relationships (IRs), we have shown that globalization takes differentiated forms within each industry. This is because the substantive regulatory content and dominant negotiating sites for certain IRs have been more subject to what Sassen terms 'rescaling' (2007: 82) than others.

Studied simultaneously as a vector for legitimization, we have also shown that globalization frequently provides actors with a powerful weapon with which to change not only the laws, policy instruments and social norms which regulate industries (Risse, 2007), but also the scale at which these are set and intended to apply (Carter and Smith, 2008). As each of the book's chapters has underlined, this activity of de- then re-institutionalization has been caused by the political work undertaken by identifiable actors. These company managers, interest group leaders, public officials and politicians have sought to reframe intra-company, collective and public 'problems' whilst building alliances of actors capable of transforming new framings into changed laws, norms and policy instruments.

By conceptualizing globalization in this way, we are not simply stating, as many others have, that globalization provokes 'divergent responses' (Bisley, 2007; Braithwaite and Dranos, 2000; Held and McGrew 2007; Levy-Faur, 2006b). Although similarly convinced that globalization is a vector for renewing diversity, we fundamentally disagree with the contention that the phenomena it encompasses can and should be studied in terms of extra-sectoral or macro stimuli and intra-sectoral 'responses'. As this book has repeatedly shown through its case studies, globalization is not an anonymous, 'structural' and exogenous force which imposes itself upon industries and sectors in consistent and predictable ways. Rather the trends, framings and processes it includes are co-produced by the private, collective and public actors who make up each industry's IO. Indeed, this book has made a central claim regarding the causal impact of 'political work' upon the regulation of industries. Through our case studies, it has then demonstrated that it is this work that has changed or maintained the institutions of each industry, and that specific translations of 'globalization' have been deployed to effect these outcomes.

Building upon this general conclusion, this final chapter reflects upon the analytical purchase of our *Politics of Industry* approach for the study of globalization. Over the last four to five years, we have developed and sought to share this approach. This book has thus constituted a concerted attempt to test its robustness and 'competitive advantages' as regards other modes of studying industries. From this perspective, this conclusion first revisits four key concepts within our approach – Institutional Orders, Institutionalized Relationships, Problematization and Politicization – from an angle which proposes them as four key stages for analysing the de-institutionalization and re-institutionalization of industries in general, and the role played therein by globalization in particular. Finally, we then present findings about the locus and type of political work which has led to change or stasis in each of the industries which feature in this book.

1. Industries as Institutional Orders

Conceptualizing industries as Institutional Orders first means distancing research from the commonly employed term 'sector' as used by statistics and economics on the one hand, and by political scientists on the other. Our concept of IO then implies developing the hypothesis that when an industry can consistently be identified as a specific and distinct entity, its dynamics can be explained only in terms of the structuration of an order, not as simply the emergence of a 'configuration'. By testing this hypothesis in their respective case studies, the contributors to this book have illustrated and demonstrated the analytical added value of this conceptual displacement.

As regards the 'sector' so dear to statisticians and economists, our fundamental proposition has been to show that beyond the constraints associated with technologies and markets, what defines industrial organization (i.e. degrees of concentration, differentiation, entry barriers, etc.) is the processes which allow actors within firms to provide order for their activities. It is these highly political processes which shape, reproduce or change how market situations or technological uncertainties are defined and influence firm behaviour. More profoundly, processes of ordering structure the distribution of roles and power within an industry through simultaneously defining, both 'objectively' and discursively, what factors, such as capacities and skills, are seen as determining each firm's competitiveness and success. From this angle, the chapters by Matthieu Montalban on pharmaceuticals and by Sylvain Moura on the US defence industry show clearly how the relative order that reigns in each of these industries – what most economists reduce to its 'industrial structure' – is in no way natural. Instead, these case studies highlight that order has been socially and politically constructed. In the case of pharmaceuticals, a key cause of change in the order of this industry has been the translation of financialization experienced by each firm. These translations continue to differ considerably from firm to firm because other institutions within the industry's IO, such as national health systems, still possess distinct properties. In the case of US arms production, despite pressures to both 'civilianize' and open up to the rest of the world, this industry remains ordered by the hegemonic power of national military funding.

When compared to the definition of a sector as used by political scientists (Hollingsworth *et al.*, 1994; Muller, 2004), or the notion of 'policy network' with which it is frequently linked (Levy-Faur, 2006a; March and Rhodes, 1992), envisaging industries as IOs equips research with a concept that better fits the social and productive realities of the 'life' of industries. Indeed, designed to study public policy-making, proponents of 'sector' and 'policy network' in political science are interested only in the daily affairs of industrial actors to the extent that the latter intervene in, or interfere with, public action. Similarly, trans-industry or inter-industry logics, such as the generalized deregulation of markets, are studied only through their relationship with the process of making public policies. Here the contribution of industrial economists and of interdisciplinary exchange is to underline that, in the daily productive life of each industry, power and politics are more pervasive than a policy-centred approach can reveal. In particular, taking on board the *acquis* of industrial economics enables one to identify how trans-industry logics necessarily impact within each industry because firms constantly experience the constraints and opportunities imposed upon them by a whole range of what political science calls 'sectors'. For example, as Andy Smith's chapter on the wine industry highlights, over the last 40 years, French growers, merchants and retailers have had to react to changes in consumption partly caused by policies on alcohol-use developed by representatives of the health sector. Similarly, as Caitríona Carter's chapter shows, the European fisheries industry has had to adapt its IO partly because of pressure from environmentalist interest groups and administrations to engage in 'sustainable fishing'. In summary, the access firms have to certain resources and certain markets is regulated in distinct negotiating arenas and according to industry-specific logics which, from the point of view of company managers, needs to be ordered both functionally and politically through a single set of institutions. At the same time, institutions and actors from these orders are in constant interaction with trans-industry regulatory orders.

In addition, this book has also highlighted the importance of distinguishing our concept of Institutional Orders from the metaphor of 'institutional configuration', which has come to be used by many political economists (Hall and Soskice, 2001). Indeed, our point of difference here is above all one of research agenda. When the term 'configuration' has been used in the study industries, the aim has generally been descriptive: to identify the type of mediation which articulates the institutions to which firms must position themselves when undertaking their productive and commercial activities. If one uses instead the concept of IO, however, the aim of research is to elucidate an order which has a certain degree of functional and political coherence because the concept contains the following underlying hypothesis: in order for an industry to reproduce itself, its actors collectively, and constantly, need to develop and maintain compromises over the complementarity between the industry's institutions which render their ordering politically and economically sustainable and legitimate. As Montalban's and Jullien's chapters recall, Fligstein's concept of 'conception of control' (2001) was originally developed from a perspective similar to our own research agenda. However, whereas Fligstein has above all been interested in how 'conceptions of control' emerge and change within firms, our concept of IOs extends this question to the scale at which an industry as a whole is ordered.

Having restated, and hopefully clarified, the concept of IOs used in this book to study the dynamics of different industries, it is now possible to identify what this also adds on to research on globalization. We hold that it possesses three major advantages.

i. The first concerns linkages between globalization and the production of institutions. The concept of IOs leads research to inscribe firms at their heart and not to consider institutions only as constraints upon them or as defining their respective 'structure of opportunities'. The orders we have identified and studied have all been co-produced and reproduced by representatives of such firms and by their interlocutors within public administrations. This certainly does not mean that we share the Hayakian evolutionist view which sees institutions as having been 'selected' over time in order to ensure that firms are provided 'efficient' solutions to their problems. On the contrary, our emphasis on the co-production and reproduction of institutions stems from findings which show that industrial production and competition are always so functionally, cognitively and politically problematic that they give rise to collective action, recourse to third parties and efforts to regularize these activities through the development of legitimate and institutionalized compromises and rules without which firms could no longer exist. Far from challenging this quest for regularity by transforming industries into anarchic spaces of interaction, all our chapters show that actors within each industry have injected globalization into ongoing intra-industry struggles to shape and 'update' its respective IO.

ii. This means that the rules and norms which structure IOs simply cannot be shown to have been imposed upon actors within an industry by 'external' forces or actors (e.g. financialization or the US government). As the cases of fisheries, wine and car distribution highlight, even when 'the legislator' has attempted to impose laws from outside an industry, negotiation of these laws during their adoption and, above all, their implementation reveal that rules take effect only through successive processes of appropriation which involve alliances of public and private actors. This finding provides yet another reason for considering that globalization never has automatic or unmediated effects upon each industry.

iii. Because the emergence of each IO can be explained only in terms of the stabilization of rules which implicate both private and public actors, and for which their non-respect can be legally and economically enforced, recourse to the concept of institutions is vitally important. Indeed, on this point we take issue with economists who consider that the organization of industry occurs 'spontaneously' in response to functional tensions and problems (Williamson, 1985). Instead, we argue that industries take a structured shape only when a process of institutional creation has been undertaken to order them as IOs. For this reason, this book shows that globalization has rarely, if ever, given rise to 'global' industries, that is ones where the entire regulation takes place on a worldwide scale. On the contrary, the regulation of industries is generally only very partially 'globalized' in this sense of the term. As Moura shows, the extreme case here is that of the US defence industry, which is still regulated almost entirely on a national basis. To some extent pharmaceuticals does provide a more clear-cut case of globalized regulation, but even here European and national IOs continue to heavily influence this industry.

Overall, the fragility and therefore dynamism of IOs is ultimately the result of their specific character, the imperfection of the functions they serve, inequality between the actors they impact upon and the contradictory demands that they contain. For this reason, although at first sight the concept appears only to be a tool for making static descriptions of an industry, when used in research it can be made to encompass a dynamic element through encouraging analysis of change. But this trait is even more apparent when IOs are used as the first step towards detailed analysis using the other three key concepts of *The Politics of Industry* model.

2. Industries ordered by their Institutionalized Relationships

Inspired by a range of heterodox economics, in particular that of conventionalists and regulationists, our *Politics of Industry* approach sets out to unpack IOs first by considering, on the one hand, that they always regulate the access of industrial actors to four main sets of resources or markets and, on the other, that the combination of these regulations is what renders production and competition in an industry durably possible. The meso-economic focus of this approach positions it alongside conceptualizations of 'institutional complementarity' such as those developed by regulationists (Amable, 2003) or, more generally, analyses of national 'Varieties of Capitalism' (Hall and Soskice, 2001) or company-type (Aoki, 2001). However, in choosing to examine regulation in terms of industries rather than companies, nations or regions, we developed our own concept of IRs. Its usage in this book and the findings it has enabled our contributors to identify and highlight establish not only the relevance of this concept, but also its 'comparative advantages' over notions developed by conventionalists and regulationists.

As developed by researchers such as Salais and Storper (1993), the conventionalist concept of 'productive worlds' of course already separated out the different activities associated with production in order to reveal their respective patterns and logics. Moreover, they also underlined that nonetheless each 'sector' tended strongly to develop coherence between these logics in order that the actors concerned could live with the 'undecidable' nature of daily productive activity. Finally, and again like ourselves and Aoki but unlike the Varieties of Captialism approach, conventionalists find no reason why the forms of co-ordination developed should be of the same type. However, as a number of regulationists have already argued (Amable and Palombarini, 2005; Lipietz, 1995), there is also no reason to consider that each of these co-ordinations is based upon equality between actors. Indeed, we consider instead that actors (be they policy-making stakeholders or business rivals) are highly unlikely to establish relationships on the basis of parity. Rather, the relationships which have been institutionalized over time have emerged in, and have often reproduced or even exacerbated, situations of inequality which have given rise to rights and modes of regulation which favour certain actors whilst disadvantaging others, thus constituting relations which are fundamentally political.

As for regulationists, their approach to relationships within the same industry is more structuralist and, above all, centred chiefly upon national modes of growth and regulation. Here its strength has been to 'consecrate' the primacy of politics over the functionality of economics. More precisely, as Amable explains (2003), regulationist theory considers that the functional dimension of the compromises at the root of 'institutional forms' (IFs) can first be seen *ex post* as having contributed, or not, to the performance of national economies. Secondly, they claim, the origins of these compromises can be seen to have been fundamentally political because they were caused by what Amable and Palombarini call 'political equilibria' between 'dominant social groups' (2005). We share the basic premises behind this approach and, consequently, consider that relationships institutionalize not because of their 'economic efficiency', but due to their industry-specific political sustainability. Similarly, we share the idea that functional problems which emerge either at the level of distinct IRs or between them in terms of 'institutional complementarity' potentially reopen the conflicts which gave rise to institutions in the first place. This said, our concept of IRs also differs from the equivalent terms employed by regulationists in three ways.

First, for reasons linked to our industry-by-industry scale of observation, the specification of IRs and that of IFs differ considerably. In particular, our approach allows one to conceptualize the position of an industry in the inter-industry division of labour and power through the Purchase IR. Whilst regulationists reduce this vital question to 'inter-firm' relations, chapters in this book on industries such as car distribution, fisheries and foie gras show the vital role played by institutions in transforming sporadic interactions between firms into relatively stable relationships. In the case of foie gras, for example, institutions invented as recently as the early 1990s have caused the expansion of what was hitherto artisanal activity into an intensive industry that is now structured around Taylorized roles for duck rearers and manufacturers.

Second, our meso-economic approach prefers to examine the diversity of ways that the four IRs are translated in different industries. This is because we focus in particular upon IRs as mediations between each industry and the economic and social spaces within which it has come to be situated. For this reason, we are able to show that in certain cases IRs can develop in line with dominant inter-industry IFs (the logic of submission), whilst, on the contrary, in other cases IRs will derogate from these IFs (the logic of subtraction). In most of our case studies, for example, the Financial IR has evolved in line with trans-industry policies and laws in favour of open frontiers and competition policy. In contrast, the Purchase IRs of industries such as car-retailing, wine, fisheries and foie gras have developed by obtaining derogations from part or all of these 'horizontal' institutions.

Finally, and as many political scientists have underlined, one of the key characteristics of making contemporary public policy which impacts upon industries is the 'multi-level' or 'multi-layered' nature of this process (Hooghe and Marks, 2001; Sassen, 2007). According to this vision, and against that of most regulationists or Hall and Soskice (2001), nation states are no longer the scale at which industries are regulated; rather this process also takes place at the level of sub-state, international region (e.g. the EU) or at the global (e.g. the WTO) level. This general assertion clearly has a good deal of empirical veracity. However, if one simply adopts the multi-level metaphor when analysing industries, one will inevitably fail to capture the more complex, but also more revealing, interplay between territory and industry which actually structures the politics of the latter (Carter and Smith, 2008).

For this reason, when beginning research on any industry, the *Politics of Industry* approach makes no *a priori* assumptions about the territorial 'scale' at which industries are governed. Moreover, as the 'empirical' chapters in this book testify, each of our case studies is based instead on the hypothesis that each IR within an industry is most likely to be governed at a scale which differs from the other three. As Table 8.1 summarizes, our research findings validate this hypothesis. Employment IRs in all our chapters still tend strongly to be regulated at the level of the state. However, in the case of European states, this regulation nonetheless also contains important EU and sub-state dimensions. In contrast, over the last 20 years, Financial IRs in most of the industries studied

Table 8.1 The territorial scaling of each industry's IRs (2007)

Case studies	Sub-state	National	EU	Global
Car-Retailing	–	Employment Purchase Commercial	Employment Purchase Commercial	Financial
Wine	Purchase	Purchase Employment Commercial	– Employment Commercial	Financial Commercial
Pharmaceuticals	–	Employment Purchase Commercial	Employment – Commercial	Financial
Defence	–	Employment Financial Purchase Commercial	–	–
Fisheries	Purchase Commercial	Purchase Employment	Purchase Employment Commercial	Purchase Financial
Foie gras	Purchase	Employment Commercial	Employment	Financial

have clearly undergone a form of change which has seen them largely reinstitutionalized in a way which has created a pattern of national, supranational (e.g. EU) and worldwide regulations which now applies to most firms on the planet. In contrast, the Purchase and Commercial IRs studied in this book tend to vary much more in their scaling from industry to industry. This is largely because these IRs have been institutionalized over time through industry-specific confrontations between representatives of firms and public action where representatives of institutionalized territories, generally states, have played key roles. Even if over the last 30 years the role of these actors has changed considerably, particularly due to decentralizations or the rise of the EU, public actors as a whole still appear to retain deeper roots in decision-making arenas where employment and the supply of raw materials are at issue.

In summary, we maintain that, as defined and used in the book, the concept of IRs enables research to generate new knowledge about the dynamics of industries in three ways:

1. by identifying with precision the arenas within which reproduction and change of IRs takes place and by considering that these are likely to overlap;
2. by encouraging research, when used in conjunction with the concept of IOs, to elucidate the hierarchy of each IR and how this may be challenged during periods of change whose causes can and must be identified;
3. by reiterating, as institutionalist theory advocates, that the construction and evolution of IRs involves private, collective and public actors in constant processes of institutional co-production.

3. Institutional change and the 'problematization' of industrial issues

When actually studying processes of change in IRs or IOs, one frequently discovers that dysfunctional or even contradictory institutions provide its initial stimuli. However, the deinstitutionalization and reinstitutionalization that lies at the heart of such change can never be reduced to the quest for economically or politically 'efficient' solutions. Instead, political work translates and 'converts' industrial dysfunctions through a process grasped in this book through the concept of 'problematization'. Adopting this concept is essential to the type of analysis we use and advocate because it obliges both economists and political scientists to break with the paradigm of 'calculus', which is nothing less than an epistemological barrier to studying change within industries.

In political science, the paradigm of calculus is particularly strongly present in theories of rational choice which attempt to explain change by focusing upon the supposed interests of individuals and groups of actors who, although they have varying resources, are all considered to be confronted with the same objective set of issues and challenges (Krasner, 1991; Shepsle, 1989). Change is then explained as a function of the interests and the resources of different actors and how they manage to influence the groups and polities to which they belong. Without overlooking the importance of the concept of 'interests', adopting that of problematization enables research to develop a quite different stance and set of hypotheses about their role in the politics of industry. Problematization is in fact a critical phase of change where nothing has been decided and during which actors, usually implicitly, realize that the issues which are preoccupying them have, to use Simon's language, no satisfactory 'solution'. It is only then that they begin to identify and debate the need for institutional change, a process during which their interests and, in passing, that of their allies or enemies, are rethought and redefined.

Similarly, in economics structuralist and/or functionalist approaches also fail to constitute pertinent perspectives from which to study the question of institutional change because they see 'objective functions' for each actor and 'structures' as 'parameters' which simply impose themselves as exogenous variables upon each industry (Williamson, 1985). In this way, for example, the law that relates to automobile distribution is often seen as simply the inevitable result of actors adapting their respective preferences to changing technologies and 'market conditions'. Instead, the concept of problematization has allowed this book's chapter on car distribution to show that the issues under debate have not been stabilized and that each attempt made by an actor to move in such a direction by requalifying these issues as institutionalized problems leads other actors to propose alternative definitions. From this perspective, the case of Scottish fisheries provides another particularly clear example. Here representatives of fishermen have explicitly sought to reframe the question at the heart of their Commercial IR around notions of sustainable and quality fishing. This not only modifies this IR, but also takes the industry as a whole away from problematizations of the rarity of fish which previously had been framed only within the Purchase IR. Indeed, this example raises a more general point: the politics of an industry is rarely driven directly by functional issues, such as rises in fuel costs. Although these often seem all consuming, these issues often turn out to be actually rather trivial and responses to them can often be found relatively quickly. Instead the politics of industry concerns much more the reaching of agreement over what poses the more underlying problems in an industry – a process that is fundamentally indeterminable and, for this reason, highly conflictual.

In summary, by giving rise to the hypothesis that phases of problematization are crucial to the politics of industry, this book's 'empirical' chapters reveal the two major advantages of adopting this concept:

1. it commits research to retracing how, within firms and during collective and public action, each actor has framed the questions it is pertinent to solve in their respective industry and how these challenges are interlinked;
2. it underlines the fundamentally uncertain nature of processes of change because their result depends upon the range of problems framed and raised by the actors concerned, and upon their respective capacity to impose these framings either as political priorities or, on the contrary, as issues which should be erased from the agendas of collective and public action.

Moreover, for economists, this conceptualization of industrial ontologies means they are faced with the following dilemma: either they remain functionalists and therefore renounce a quest for relevance to actors in order to save their goal of 'predictability'; or they study phases of problematizaion and leave the question of deciding which economic questions they should regulate to the actors themselves. Our approach clearly leads to the second choice.

4. Institutional change through politicization and depoliticization

When one considers that political work is the principal vector for change in the IOs which structure each industry's routine dynamics, discovering how the problems its actors define are politicized takes on crucial importance. In order to grasp this process, the contributions to this book have first sought to identify the reasons why issues originally linked to production, processing or marketing were made political. Secondly, they have striven to show more precisely the political work behind these politicizations.

4.1. The incomplete nature of productive systems and the role of politics

As many behaviourist studies of the firm have shown, in most cases actors within industries cannot cope with situations where the only way of finding satisfactory solutions to their problems is to modify their goals. For this reason, Kandil advocates analysis in terms of 'the logical primacy of judgements over meaning' (1998: 161). More precisely, in seeking to identify the judgement criteria used in intra-firm deliberations prior to action, she has shown that calculus alone is never sufficient. For Kandil, those 'who conceptualise institutions only from the angle of their functionality' end up examining institutions 'instrumentally' (1998: 150). Instead, she concludes, such deliberations 'also include reflection about the goals being pursued' which are never purely individual and which, consequently, are linked to what is instituted (thus contributing to both making institutions 'live' and changing them). Ultimately, it is within this dimension of economic activity that the reproblematizations which mark industries both take place and structure the politicization of productive systems.

Because actors in such industries are constantly led to ask themselves questions about their own respective goals, motives and intentions, institutions take on the role of 'signposts of meaning' which, in Thévenot's words, allow these practitioners to 'put an end to their quest for intention' (1989). To return to Kandil, action is subject to a plurality of forms of judgement because, contrary to what Simon maintained, the obstacles to action are not only cognitive or epistemic. Instead, beyond question of functionality, the criteria for judgement also include issues of meaning and what Kandil calls 'morality'.

This book has shown that it is around this question of goals and of the need to find responses to the issues of industry that are socially tenable, both for representatives of the industry and for its inscription in wider society, that processes of politicization emerge. Indeed, both the definition of the productive problems judged worthy of collective and public treatment and the solutions proposed for them are fundamentally conflictual and therefore undecidable. It is therefore always highly unlikely that actors will manage to even regularize these problems 'spontaneously' without bringing into play a third party who is both capable of legitimizing the problem through highlighting its extra-industry relevance and of developing the resources necessary to impose this point of view. It is precisely because the reproblematizations of productive issues which mark the changes of IOs redefine the aims of their action and redistribute power within industries that they cause politicizations which, from the point of view of research, are revealing of the social and cognitive incompleteness of productive systems.

4.2. Globalization and processes of politicization

As our case studies underline, considering that actors are confronted by 'the question of goals' does not mean that they constantly speculate or philosophize. Rather what becomes apparent in a case such as foie gras is that actors are frequently confronted with issues which seem insoluble within their respective IO. Consequently, they begin to question the legitimacy of its institutions and/or appeal to public authority in order to obtain the resources they fail to possess. This initial stage involves the publicization of a productive issue which the parties concerned consider they are facing. In this way the faculty of an IO's or an IR's rules to regulate such issues are constantly being tested: whenever the conflicts within these relationships are irreconcilable, the rules which make up their constantly provisional modes of regulation necessitate the intervention of public guarantors.

In cases where open conflict persists beyond this initial phase of publicization, actors begin to seek changes in the rules in order to obtain a redistribution of the resources they consider they need to survive and/or prosper. In the case of foie gras, in the late 1980s, globalization in the form of international competition was a new issue for which the classical solution of import restrictions was no longer legally available. By reformulating the problem as one of 'usurpation', this issue was able to be inscribed on the agenda of the EU in such a way as to generate new rules. These rules were linked to other goals which, in turn, enabled the actors concerned to engage in further political work that would provide them with new forms of legitimacy.

From a cognitive point of view, this type of displacement is always highly contentious because it modifies the meaning of collective and public action, institutionalized modes of reasoning and ways of anticipating both the future of an industry and the actions–reactions of its participants. It is therefore also problematical from the point of view of the distribution of power because a redistribution of rights or resources tends to unveil conflicts which the IO had previously kept behind closed doors. For all these reasons, carrying a productive issue into the public domain in order to find solutions that are both politically defendable and likely to propose a positive, or simply better, future for a productive system involves what we call 'political work'. Like all other types of work, this consumes resources and prevents those who carry it out from simultaneously engaging in other work. Moreover, political work is quintessentially dual in nature.

On the one hand, it is intra-industry because one must convince fellow operators that the new productive problem is the right one to tackle and not, as the case of wine shows, just the same set of issues as before. Here politico-productive solutions need to be developed and promoted by recruiting allies to their 'cause'. Given that this process generally implies a redistribution of power, forging coalitions around new rules has to be made to fit with a new ordering of rights and resources which, if the political enterprise succeeds, will render the new rules effective.

On the other hand, and because the attribution of rights cannot generally be obtained solely through intra-industry negotiations, political work also contains an external dimension. Here work is dominated by the importation of politico-productive solutions from beyond the industry itself in question in order to inscribe it within a 'meta', trans-industry IO. Here general principles from the latter, for example EU competition law, can confer legitimacy upon an industry's solutions. Moreover, it is the trans-industry order which allows actors from specific industries to obtain the resources that are necessary for, in the first instance, their political victory and subsequently the durable guarantee of their solution, notably through the threat of legal action.

In summary, in this book politicization has been conceptualized and studied around attempts to extend the sharing of judgements about meaning in the daily life of industries. In most cases, this process begins within an industry itself when all or some of the actors involved in its IO start to question its institutions and no longer manage to find within its rules acceptable solutions to their respective productive problems. This was clearly the case for foie gras, where not only representatives of other labelled foodstuff were enrolled, but also the French government and the European Commission. But politicization can also occur because external allies are no longer there, thus amputating actors within an industry from the political resources they need in order to perpetuate the IO that had previously shored up their domination. For example, the objective of spending less on public health or defence, or liberalizing car-retailing and no longer tolerating large price differences across

Europe, or plans to stop the exhaustion of fish stocks have all engendered politicizations of this second type. In each case, they have given rise to intra-industry politicizations which have either organized resistance to trans-industry regulation through a logic of extraction from its meta-principles, or caused an industry to submit to such principles (logic of submission).

Conversely, other parts of the book have also shown that change or stasis can also be politically worked towards through adopting the depoliticizing of industrial issues. Here the power of supermarkets in industries such as wine or foie gras provides empirical examples of this point. In both cases, the capacity of supermarkets to choose their suppliers and determine prices has of course provoked constant grumbling among producers and processors. However, in neither instance have concerted attempts been made to reframe these issues as anything other than the 'natural consequence' of markets, mergers and acquisitions. More precisely still, sporadic attempts to problematize these issues in such a way have yet to succeed in systematically politicizing the power of supermarkets in terms of the social values they bring into question.

Overall, when mobilized as a political enterprise, globalization clearly can encourage the spreading of fatalistic perceptions amongst actors within industries, which leads them to consider 'markets' or 'technology' as unopposable motives for institutionalized change within their respective industries. Nonetheless, and as our case studies highlight, such actors are even more likely to work politically to institutionalize a logic of subtraction from the norms of globalization than they are to simply submit to them.

5. Political work, 'contamination effects' and institutional change

On the basis of the concepts defined and the arguments made above, writing this book has also been driven by the hypothesis that political work is the key explanatory variable for analysing change within industries. Indeed, these principles and arguments are all part of an ontology of economic action which considers the political content of industrial dynamics to be essential. Our challenge has been to transform this viewpoint into a research method which enables one to capture the dynamism of each industry studied through grasping its causal mechanisms. Applied to six industries which, over the last 20 years, have all undergone significant pressure for reform, and in many cases substantial change, our approach has on the whole met this challenge. By disciplining our study of these industries, this approach has encouraged identification of what has given rise to criticism, and often vilification, of existing IOs. In particular, this has been achieved by encouraging examination of the possible 'contamination effects' when change within one of its IRs affects others and, in this way, the industry as a whole. As we have seen, the complementary and hierarchical nature of the relations which link the IRs to each other also enables one to grasp the dynamics of an industry as a whole. More precisely, one is able to explain the contamination effects which are susceptible to emerge when, after being politically worked by actors, one of the IRs changes. In certain cases, change will remain limited and therefore the identity of the industry will be unchanged. In other cases, however, from the point of view of firms, their competitive strategies and also those of collective and public actors, change in one IR will provoke modifications in access to resources and/or markets in the other three. In such cases, change through contamination will thus be synonymous with the restructuration of the industry, and therefore of the distribution of roles and power within it.

Consequently, and compared to very general commentary on industries which synthesize their change and restructuring by evoking 'globalization', 'financialization', the impact of new information technologies or even the increased power of large retailers, the *Politics of Industry* approach offers a means of systematically examining all the key dimensions of an industry's 'life'. In this way, when we examine the effects of what is presumed to be a meta-trend upon an industry, for example globalization or 'the information revolution', we set out to locate and discern its actual impact upon each of the industry's four IRs. Similarly, whenever our initial angle of study is through one of these relationships, for example, the Financial IR when examining the hypothesis of financialization or the Commercial IR when tackling that of supermarket power, our overall analytical grid obliges us to measure, contextualize and often relativize the impact of these trends by discerning whether they had contamination effects upon the industry's other three IRs.

In promoting this point of view, it should be recalled that in the social sciences, and notably in industrial economics, the Financial and Commercial IRs have largely been understudied. One of the merits of our approach has therefore been to give these IRs the same theoretical importance as the Purchase and Employment IRs. Indeed, in our view, the recent success of literature on financialization or 'the power of the retailer' is akin to the rather naïve discovery of parts of industrial life which hitherto had largely been neglected. As highlighted by the chapters by Montalban on pharmaceuticals and Moura on defence – two industries often seen as emblematic examples of financialization – the *Politics of Industry* approach enables research to take this trend seriously first by transforming it into a carefully defined object for research. Secondly, the approach then disciplines empirical study of not only how such trends have changed the dynamics of an industry, but also what effects this then had upon its 'institutional complementarity'. Thirdly, the approach generates knowledge of how these effects either led to fundamental change of the industry's IO (as in pharmaceuticals) or relatively little change (the case of defence). In summary, here our approach allows research to discern whether previously existing hierarchies between institutions in the IO have continued to give one IR a structuring role over the others, thus channelling and limiting the contamination effects that are possible within the industry. It is in this way that trends such as financialization or globalization, so in vogue in contemporary social science, can be rigorously studied. In short, the inference here is not that one can claim that 'nothing has changed'; rather, it is only through identifying the nature and impact of political work in the IR concerned, and then its capacity to induce change in the IO as a whole, that one can actually identify the impact of meta-trends within each industry.

This claim can be further illustrated by revisting briefly how our case studies on automobile distribution, wine and foie gras all shed light upon both the institutional thickness and the possible contamination effects of change in the Commerical IR. In the EU, the importance accorded to the Single Market and to competition policy as a means of 'facing up to globalization' has tended to confer a central role upon the Commercial IR in each of these industries' IOs. In addition, the accent placed in the world of management upon 'the client' and the need to satisfy them has also contributed to questions of 'demand' and commerce being taken more seriously by private, collective action and public decision-makers. While this has occurred, however, much of social science dogmatically remains more interested in questions relating to production and industrial relations. It has therefore largely failed to generate the conceptual tools and empirical research capable of systematically studying the actual effects of 'the rise' of the Commerical IR. Here again the *Politics of Industry* approach offers some solutions to this analytical challenge. In the case of wine, for example, whilst recognizing that productive problems have been increasingly marked by change in the industry's Commerical IR, we have shown how and why the latter has thus far given rise to so little politicization. Similarly, our analysis of car-retailing also shows that if European Commissioner Mario Monti claimed to be 'putting the consumer in the driver's seat', as in the case of wine, the centre of political work carried out in this industry remains clearly within the Purchase IR. Finally, in the case of foie gras, although the introduction of legal protection for geographical indications was often justified as a means of 'protecting the consumer', within this industry the Commercial IR has not taken on a central role. Rather the Purchase IR continues to 'house' the arenas within which most key decisions are taken. Conversely, in the case of fisheries, political work originally concentrated in the Purchase IR has recently spilled over into the Commercial IR, where considerable change has taken place. In short, such contamination effects can be studied with precision and merit greater research in the future.

Conclusion

The *Politics of Industry* approach at the heart of this book has essentially been used here to generate knowledge about the regulation of industries, the role played therein by globalization and what we consider we have added to existing ways of studying these subjects. However, conceptualizing change within industries as we have is not just a means of 'liberating' academics from disciplinary or theoretical blinkers and cages. So long as researchers maintain a posture of 'elucidation' that attempts to open practitioners up to thinking more objectively about their respective autonomy, and do not fall into the trap of the expert who tells them what to think and do (Jullien, 2004), we strongly believe our approach can also participate in the displacement of the way collective and public problems are defined and tackled.

From the point of view of collective action (e.g. wine interprofessions), the analytical perspective put forward here can be used to reframe debates by rendering issues more explicit. This is particularly so for controversies which are often seen by the actors themselves as 'unmentionable' and impossible to discuss. Similarly, from the point of view of actors who are employed to defend the public interest within public administrations, this form of analysis can allow them to develop some distance between their own thinking and the way public problems are defined by their habitual socioprofessional interlocutors. In other words, analysis of political work within each industry can provide a means for the actors themselves to escape from the constraints of neo-corporatist forms of regulation.

More generally, the research approach developed in this book encourages revisiting the question of the link between reflexivity about, and change of, industrial practices. It would of course be naïve to claim that if one changes the representations of reality of certain actors then the force and inertia of power relations can be overcome. Nevertheless, we maintain that the new information and interpretations generated by rigorous analysis of the link between industrial organization and political work is more likely to be heard by practitioners than research approaches which continue to perpetuate the idea that the regulation of industries, and therefore their globalization, are disincarnated and a-political processes which simply impose themselves upon industries and the actors they encompass.

Notes

1. Introduction: Industries, Globalization and Politics

1. In contrast to representations of industries in terms of 'productive worlds' proposed by the 'Economy of Conventions' (Salais and Storper, 1993), *The Politics of Industry* approach considers that IRs are highly unlikely to feature parity between the actors they contain. Rather, the regulation of these IRs almost always features the domination of one actor by another.

2. European Automobile Distribution: Globalization and Incomplete Liberalization

1. From the point of view of public authorities, the EU's dynamic of integration relies mainly on its competence in relation to the regulation of competition through the European Commission's DG Competition. The latter is nonetheless supported by DG Internal Market when issues related to the question of spare parts and related intellectual property rights are being considered.
2. Sloan in the United States initially presented General Motors as far more respectful of its dealers in the 1920s than its main competitor Ford (Tedlow, 1996). However, he subsequently came to understand the depth of such relationships and the asymmetries of power that they generally entail (Jullien, 2003).

3. Globalization Within the European Wine Industry: Commercial Challenges but Producer Domination

1. The empirical analysis synthesized here has been published in book form (Smith, de Maillard and Costa, 2007). Research data was compiled using a range of statistics, analysis of the specialized press and more than 60 interviews with representatives of the wine sector. I take this opportunity to thank Jacques de Maillard and Olivier Costa for their contribution to this research.
2. Bevir and Rhodes consider that narratives of this type explain social action by 'pointing to the conditional and volitional links between the relevant beliefs, preferences, intentions and actions' (2003: 20). In the wine industry, examples of the narrative I am about to describe include the journalism of Deroudille (2003) and the geography of Hinnewinkel (2004).
3. Réjalot (2003) underlines that it is impossible to isolate out the Bordelais component of figures on turnover for these companies.

4. Shareholder Value, Political Work and Globalization in the Pharmaceutical Industry

1. At around the same time – 1941 – in France a state-run *visa* system for the control of drug safety was also created (Chauveau, 1999).
2. Health is also a difficult concept to define: what is 'good' or 'normal' health? For example, should we consider that 'hyperactivity' problems of children are 'health care' problems? In reality, the definition of what constitutes a disease or pathology is constructed by the effects of drugs detected in clinical trials (Pignarre, 2003; PLOS Medecine, 2006).
3. To avoid competition, sometimes *Big Pharma* develop agreements with generic firms. Called 'brand payments', these give royalties to generic firms if they accept to enter the market later by signing a licence of exclusivity for the branded company.
4. The US is the only country, other than New Zealand, where direct-to-consumer advertising for ethical drugs is authorized.
5. Here 'public' is a misnomer because the French health care system is a hybrid between a Bismarckian health care system and a Beveridgian one. In addition, this model also contains *mutuelle* insurance companies.
6. The report underlined 'that the decline of European competitiveness in pharmaceuticals is linked to the persistence of a fragmented market and, at the same time, to major 'non-market' and 'bureaucratic failures in public intervention and in price regulation'. The solutions proposed by Gambardella *et al.* (2000) were 'Upgrading scientific research and favouring the integration between scientific and industrial research' (by increasing funding, creating and integrating a European research system, etc.), 'strengthening industrial R&D' and 'strengthening market-based competition within an integrated environment'.
7. Surprisingly this DG is in charge of drugs. One might have thought this would be an issue for the Health DG.
8. Hank McKinnel from Pfizer, Raymond Gilmartin from Merck & Co, Peter Dolan from Bristol-Myers Squibb. But, of course, these men were fired whilst still receiving very comfortable compensation (e.g. $180 million in stock options, pension and salaries for McKinnel).

5. The US Defence Industry Since 1945: Globalization Refused

1. The most relevant recent example is the Internet. This was spawned by military research on communication supported by the Defense Advanced Research Projects Agency (DARPA) of the Pentagon.
2. Dual-use technology has been increasingly challenged because its results are far from convincing. In fact, few technologies developed and used in the military sector actually fit with civilian ones. This is largely due to the specific type of skills attached to production processes in the military (Cowan and Foray, 1995).
3. According to the Buy American Act, a product is American proven when at least 50% of it is made in the US.

6. Globalization, Scottish Fisheries and 'Political Work': Global–EU–Local Dialectics

1. By contrast, limited political work is found in the *Employment* and *Finance IRs*. Clearly, this does not mean that these *IRs* had had no effect on the industry during this time. For example, central provisions of the EU working time directive threatened to affect the share-system working practices of Scottish fishers in the northeast and caused political reaction within Scotland (Nuttall, 2000: 111). Similarly, EU financial support to redress losses of earnings related to declining stocks and falling prices had important effects. This is because, although the price of fish influences the volume of fishing activity (Friis, 1996: 177), this can be offset by local decisions over usage of EU monies for de-commissioning or 'tying-up' of vessels. Debates over these issues have taken place in Scotland; however, they have been episodic. Instead, it has been political work conducted to destabilize and rebuild the *Purchase* and *Commercial IRs* which has driven change across the industry and towards a sustainable fisheries production model. Consequently, whilst recognizing the importance of the *Employment* and *Finance IRs* to the industry as a whole, I have chosen not to focus on these in the remainder of this chapter.

Bibliography

Aglietta, M. and Rébérioux, A. (2005) *Dérives du capitalisme financier*, Paris: Albin Michel.
Albert, P. and Martin, M. (2001) 'Transformation des formes organisationnelles des firmes. Une application à l'industrie des vins et spiritueux', *Economie rurale*, n° 264–265: 60–75.
Allain, M-L. and Chambolle, C. (2003) 'Approches théoriques des rapports de force entre producteurs et distributeurs', *Economie rurale*, n° 277–278: 183–191.
Amable, B. (2003) *The Diversity of Modern Capitalism*, Oxford: Oxford University Press.
Amable, B. and Palombarini, B. (2005) *L'économie politique n'est pas une science morale*, Paris: Auber.
Aoki, I. (2001) *Towards a Comparative Institutional Analysis*, Cambridge (MA): The MIT Press.
Arena, R. Benzoni, L., de Bant, J. and Romani, P. (1990) *Traité d'Economie Industrielle*, Paris: Economica.
Arnaud, L. and Guionnet, C. (2005) 'Introduction. Les frontières du politique', in L. Arnaud and C. Guionnet (eds) *Les frontières du politique. Enquête sur les processus de politisation et de dépolitisation*, Rennes: Presses universitaires de Rennes.
Arrow, J. K. (1962) 'Economic welfare and allocation of resources for invention', in R. R. Nelson (ed.), *The Rate and Direction of Inventive Activity*, Princeton: Princeton University Press.
Ball, N. and Leintenberg, G. (1983) *The Structure of the Defense Industry*, New York: St Martin's Press.
Ballot, E., Segrestin, B. and Weil, B. (2006) 'La diversité comme vecteur de croissance? Interrogation sur l'impact économique de la diversité chez les constructeurs automobiles', Paper presented to the *14th GERPISA International Colloquium*, Paris, June 12–13.
Batsch, L. (2002) *Le capitalisme financier*, Paris: La Découverte.
Behr, N. (2004) *Distribution de la variété, incertitude sur la demande et relations verticales dans l'industrie automobile*, PhD dissertation, Ecole des Mines de Paris, June.
Bélis-Bergouignan, M-C. and Montalban, M. (2006) 'L'industrie pharmaceutique face aux mutations', in G. Colletis and Y. Lung (eds) *La France industrielle en questions*, Paris: La Documentation Française.
Berger, S. (2006) *Made in Monde*, Paris: Seuil.
Bergès-Sennou, F. and Caprice, S. (2003) 'Les rapports producteurs-distributeurs: fondements et implications de la puissance d'achat', *Economie rurale*, n° 277–278: 192–205.
Berle, A. and Means, G. (1932) *The Modern Corporation and Private Property*, London: MacMillan.
Berthomeau, J. (2001) *Comment mieux positionner les vins français sur les marchés d'exportation?*, report commissioned by French Ministry of Agriculture.

Bevir, M. and Rhodes, R. (2003) *Interpreting British Governance*, London: Routledge.
Bisley, N. (2007) *Rethinking Globalization*, Basingstoke: Palgrave.
Bourdieu, P. (2000) *Les structures sociales de l'économie*, Paris: Liber.
Boyer, R. (2003) 'Les analyses historiques du changement institutionnel: quels enseignements pour la théorie de la régulation', *L'Année de la Régulation*, n° 7: 167–203.
Boyer, R. and Freyssenet, M. (2000) *Les modèles productifs*, Paris: La Découverte. (version in English: *Productive models:The Conditions of profitability*, London: Palgrave, 2002).
Boyer, R. and Freyssenet, M. (2002) 'Entre innovations historiques et contraintes structurelles: éléments d'une théorie des modèles productifs', Document du travail CEPREMAP, n° 2002–05.
Braithwaite, J. and Drahos, P. (2000) *Global Business Regulation*, Cambridge: Cambridge University Press.
Briquet, J.-L. (1994) 'Communiquer en actes. Prescriptions de rôle et exercise quotidien du métier politique', *Politix*, 28 (4): 16–26.
Buzan, B. and Herring, E. (1998) *The Arms Dynamic in World Politics*, Boulder: Lyne Rienner.
Capus, J. (1947) *L'Evolution de la législation sur les appellations d'origine. Genèse des appellations contrôlées*, Paris: INAO– Editions Louis Larmat.
Carpenter, M., Lazonick, W. and O'Sullivan, M. (2003) 'The Stock Market and Innovative Capability in the New Economy: The Optical Networking Industry', *Industrial and Corporate Change*, 12 (5): 963–1034.
Carter, C. (2007) 'EU Fisheries, 'Better Regulation Strategy' and the (Re-)Defining of Regional Governance: the UK Experience', paper presented to seminar *Le Gouvernement Européen de l'Industrie*, Paris, 23rd March.
Carter, C. and Smith, A. (2007) 'Is Scottish Devolution Pluralist? Sectors, Territory and Domination', paper presented to the seminar series of the *Territorial Politics Research Group*, University of Edinburgh, 8 November, 2007.
Carter, C. and Smith, A. (2008) 'Revitalizing Public Policy approaches to the EU: Territorial institutionalism, fisheries and wine', *Journal of European Public Policy*, 15 (2): 263–281.
César, G. (2002) *Rapport d'information de la Commission des affaires économiques et du Plan du Sénat sur l'avenir de la viticulture française*, The French Senate.
Chauveau, S. (1999) *L'invention pharmaceutique. La pharmacie française entre l'Etat et la société au XXeme siècle*, Paris: Institut d'éditions Sanofi-Synthélabo.
Combes, J. and Myers, M. (2004) *A Traceability and Responsible Fishing Demonstration in the Nephrops Supply Chain*, Seafish Report No. SR560, Edinburgh: Sea Fish Industry Authority.
Commons, J. R. (1934) Institutional Economics. Its Place in Political Econmy, New York: MacMillan.
Coriat, B. and Orsi, F. (2003a) 'Droits de propriété intellectuelle, marchés financiers et innovation, une configuration soutenable?', *Lettre de la Régulation*, n° 45, July.
Coriat, B. and Orsi, F. (2003b) 'Brevets pharmaceutiques, génériques et santé publique. Le cas de l'accès aux antirétroviraux', *Economie publique*, n° 12: 153–177.
Coull, J. (1999) 'Changing Balance of Fish Production in Scotland' *Marine Policy*, 23 (4–5): 347–358.

Couper, A. and Smith, H. (1997) 'The Development of Fishermen-Based Policies', *Marine Policy*, 21 (2): 111–119.

Cowan, R. and Foray, D. (1995) 'Quandaries in the Economics of Dual Technologies and Spillovers from Military to Civilian Research and Development', *Research Policy*, 24 (6): 851–868.

Crean, K. and Wisher, S. (2000) 'Is there the will to Manage Fisheries at Local Level in the European Union? A Case Study from Scotland', *Marine Policy*, 24: 471–481.

Cuntigh Ph., Jullien B. and Smith A. (2005) 'Le contenu politique des régulations sectorielle et les méfaits de sa dénégation: le cas de la gestion publique des produits palmipèdes périgourdins', *Politique et management public*, 23 (3): 175–195.

Cuntigh, Ph. and Smith, A. (2005) 'Des racines et des plumes en Périgord: la gestion publique des canards entre logiques de filière et de Territoire', in J. Palard, E. Kerrouche, L. Bherer, J-P. Collin (eds) *Jeux d'échelle et transformation de l'Etat: le gouvernement des territoires au Québec et en France*, Sainte-Foy (Québec): Presses de l'Université de Laval.

Davis, K. (1971) *Arms, Industry and America*, New York: H. W. Wilson.

Deas, B. (2006) 'Regional Advisory Councils and the Future of Fisheries Policy', unpublished Buckland lecture.

Degnbol, P. (2003) 'Science and the Use Perspective: the gap co-management must address' in D. Wilson, J. Nielsen and P. Degnbol (eds) *The Fisheries Co-Management Experience Accomplishments, Challenges and Prospects*, Amsterdam: Kluwer, 31–49.

Deroudille, J.-P. (2003) *Le vin face à la mondialisation*, Paris: Hachette.

Di Masi, J. A., Grabowski, H. G. and Hansen, R. W. (2003) 'The Price of Innovation: New Estimates of Drug Development Costs', *Journal of Health Economics*, 22: 151–185.

Dobbin, F. and Zorn, D. (2005) 'Corporate Malfeasance and the Myth of Shareholder Value', *Political Power and Social Theory*, 17: 179–198.

Dore, R. (2000) Stock *Market Capitalism: Welfare Capitalism. Japan and Germany versus the Anglo-Saxon*, Oxford: Oxford University Press.

Dubois V. and Dulong D. (eds) (1999) *La question technocratique: de l'invention d'une figure aux transformations de l'action publique*, Strasbourg: Presses universitaires de Strasbourg.

Duménil, G. and Lévy, D. (2004) *Capital Resurgent. Roots of the Neoliberal Revolution*, Harvard: Harvard University Press.

European Commission (2006) *Vin: Economie du secteur*, Document de travail, February.

Eymard-Duvernay, F. (1989) 'Conventions de qualité et formes de coordination', *Revue Economique*, 40 (2): 329–359.

Farnell, J. and Elles, J. (1984) *In Search of a Common Fisheries Policy*, Aldershot: Gower.

Federal Trade Commission (2002) *Generic Drug Entry Prior to Patent Expiration: An FTC Study*, July.

Filder, B. (2005) '2005 Outlook: Nice volumes, shame about the $', *Industry Update: Aerospace sector*, Deutsche Bank, 13th January.

Fligstein, N. (1990) *The Transformation of Corporate Control*, Cambridge (MA): Harvard University Press.

Fligstein, N. (1996) 'Markets as Politics: A Political-Cultural Approach to Market Institutions', *American Sociological Review*, 61 (August): 656–673.

Fligstein, N. (2001) *The Architecture of Markets. An Economic Sociology of Twenty-First-Century Capitalist Societies*, Princeton: Princeton University Press.

Fligstein, N. and Choo, J. (2005) 'Law and Corporate Governance', *Annual Review of Law and Social Science*, 1: December.

Fløysand, A. and Lindkvist, K. (2001) 'Globalisation, Local Capitalism and Fishery Communities in Change' in *Marine Policy*, 25: 113–121.

Friis, P. (1996) 'The European fishing industry: deregulation and the market', in K. Crean and D. Symes (eds) *Fisheries Management in Crisis*, Oxford: Fishing News Books, pp. 175–186.

Froud, J., Johal, S., Leaver, A. and Williams, K. (2006) *Financialisation and Strategy: Narrative and Numbers*, London: Routledge

Gambardella, A. (1995) *Sciences and Innovation in the US Pharmaceutical Industry*, Cambridge: Cambridge University Press.

Gambardella, A., Orsenigo, L. and Pammoli, F. (2000) *Global Competitiveness in Pharmaceuticals. A European Perspective*, Report for European Commission (DG Enterprise).

GAO (General Accounting Office) (2006) 'Defense Trade Data', *Briefing to senate committee on armed services*, Washington DC: US Government Printing Office.

Genieys, W. (1998) 'Le retournement du Midi viticole', *Pôle Sud*, n° 9: 7–25.

Gibbs, M. (2008) 'Network Governance in Fisheries', *Marine Policy*, 32: 113–119.

Gleditsch, N. and Njolstad, O. (1990) *Arms Races. Technological and Political Dynamics*, London: Sage.

Green, R. R., Rodriguez Zniga, M. and Pierbattissi, L. (2003) 'Global market changes and business behaviour in the wine sector', in S. Gatti, E. Giraud-Héraut and S. Milli (eds) *Wine in the Old World. New Risks and Opportunities*, Milan: FrancoAngeli, pp. 157–169.

Gourevitch, P. A. and Shinn, J. (2005) *Political Power & Corporate Control. The New Global Politics of Corporate Governance*, Princeton: Princeton University Press.

Haas, P. (1992) 'Introduction: Epistemic Communities and International Policy Co-Ordination', *International Organization*, 46 (1): 1–35.

Hall, P. and Soskice, D. (eds) (2001) *Varieties of Capitalism. The Institutional Foundation of Comparative Advantage*, Oxford: Oxford University Press.

Hanna, S. (1998) 'Parallel institutional pathologies in fisheries management' in D. Symes (ed.), *Northern Waters: Management Issues and Practice*, Oxford: Fishing News Books, pp. 25–35.

Hartley, K. and Sandler, T. (1995) *The Economics of Defense*, Cambridge: Cambridge University Press.

Harvey, D. (2003) *The New Imperialism*, Oxford: Oxford University Press.

Hatcher, A., Pascoe, S. and Banks, R. (2002) 'Future options for UK fish quota management', CEMARE Report 58, June.

Hay, C. (2006) 'What's Globalization Got to Do With It? Economic Interdependence and the Future of European Welfare States', *Government and Opposition*, 41 (1): 1–22.

Hay, C. and Marsh, D. (2000) 'Introduction: Demystifying globalization', in C. Hay and D. Marsh (eds) *Demystifying Globalization*, Basingstoke: Palgrave-Macmillan.

Hay, C. and Marsh, D. (2001) 'Introduction: Demystifying globalization', in C. Hay and D. Marsh (eds) *Demystifying Globalization*, London, Palgrave.
Held, D., McGrew, A., Goldblatt, D. and Perraton, J. (1999) *Global Transformations*, Cambridge: Polity Press.
Held, D. and McGrew, A. (eds) (2007) *Globalization Theory. Approaches and Controversies*, Cambridge: Polity Press.
Hinnewinkel, J.-C. (2004) *Les terroirs viticoles. Origines et devenirs*, Bordeaux: Editions Féret.
Hollingsworth, J., Schmitter, P. and Streek, W. (eds) (1994) *Governing Capitalist Economies*, Oxford: Oxford University Press.
Hooghe, L. and Marks, G. (2001) *Multi-Level Governance and European Integration*, Maryland: Rowman & Littlefield.
Höpner, M. (2001) *Corporate Governance in Transition: Ten Empirical Findings on Shareholder Value and Industrial Relations in Germany*, working Paper Max Planck Institute.
Hughey, K., Cullen, R. and Kerr, G. (2000) 'Stakeholder Groups in Fisheries Management' *Marine Policy*, 24: 119–127.
Imaï, K. I. and Itami, H. (1984) 'Interpenetration of Organization and Market: Japan's Firm and Market in Comparison with the US', *International Journal of Industrial Organization*, n° 2: 285–310.
Jabko, N. (2006) *Playing the Market: A Political Strategy for Uniting Europe, 1985–2005*, Ithaca: Cornell University Press
Jesus Oliveira Coelho, A.-M. and Rastoin, J.-L. (2001) 'Globalisation du marché du vin et stratégies d'entreprise', *Economie rurale*, n° 245–265: 16–34.
Joana, J. and Smith, A. (2002) *Les commissaires européens. Technocrates, diplomates ou politiques?*, Paris: Presses de Sciences Po.
Jobert, B. and Muller, P. (1987) *L'Etat en action. Politiques publiques et corporatismes*, Paris: Presses Universitaires de France.
Jensen, M. C. and Meckling, W. H. (1976) 'Theory of the Firm: Managerial Behavior, Agency Costs and Ownership Structure', *Journal of Financial Economics*, 3: 305–360, Octobre.
Jullien, B. (2000) 'La distribution automobile en 2000: vers le partenariat ou la taylorisation', Paper to Huitièmes Rencontres Internationales du GERPISA, Paris, 8–10 June.
Jullien, B. (2001) 'La distribution automobile en 2000: vers le partenariat ou la taylorisation', *Actes du GERPISA Réseau international* (Université d'Evry-Val d'Essonne), n° 31: 130–141.
Jullien, B. (2002) 'Consumer vs Manufacturer or Consumer vs Consumer? The Implication of a Usage Analysis of Automobile Systems', *Competition and Change*, 6: 113–125.
Jullien, B. (2003a) 'L'après-vente- Derrière l'occasion, la pièce, l'entretien et la réparation, la réalité des consommations et des offres automobiles: la diversité et la difficulté des constructeurs à y faire face' in EBG, *L'Automobile*, Paris: Elenbi Editeur.
Jullien, B. (2003b) 'Ford's distribution network in Europe: Recent developments in the context of the history of automobile retailing', in H. Bonin, Y. Lung and S. Tolliday (eds), *Ford, The European History, 1903–2003*, Paris: P.l.a.g.e., pp. 417–442.

Jullien, B. (2004) *Pour une méso-économie politique – Eléments d'une approche institutionnaliste du changement dans les industries, rapport pour l'HDR,* University of Bordeaux IV: Roneo.

Jullien, B. (2005a) 'Comment comprendre les transformations de la distribution automobile en Europe? Une épreuve de pertinence pour les institutionnalismes', Paper presented to conference *Analyse des changements institutionnels,* La Rochelle, 14–17 September.

Jullien, B. (2005b) 'L'après-vente en France après 2002: les raisons d'une mutation' paper presented to the 151th GERPISA seminar, Paris, 15th Avril.

Jullien, B. (2006a) 'La place renouvelée des services dans les systèmes automobiles', Paper presented to the *14th GERPISA International Colloquium,* Paris, June 12–13.

Jullien, B. (2006b) 'What a European Competition Policy can or cannot be, and/or what should it try or not try to be? Comments on the 'Developments in car retailing and after-sales markets under Regulation 1400/2002 report1 received by N. Kroes', *La Lettre du Gerpisa,* n° 192, September–October: 2–8.

Jullien, B. (2007) 'The Industrial and Automobile Policies of the European Union', *La Lettre du GERPISA,* n°196, March–April.

Jullien, B. and Smith A. (2004) *Organisation industrielle et politique des Indications géographiques protégées,* report commissioned by the Aquitaine Regional Council, July.

Jullien, B. and Smith, A. (2008a) 'Conceptualizing the Politics Behind Capitalist Variety: Industries and their Institutionalizations', forthcoming.

Jullien, B. and Smith, A. (2008b) 'Studying the Politics of Industry', forthcoming.

Kandil, F. (1998.) 'De la rationalité à la raison pratique dans les actes économiques', in R. Salais *et al.* (eds) *Institutions et conventions – La réflexivité de l'action économique,* Paris: Editions de l'Ecole des Hautes Etudes en Sciences Sociales, pp. 145–169.

Kandil, F. (2003) 'L'économie des conventions aujourd'hui et demain: science économique ou économie politique?', paper given to conference *Conventions et institutions: approfondissements théoriques et contributions aux débats politiques,* Paris, 11–12 December.

Kingdon, J. (1984) *Agendas, Alternatives and Public Policies,* Glenview, Illinois: Harper-Collins.

Krasner, S. (1991) 'Global Communications and National Power: Life on the Pareto Frontier', *World Politics,* 43 (April): 336–366.

Krippner, G. (2005) 'Financialization of the American Economy', *Socio-Economic Review,* n° 3: 173–208.

Kucera, R. (1974) *The Aerospace Industry and the Military: Structural and Political Relationships,* Beverly Hills: Sage.

Lagroye, J. (1994) 'Etre du métier', *Politix,* 28 (4): 1–15.

Lagroye, J. (2003a) 'Avant propos', in J. Lagroye (ed.), *La politisation,* Paris: Belin.

Lagroye, J. (2003b) 'Les processus de politisation', in J. Lagroye (ed.), *La politisation,* Paris: Belin.

La Porta, R., Lopez-De-Silanes, F., Shleifer, A. and Vishny, R. (1999) 'Corporate Ownership Around the World', *The Journal of Finance,* 54: 471–517.

Laporte, J.-P. and Touzard, J.-M. (1998) 'Deux décennies de transition viticole en Languedoc Roussillon: de la production de masse à une viticulture plurielle', *Pôle Sud,* n° 9: 26–47.

Lascoumes, P. and Le Galès, P. (2007) 'Introduction: Understanding Public Policy through its Instruments', *Governance*, 20 (1): 1–21.

Launay, R., Le Meur, J. C. and Moreau, E. (2004) *L'industrie pharmaceutique indienne: de la copie aux génériques...et au-delà?*, Paris: Conseil Général des Mines.

Lazonick, W. (2005) 'Evolution of the new economy business model', de Brousseau Eric and Curien Nicolas (eds) *the Economics of the Internet*, Cambridge: Cambridge University Press.

Lazonick, W. and O'Sullivan, M. (2000) 'Maximising Shareholder Value: A New Ideology for Corporate Governance', *Economy and Society*, 29: February: 13–35.

Leigh, M. (1983) *European Integration and the Common Fisheries Policy*, London: Croom Helm.

Les Entreprises du Médicament (2003) *L'essentiel: le medicament dans la santé et l'économie*.

Levy-Faur, D. (2006a) 'Varieties of Regulatory Capitalism: Getting the Most Out of the Comparative Method', *Governance*, 19 (3): 367–382.

Levy-Faur, D. (2006b) 'Regulatory Capitalism: The Dynamics of Change Beyond Telecoms and Electricity', *Governance*, 19 (3): 497–525.

Lipietz, A. (1995) 'De la régulation aux conventions: Le grand bond en arrière', *Actuel Marx*, n° 17: 39–48.

Long, A. (1999) 'The marine stewardship council initiative: The development of a market incentive approach to achieving sustainable fisheries' in D. Symes (ed.), *Alternative Management Systems for Fisheries*, Oxford: Fishing News Books, pp. 146–156.

Lorell, M. (1995) 'Troubled Partnership: A History of U.S. – Japan Collaboration on the FS-X fighter', *Report for the United States Air Force*, Santa Monica: RAND.

Loubet, J.-L. (1995) *Citroën, Peugeot, Renault et les autres. Soixante ans de stratégie*, Paris: Le Monde Editions.

Maillard (de), J. (2001) 'La Commission, le vin et la réforme', *Politique européenne*, n° 5: 70–86.

Makinson, L. (2004) 'Outsourcing the Pentagon, Who benefits from the Politics and Economics of National Security?', *Pentagon Spending Project*, Washington DC: Center for Public Integrity.

Majone, G. (1996) *L'Union européenne, un Etat régulateur*, Paris: Montchrétien.

Marette, S. and Raynaud, E. (2003) 'Applications du droit de la concurrence au secteur agroalimentaire', *Economie rurale*, n° 277–278: 9–22.

Marmot, J. (2004) *L'attractivité de la France pour les industries des biens de santé*, Report to French Ministry of the Economy and Finance.

Masson, A. (2004) *PharmaFrance 2004. S'inspirer des politiques publiques étrangères d'attractivité pour l'industrie pharmaceutique innovante*, Report to the French Conseil Général des Mines.

Marsh, D. and Rhodes, R. (eds) (1992) *Policy Networks in British Government*, Oxford: Clarendon.

McKelvey, M. and Orsenigo, L. (2001), *Pharmaceuticals as a Sectoral Innovation System*, working paper for project Sectoral Systems in Europe: Innovation Competitiveness and Growth.

Melman, S. (1975) 'Twelve Propositions on Productivity and the War Economy', *Challenge*, March/April: 7–11.

Mikalsen, K. and Jentoft, S. (2008) 'Participatory Practices in Fisheries Across Europe: Making Stakeholders More Responsible', *Marine Policy*, 32: 169–177.

Ministère de l'économie et des finances (2004) *Le financement public des entreprises de biotechnologies*, internal note, April.

Montalban, M. (2007) *Financiarisation, dynamiques des industries et modèles productifs: une analyse institutionnaliste du cas de l'industrie pharmaceutique*, PhD dissertation, University of Bordeaux (IV).

Moran, T. (1990) 'The Globalization of America's Defense Industries', *International Security*, 15 (1): 57–99.

Moreau, A. Rémont, S. and Weinmann, N. (2002) *L'industrie pharmaceutique en mutation*, Paris: La Documentation française.

Morin, F. (2006) *Le nouveau mur de l'argent. Essai sur la finance globalisée*, Paris: Editions du Seuil.

Muller, P. (1995) 'Les politiques publiques comme construction d'un rapport au monde', in A. Faure, G. Pollet, Ph. Warin (eds) *La construction du sens dans les politiques publiques*, Paris: l'Harmattan.

Muller, P. (2004) 'Secteur', in L. Boussaguet *et al.* (eds) *Dictionnaire des politiques publiques*, Paris: Presses de Sciences Po.

Nautilus Consultants Ltd (2006) *A Review of UK Producer Organisations*, Report prepared for the UK Fishery Administrations, August.

Nielsen, J., Degnbol, P., Viswnathan, K., Ahmed, M., Hara, M. and Abdullah, N. (2004) 'Fisheries Co-Management – An Institutional Innovation? Lessons from South East Asia and Southern Africa' *Marine Policy*, 28: 151–160.

Nielsen, N. (2005) 'The Competition Between the U.S. National Security Regime: A Study of the U.S. Aerospace Sector', Conference to Fox School of Business BIBER, Temple University, Philadelphia, April 2nd.

Nuttall, M. (2000) 'Crisis, risk and deskilment in North-east Scotland's Fishing Industry' in D. Symes (ed.), *Fisheries Dependent Regions*, Oxford: Fishing News Books, pp. 106–115.

OTA (Office of Technology Assessment) (1991) *Redesigning Defense, Planning the Transition to the Future US Defense Industrial Base*, Congress of the United States, Washington DC: US Government Printing Office.

OTA (Office of Technology Assessment) (1992) *After the Cold War: Living With Lower Defense Spending*, Congress of the United States, Washington DC: US Government Printing Office.

Orsi Fabienne (2002) 'La constitution d'un nouveau droit de propriété intellectuelle sur le vivant aux Etats-Unis: origine et signification économique d'un dépassement de frontières', *Revue d'Economie Industrielle*, 99, n° 2 trimestre, pp. 65–86.

Padioleau, J.-G. (1982) *L'Etat au concret*, Paris: Presses Universitaires de France.

Pardi, T. (2006) 'Entre déréglementation et contrôle du marché: la distribution automobile en Europe, 1962–2005', paper presented at the the 2nd Colloquium of the French Sociology Association, Bordeaux.

Pharmaceutical Shareowner Group (2004) *The Public Health Crisis in Emerging Markets. An Institutional Investor Perspective on the Implication for Pharmaceutical Industry*, report, September.

Pharma Futures (2004) *The Pharmaceutical Sectors. A long term value outlook*, report, December.

Phillipson, J. (1999) 'The fish producers' organisations of the UK: A strategic analysis' in D. Symes (ed.), *Alternative Management Systems for Fisheries*, Oxford: Fishing News Books, pp. 79–92.

Pignarre, P. (2003) *Le grand secret de l'industrie pharmaceutique*, Paris: La Découverte.

PLOS Medecine (2006) The fight against disease mongering: Generating Knowledge for Actions, 4 (3): April.

Polanyi, K. (1944) *The Great Transformation*, Boston: Beacon.

Pomarici, E. (2005) 'Recent evolution in the world wine market: supply, demand and new actors', paper presented to the annual conference of the Vineyard Data Quantification Society, Macerata, May.

Posen, B. (2005) 'Command of the commons: The military foundations of the US hegemony', in P. J. Bolt, D. Coletta, and C. Shackleford (eds) *American Defense Policy*, 248–269, Baltimore: The Johns Hopkins University Press.

Prescrire (2006) 'Alerte citoyenne', *Prescrire*, tome 2, n° 271, p. 241.

Radaelli, C. (1999) *Technocracy in the European Union*, London: Longman.

Radaelli, C. (2001) 'The Domestic Impact of European Union Public Policy: Notes en Concepts, Methods and the Challenge of Empirical Research', *Politique européenne*, n° 5: 107–142.

Ramirez, S. (2006) 'Anti-trust ou Anti-US? Industrie automobile européenne et les origines de la politique de la concurrence de la CEE?', in E. Bussière, M. Dumoulin and S. Schirmann (eds) *Europe organisée, Europe du libre-échange*, Bruxelles: Pieter Lang, pp. 203–229.

Ramirez, S. (2007) 'Multinational corporations and European integration: The case of the automobile industry', forthcoming in *Enterprise and Society*.

Ramírez, S. M. (2008) 'The European search for a new Industrial Policy (1968–1992)', in S. Baroncelli, C. Spagnolo, and L. S. Talani (eds) *Back to Maastricht: Obstacles to Constitutional Reform in the EU Treaty (1999–2007)*, Newcastle: Cambridge Scholars Publishing, pp. 303–325.

Réjalot, M. (2003) *Le modèle vitivinicole bordelais dans sa filière (1980–2003). Un idéal français dans la tourmente*, PhD Dissertation (Geography), Université de Bordeaux III.

Reppy, J. (1983) 'The United States', in N. Ball and M. Leitenberg (ed.), *The Structure of the Defense Industry*, New York: St Martin's Press, pp. 21–49.

Rexecode (2004) *Les enjeux de l'industrie du medicament pour l'économie française*, Study for Les Entreprises du Médicament.

Rhodes, R. (1996) *Understanding Governance*, Buckingham: Open University Press.

Risse, T. (2007) 'Social constructivism meets globalization', in D. Held and A. McGrew (eds) *Globalization Theory. Approaches and Controversies*, Cambridge: Polity Press, pp. 126–147.

Rochefort, D. and Cobb, R. (1994) *The Politics of Problem Definition*, Lawrence: University Press of Kansas.

Roe, M. (2000) 'Political Preconditions to Separating Ownership from Corporate Control', *Stanford Law Review*, 53 (3): 539–606.

Roe, M. (2001) *The Shareholder Wealth Maximization Norm and Industrial Organization*, Harvard Law School of Public Law, Working Paper n° 019.

Salais, R. and Storper, M. (1993) *Les Mondes de Production: enquête sur l'identité économique de la France*, Paris, Editions de L'Ecole des hautes etudes en sciences sociales.

Salais, R. (1994) 'Incertitude et interaction de travail: des produits aux conventions', in A. Orléan (ed.), *Analyse économique des conventions*, Paris: PUF.
Sarkesian S. Williams J. and Cimbala S. (2005) 'The Military Establishment, the President and the Congress', in P. J. Bolt et al. (eds) *American Defense Policy*, Baltimore: Johns Hopkins University Press: 139–150.
Sassen, S. (2007) 'The places and spaces of the global: an expanded analytical terrain', in D. Held and A. McGrew (eds) *Globalization Theory. Approaches and Controversies*, Cambridge: Polity Press, pp. 179–105.
Schwach, V. *et al.* (2007) 'Policy and Knowledge in Fisheries Management: A Policy Brief', *ICES Journal of Marine Science*, 64(4): 798–803.
Seafish, (2003) *2003 Economic Survey of the North Sea and West of Scotland Whitefish Fleet*, Edinburgh: Sea Fish Industry Authority.
Seafish, (2005) *Seafood Industry Value Chain Analysis: Cod, Haddock and Nephrops*, Edinburgh: Sea Fish Industry Authority.
Seafish, (2006) *West of Scotland Nephrops Industry: Review of Issues Facing the Industry*, Edinburgh: Sea Fish Industry Authority.
Shepsle, K. (1989) 'Studying Institutions: Some Lessons from the Rational Choice Approach', *Journal of Theoretical Politics*, 1 (2): 131–147.
Sihanya, B. (2007) *Patents, Parallel Importation and Compulsory Licensing in HIV/AIDS Drugs: The Experience of Kenya,* Managing the Challenges of WTO Participation, case study n° 19.
SIPRI, various years, *SIPRI Yearbook*, Oxford: Oxford University Press.
Smith, A. (2004a) *Le gouvernement de l'Union européenne. Une sociologie politique*, Paris: LGDJ.
Smith, A. (ed.) (2004b) *Politics and the European Commission. Actors, interdependence, legitimacy*, London: Routledge.
Smith, A. (2007) 'Un problème communautaire faiblement européen: l'alimentation sous Indication géographique protégée', in A. Campana, E. Henry and J. Rowell (eds) *La construction des problèmes publics en Europe*, Strasbourg: Presses universitaires de Strasbourg, pp. 155–174.
Smith, A. (2008) 'What constitutes a legitimate interest? The politics of food labelling in Europe, the New World and at the WTO', in M. Smyrl and W. Genieys (eds) *Accounting for Change*, London: Palgrave.
Smith, A. (de) Maillard, J. and Costa, O. (2007) *Vin et politique. Bordeaux, la France et la mondialisation*, Paris: Presses de Science Po.
Stanziani, A. (2003) 'Produits, normes et dynamiques historiques', *Sociologie du travail*, 45: 259–266.
Stanziani, A. (2005) *Histoire de la qualité alimentaire XIXe-Xxe siècles*, Paris: Seuil.
Swidler, A. (1986) 'Culture in Action: Symbols and Strategies', *American Journal of Sociology*, 51 (2): 273–286.
Symes, D. (1998) 'Northern waters: common denominators and regional differences' in D. Symes (ed.), *Northern Waters: Management Issues and Practice*, Oxford: Fishing News Books, pp. 254–257.
Symes, D. and Crean, K. (1995) 'Historic Prejudice and Invisible Boundaries: Dilemmas for the Development of the Common Fisheries Policy' in G. Blake, W. Hildesley, R. Pratt, R. Ridley and C. Schofield (eds) *Peaceful Management of Transboundary Resources*, London: Graham and Trotman.

Tedlow, R. (1996) *New and Improved: The Story of Mass Marketing in America*, Boston: Harvard (2nd edition).
Telser, L. G. (1960) 'Why should Manufacturers want Fair Trade?', *Journal of Law and Economics*, 3: 86–105.
Thelen, K. and Steinmo, S. (1992) 'Historical Institutionalism in Comparative Politics', in S. Steinmo, K. Thelen and K. Longstreth (eds) *Structuring politics. Historical Institutionalism in Comparative Analysis*, Cambridge: Cambridge University Press.
Thévenot, L. (1989) 'Economie et politique de l'entreprise: économies de l'efficacité et de la confiance', in L. Boltanski et L. Thévenot (eds) *Justesse et justice dans le travail*, Paris: Cahiers de Centre d'Etudes de l'Emploi (Presses universitaires de France), pp. 135–207.
Théret, B. (2001) 'Saisir les faits économiques: une lucture structuraliste génétique de la méthode Commons', *Cahiers d'Economie Politique*, n° 40–41: 79–138.
Tirman, J. (1984) *The Militarization of High Technology*, Cambridge: Ballinger.
Torre, A. (2000a) 'Introduction. Activités agricoles et agro-alimentaires et processus de développement local', *Revue d'Économie régional et Urbaine*, n° 3: 1–19.
Torre, A. (2000b) 'Économie de proximité et activités agricoles et agroalimentaires. Éléments d'un programme de recherche', *Revue d'Économie régional et Urbaine*, n° 3: 121–141.
Torrès, O. (2005) *La guerre des vins: 'l'affaire Mondavi'*, Paris: Dunod.
US Congress (1990) *Arming Our Allies: Cooperation and Competition in Defense Technology*, Office of Technology Assessment, Washington DC: US Government Printing Office.
Vitols, S. (2004) 'Negociated Shareholder Value: The German Variant of an Anglo-American Practice', *Competition and Change*, 8 (4): 357–374.
Wiber, M. (2005) 'Mobile law and globalism: Epistemic communities versus community-based innovation in the fisheries sector', in F. Von Benda-Beckmann, K. Von Benda-Beckmann and A. Griffiths (eds) *Mobile People, Mobile Law: Expanding Legal Relations in a Contracting World*, Aldershot: Ashgate, pp. 131–151.
Williamson, O. (1985) *The Economic Institutions of Capitalism*, New York: Free Press.
Wilson, D. and Hegland, T. (2005) 'An Analysis of Some Institutional Aspects of Science in Support of the Common Fisheries Policy' Project Report for Policy and Knowledge in Fisheries Management, CEC 5th Framework Programme No. Q5RS-2001-01782. Working paper no. 3-2005, Institute for Fisheries Management & Coastal Community Development.
Wine and Spirits Intelligence service Ltd (2002) *L'avenir des vins du Nouveau Monde. La fin de l'âge d'or?*, Report presented at London International Wine & Spirits Fair, 21–23 May.
Wise, M. (1984) *The Common Fisheries Policy of the European Community*, London: Methuen.

Index

Commercial IR, 4, 6, 9, 12, 23–7, 29, 32–3, 46–7, 62, 66–7, 71, 76–7, 79–82, 89–90, 94–6, 100–1, 108, 114, 118, 123, 127, 129–30, 134–5, 137–8, 143–4, 146–7, 152–3, 161–2, 164, 169, 172–7, 178–81, 184, 189, 193–6, 199–200, 210–11, 217–19
Common Fisheries Policy (CFP), 26, 149–50, 152–3, 156, 159–61, 164, 168, 180
competition policy, 12, 16, 27, 37–8, 41, 63–4, 183, 201, 208, 218
conception of control, 9, 32, 34, 128, 204
constructivist, 21
corporate governance, 3, 93, 102, 105

deinstitutionalization, 3, 15, 25, 42, 44, 46, 63, 71, 94, 122–3, 127, 136, 138, 162, 202, 210
DG Competition, 30, 37, 39, 49, 50, 56, 59–60, 63–4, 221
domination, 9, 31, 33, 36, 60, 86–7, 94, 97, 100, 107, 116–17, 128, 133, 140, 144, 162, 180, 184, 189, 192–3, 200, 215

Employment IR, 4, 5, 13–14, 24, 33, 44, 46, 66, 72, 76, 127, 189, 209, 217
European Union (EU), 10, 16, 18, 23, 25–7, 30, 37–41, 42, 49, 51, 67, 70, 72, 75–6, 78, 83–6, 90, 94, 114, 118, 120–1, 149–64, 167–9, 171–3, 175, 178, 180–1, 182–4, 187, 192, 200, 209–10, 214, 218, 221

Finance IR, 4, 5, 12–14, 25–6, 46–7, 72–3, 89–90, 94, 101, 106–7, 114, 116–17, 126–7, 129–30, 133, 135–7, 139, 141, 143, 146, 148, 190, 208–9, 217

financial markets, 92–3, 101, 115
financialization, 93, 101, 119, 127, 201, 203, 205, 217–18

globalization, 1–3, 7, 11, 13, 23–4, 26–7, 29–30, 42, 63, 65, 72, 89, 91–4, 101, 117, 122, 127–30, 132, 134–9, 143–8, 153, 180–1, 183–4, 199–202, 205–6, 214, 216–20

households, 32, 36, 43

identity, 8, 11, 13, 65, 67, 87, 90, 165–6, 217
institutional complementarity, 6, 207–8, 218
institutional investors, 93, 101–5, 107, 125–6, 141
institutionalization, 3, 8, 15, 30, 38, 90, 92, 94, 96, 100, 108, 110, 117, 119, 129, 146, 182–4, 187, 189
intellectual property rights (IPR), 32, 77, 93, 95, 99, 100, 116, 121, 122, 128, 191, 196, 198, 200

legitimization, 30, 38, 41, 90–1, 107, 116, 122, 124, 168, 183, 196, 199–201

patents, 95, 97, 99, 100, 106, 114–15, 117–18, 120–4, 127–8
politicization, 17, 19, 20–1, 27, 41, 68–70, 76, 81–2, 84–5, 89, 107, 115, 119, 127, 140, 151, 155–6, 164–6, 169, 174–8, 180, 182, 188, 193, 202, 212–16, 219
problematization, 17, 20, 22, 27, 37, 41–2, 58, 68–70, 76, 79, 80–1, 84–9, 114, 128, 135, 138, 141, 151, 154, 157–8, 163–5, 174–5, 180, 188, 193, 198, 202, 210–14, 216–20

productive systems, 75, 221
property rights, 6, 160, 171, 179, 187, 213–14
Purchase IR, 4–6, 11–12, 24, 26–7, 30–2, 34, 36, 38, 41, 44–5, 54, 63, 66–7, 71, 82–7, 89–90, 115–16, 127, 152–9, 161, 164, 169, 172–3, 175, 178–80, 185–6, 189–91, 196–7, 182, 208, 211, 219

regulation, 2–5, 8–23, 26–7, 30, 63, 66, 69, 83, 85–91, 94–9, 107, 117, 120, 128, 130, 132, 139, 151, 154–9, 161, 169, 172, 180, 183–4, 187, 198, 202, 206–10, 214, 216, 219–20, 221
reinstitutionalization, 3, 12, 24–5, 27, 44, 63, 71–2, 138, 141, 143, 150, 153, 156, 158–9, 163, 184, 189, 201–2, 210

retailing, 14, 29, 31, 36, 45, 49, 62, 76, 81–2, 161–2, 168, 177–9, 182, 184

scientific advice, 155, 166
shareholder value, 25–6, 93–4, 101–2, 105–7, 114, 116–19, 126–7, 142
sustainable, 26, 150, 152, 163–4, 168, 173, 175, 177–81, 204, 211, 220

technicization, 17, 21, 116
territorial, 2, 10, 13, 25, 88–9, 154, 168, 173, 209
territory, 6, 27, 34, 35, 38–9, 52, 66, 70, 72, 83, 87, 90, 153–4, 157, 165, 170, 183, 209

varieties of capitalism, 2, 12, 207

World Trade Organization (WTO), 14, 18, 23, 27, 75, 90, 117, 121–2, 183, 200–1, 209